Practice with Student-Involved Classroom Assessment

A Workbook and Learning Team Guide

To be used in conjunction with
Student-Involved Classroom Assessment, 3d ed.
by Richard J. Stiggins

Judith A. Arter and Kathleen U. Busick

Assessment Training Institute

50 SW Second Avenue, Suite 300
Portland, Oregon 97204

(503) 228-3060 • Fax: (503) 228-3014 • http://www.assessmentinst.com

ASSESSMENT TRAINING INSTITUTE

67240

Project Coordination: Barbara Carnegie
Copy Editing: Robert Marcum
Production: Jennifer Letter
Design and Typesetting: Heidi Bay

2001 First Printing
Printed in the U.S.A.
ISBN 0-9655101-2-3
Library of Congress Control Number: 00-132772

To teachers, for whom we have the highest respect.

Acknowledgments

This *Workbook* would not have been possible without the assistance of many dedicated and talented people. Foremost among these are the staff at the Assessment Training Institute: Dr. Rick Stiggins (classroom assessment role model), Barbara Carnegie (design and development), Jennifer Letter (production), Sharon Lippert (proof-reader) Nancy Bridgeford (proof-reader and reality-checker). Additional proofing, design and production support was provided by Robert Marcum, and Heidi Bay (Bay Design, Portland, Oregon).

Early versions of the *Workbook* were reviewed for content by Jan Chappuis (Silverdale, Washington), classroom assessment in-service professional development specialist, and Dr. Susan Brookhart (Duquesne University, Pittsburgh, Pennsylvania), pre-service teacher educator and educational researcher. Their comments and insights were invaluable during the revision and fine-tuning process. Kris Bridgeford (first year middle school science teacher) also reviewed drafts.

We would also like to thank the hundreds of educators—classroom teachers, building principals, district staff, regional office and state department of education staff, and college and university staff—with whom we have worked, learned, and shared ideas over the years.

Table of Contents

Chapter 3   Defining Achievement Standards

Chapter 4   Understanding Our Assessment Alternatives

End Part I   Activities

PART II   Understanding Assessment Methods

Chapter 5   Selected Response Assessment: Flexible and Efficient

Chapter 6 Essay Assessment: Subjective and Powerful

Chapter 7 Performance Assessment: Rich with Possibilities

Chapter 8 Personal Communication: Immediate Information About Achievement

End Part II Activities

APPENDICES

Introduction

What to Do First

Welcome to the *Workbook* that accompanies the textbook, *Student-Involved Classroom Assessment*, 3d ed. This *Workbook* contains practice activities designed to enhance, extend, and apply the learning from the textbook.

You are probably a member of one of two groups using this *Workbook*—educators studying classroom assessment individually or in a learning team as part of inservice professional development, or students involved in assessment coursework in a preservice teacher training setting. Depending on your group, here's how to proceed:

Inservice

- Read sections "Introduction" through "The First Team Meeting" of the *Workbook*. This will tell you how to set up and run a learning team, how to use the *Workbook* in an inservice setting, and the various options for conducting team meetings.

- Work with your team to decide on the schedule for your team meetings—see "Learning Team Meeting Schedules and Formats" schedule.

- Set up the first team meeting—see "First Team Meeting" section.

- Decide if you will use the Assessment Training Institute videos that are designed to accompany the textbook and this *Workbook*. If so, it's a good idea to order them ahead so they'll be on hand when you need them. This is especially the case if you'll be running several learning teams at the same time—one set of videos can go in a lending library. Figure 1 lists the videos and the chapters with which they are used.

Imagine! Assessments That Energize Students—Use with textbook Chapter 2

This video workshop is vital to understand how student-centered classroom assessment enhances teacher effectiveness and student motivation. Rick Stiggins argues that the key to success for students and teachers in today's standards-driven educational environment hinges on our ability to maintain and rebuild student confidence through intensive student involvement in classroom assessment.

Creating Sound Classroom Assessments—Use at the end of textbook Part I

This video is designed for both teachers and administrators. First, you'll learn what quality assessment means. Then, you'll discover how to achieve it in your own school or district. Rick Stiggins reveals five, critical quality assessment standards that you can use to check the reliability of your assessments and to turn the assessment process into an effective teaching tool.

Common Sense Paper and Pencil Assessments—Use with textbook Chapter 5

Implementing student-centered assessment methods doesn't mean you have to toss out traditional paper and pencil tests. This interactive video shows you how to design better paper and pencil tests and use them to build student motivation and achievement.

Assessing Reasoning in the Classroom—Use with textbook Chapter 9

Building on the information in *Creating Sound Classroom Assessments*, this video provides valuable insights into exactly what it means for students to be proficient reasoners and effective problem-solvers. Using clear illustrations and focused instruction, the video guides you through a variety of practical, effective ways to use assessments to teach reasoning skills to your students and to help them succeed at problem-solving.

Report Card Grading—Use with textbook Chapter 13

Through insightful discussion and valuable, hands-on activities, you'll explore the 'ins and outs' of report card grading. You'll examine a variety of student grading factors and discover which ones are key to accurate grading. Rick Stiggins will guide you through a discussion of the most effective evidence of achievement. Is it tests and quizzes? Performance assessment ratings? Homework scores? Class participation? Or even your own intuition about the student? You'll discover the answers with the help of this highly interactive video.

Figure 1
Videos That Support *Student-Involved Classroom Assessment*, 3d ed.

***Student-Involved Conferences*—Use with textbook Chapter 15**

This engaging video workshop will help you take maximum advantage of student-involved conferences to help students learn. Guided by Rick Stiggins and Anne Davies, both well-respected assessment trainers, consultants, and authors, you'll learn the most effective ways to involve students in and prepare students for conferences with parents.

All videos are available from the Assessment Training Institute, 50 SW 2nd St., Suite 300, Portland, Oregon 97204, 800-480-3060.

Figure 1
Continued

Preservice

- If you are using the text and this *Workbook* in a course of study, your professor probably has devised plans for its integration into your course. Follow your professor's instructions in this regard.

- If your professor has not developed specific plans, you can follow your course syllabus through the chapters of the text, completing the exercises offered herein chapter by chapter as you study.

- In either situation, it will be to your advantage to form a study group of classmates who agree to complete the same *Workbook* exercises, so you can share the learning.

Workbook Overview

We developed this *Workbook* specifically to accompany Rick Stiggins' textbook, *Student-Involved Classroom Assessment*, 3d edition. This textbook is not merely a book to read and discuss. It is a book to read, reflect on, work through, experiment with, discuss, and cull for ideas that work in each individual reader's classroom. You might be thinking, "That's all well and good, but what exactly do I reflect on, work through, and experiment with?" That's the goal of this *Workbook*—we provide specific, practical, hands-on activities designed to extend understanding and apply ideas.

The fact that you're looking at this *Workbook* means that you are embarking on a study of classroom assessment. You may be a currently practicing teacher or administrator who wants to (or has been told to) learn more about assessment. You may be a preservice teacher or administrator who is taking a course because it is part of the curriculum. You may be working individually or in a learning team.

Whether you're approaching the study of classroom assessment from a felt need, to fulfill a licensing requirement, or as a course assignment, the truth of the matter is that a combination of forces is making a strong understanding of classroom assessment essential for the success of all educators:

- Standards-based instruction which requires that teachers have a crystal clear view of student learning targets and how to get all students there

- Changes in the types of achievement targets being taught and assessed

- Changes in the purposes for and uses of assessment, including tracking student progress toward important learning targets and involving students in their own assessment

- The emerging realization that we can use assessment to turn students on or turn them off to learning

Everyone would like learning about assessment to be quick and easy; but, like any other complex skill, it does take time and practice. If you can ante up the time, the textbook presents common sense guidelines as efficiently as possible. We designed this *Workbook* to provide the practice. Your investment in learning about student-involved assessment will pay large dividends in lowered teacher and student anxiety (we all need that!), adding efficiency to the assessment process (saving you time!), and improving student achievement (our ultimate goal!).

Intended Audiences

The textbook, *Student-Involved Classroom Assessment*, 3d ed., and this accompanying *Workbook* are intended for beginning and middle-level learners about classroom assessment. Here is the classroom assessment challenge in a nutshell (also see Figure 2). We will help you find the answers to these questions:

- Do you know and understand what it means to succeed academically in your classroom—what it looks like when your students are making adequate progress toward success?

- Can you transform your vision of success into assessment exercises and scoring schemes that provide dependable information about student success? This includes having a clear idea of what is to be assessed, knowing how the results will be used and who will use them, matching targets and uses to assessment methods, sampling well, and avoiding factors that might bias or distort your judgment of student competence.

- Do you know and understand how to use both the assessment process and its results to help students learn, to believe in themselves as learners, and to strive for academic success?

- Do you understand and can you apply principles of effective communication about student achievement?

If your answers to all these questions are an unqualified "yes," then you're ready to move beyond this book. If your answer to any of these questions is "no," "somewhat" or "I don't know," then this textbook and *Workbook* combination is for you.

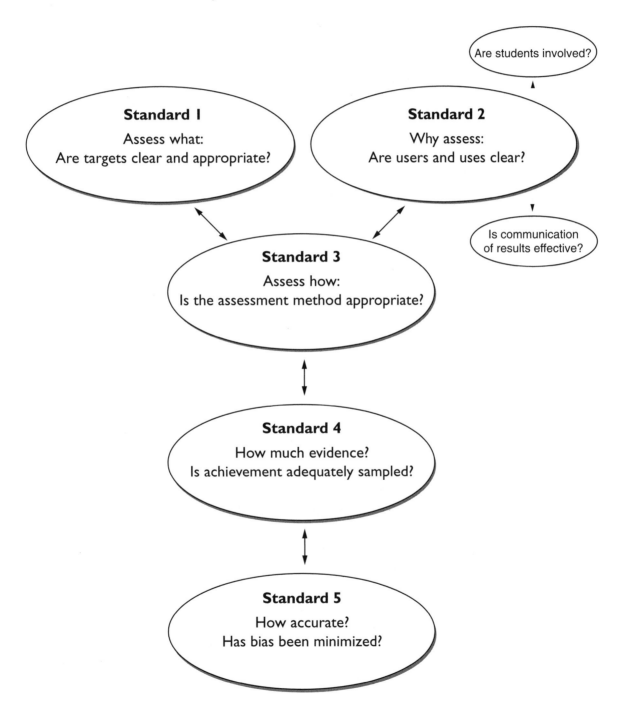

Figure 2
Five Standards of Quality Assessment

Learner Targets

To help you meet the assessment challenge, we establish the following learning objectives:

1. *You will understand the differences between sound and unsound assessment practices, and will be committed to meeting key quality standards.* We want you to know and understand the standards of assessment quality depicted in Figure 2. We want you to understand why student academic well-being hinges on our day-to-day, week-to-week, and term-to-term classroom assessments of their achievement. We also want you to see that students and their families count on these classroom assessments to provide accurate information about student learning, help them set realistic academic expectations, allocate personal resources, and be motivated to strive for success.

2. *You will master assessment development to meet standards of quality in all classroom, school, and district assessment contexts, including diverse classrooms.* We want you to learn to apply the standards depicted in Figure 2, not just understand them. This objective addresses the fact that many educators have had little experience in designing and developing assessments. You cannot meet standards of assessment quality if you don't know what those standards are.

3. *You will learn to use assessment to inform instructional decisions and as a teaching tool to motivate students to strive for excellence.* Students are the most important users of assessment processes and information; therefore, student involvement is included as an important side bubble from the users and uses standard depicted in Figure 2. When students are drawn into the assessment process, the results become far more than a source of data—they become one of the most powerful motivators and teaching tools we have. In addition, integrating assessment and instruction saves time and simplifies the teacher's job.

4. *You will learn to apply standards of sound communication about student achievement.* Learning how to recognize and develop quality assessments and use them for your own classroom decision making is important. But, so is the ability to communicate accurately and productively to other users of student achievement information. Therefore, we have included communication as an important side bubble to the users and uses standard in Figure 2. We want you to understand how to communicate effectively.

Our Professional Development Philosophy

We try to practice what we preach. We want you to help your students go on internal control and take responsibility for their own learning. So as your "teachers" we want you to do the same. Our success in attaining this goal hinges on the factors noted here.

Clear Targets

We believe that the chances of academic success increase in direct proportion to the clarity of the learning targets to be hit. This is a basic premise *of Student-Involved Classroom Assessment*. The more ways one can make learning targets clear to students, the better. In this *Workbook* we've modeled several strategies for making our targets clear:

- We describe the classroom assessment knowledge and skills educators need—in the assessment challenge outlined above, in Figure 2, and in the "Classroom Assessment Confidence Questionnaire" in Appendix A.

- Appendix B includes rubrics for quality assessment—performance criteria that describe quality classroom assessments.

- Appendix B provides "anchor" assessments illustrating different levels of quality. These sample assessments will be used throughout the *Workbook* as opportunities to refine your skills in analyzing and improving assessments.

- Appendix C describes developmental levels of learning about classroom assessment.

Learning Teams

The single most frequent comment we've heard about experiences that help to change practice is the opportunity to work with peers. Therefore, we encourage the formation of learning teams in the inservice setting and study groups with classmates in the preservice setting. Complete guides for collaborative learning teams appear later in this Introduction.

Growth Portfolios

In Chapter 14 of the text, Rick discusses the power of portfolios. We ask you to experience that power by assembling a portfolio of your classroom assessment learning. Not only will this help you learn, but will help you discover the challenges and benefits of the portfolio as an information management and communication system before you try it with students in your own classroom. The procedures for developing your own growth portfolio are described in more detail later in this Introduction.

Self-Assessment and Self-Reflection

Research has shown that self-assessment and self-reflection speed and deepen learning. Therefore, we encourage use of learning logs, provide guidance on "showing what you know," and encourage self-reflection and self-assessment as part of portfolio building. We describe these in more detail later in this Introduction.

Activities Designed for Different Learning Styles

We realize that this *Workbook* will have a diverse audience. Therefore, we have tried to honor different learning styles—visual, auditory, and verbal; inductive and deductive; and so on. We have also tried to honor the needs of users from various cultural groups. We realize that such things as the appropriate ways to conduct discussions and ways to provide feedback to others varies with culture. We have attempted to provide learning options that will feel safe to all *Workbook* users.

As authors, we are also on a journey of learning—in this case how best to provide educators with experiences that will make their assessments faster, easier, and better. Therefore, we regard this *Workbook* as a work in progress. We welcome feedback and ideas from our collaborators in this process—you, the users. Let us know what works for you.

Navigating the *Workbook*

Activity Types

The *Workbook* provides several kinds of activities to assist users to understand and use the ideas in the textbook. Each type of activity has an icon near the title, so that you can find what you want quickly.

Quick Check—Activities designed as refreshers to activate prior knowledge.

Consolidate Understanding—Activities designed to explore and deepen understanding of topics and issues. "Consolidation" activities include such things as real-life dilemmas (cases) that you will help solve, guided discussion about videos, guided analysis of sample assessments to recognize strengths and make them better, comparing past practice to current ideas, and brainstorming solutions to problems.

Apply Learning—Activities that extend understanding to your own classroom, such as building an instructional unit incorporating assessment ideas in the text, developing rubrics, and activities to try with students to involve them in their own assessment.

Self-Reflect—Activities to track your own learning progress, show what you know, and build a growth portfolio.

Chapter Layout

There is a chapter in the *Workbook* devoted to each chapter and section end in the textbook. Each *Workbook* chapter follows the same format, as outlined here.

Chapter Introduction—This is a very brief reminder of how the *Workbook* activities connect to the textbook. Each introduction has the following parts:

- *Big ideas in the chapter.* A summary of key points and major learnings from the textbook chapter.

- *Links of key points to previous textbook chapters.*

- *Links of key points to subsequent textbook chapters.*

- *Roadmap.* We describe briefly each activity in the *Workbook* chapter. These descriptions include the time the activity takes and its intent—quick check, consolidate understanding, apply/ try with students, or self-reflect.

- *Portfolio reminder.* Because we recommend that users keep a growth portfolio to track their progress in learning about classroom assessment, we include a reminder at the beginning of each chapter to keep material for potential portfolio entries close at hand.

Practice Activities—After each chapter introduction you will find the learning activities for that chapter. All activities (with only a few clearly labeled exceptions) come complete with all materials needed to successfully complete the activity. All activities are presented in the same format:

1. Activity title and relevant descriptive icons

2. Goals and rationale for the activity

3. Cross-reference to the text, telling you which specific textbook concept(s) come into play

4. Additional materials needed to complete the activity

5. Approximate time required to complete the activity

6. A complete set of instructions for doing the activity—what to do, individual reflection questions, group processing questions, and so on

End-of-Section Activities

The textbook is divided into four parts or sections—(I) the basics of high-quality, student-involved assessment, (II) assessment methods, (III) classroom applications, and (IV) communicating about student achievement. We have included "end of part" activities intended to consolidate understanding across all chapters in each part and to provide opportunities to apply and reflect on learning:

- *Case Discussions and Other Summary Activities* requiring synthesis and application of material covered in several chapters.

- *Show What You Know.* Just as we all, as teachers, give students in the classroom a chance to "show what they know" as a way to consolidate and refine understanding, we have included this type of activity at the end of each section of the *Workbook*.

- *Portfolio Work.* We don't want your portfolio assembly experience to be overwhelming. We want it to be a useful consideration of this method for self-assessment and potential use in the classroom. Therefore, we put it *only at the end of each part*. Of course, we suggest that you continuously gather evidence of your competence as you progress through the chapters of each section. But we do ask you to cull these materials for your growth portfolio at the end of each part of the text.

Tracking Your Own Learning

As Rick points out in the textbook, the most important instructional decisions are made by learners themselves. In this *Workbook* the learner is *you*. The decisions that learners make include the following: Do I stand a chance of succeeding? How am I progressing toward mastery? Is this worth the time devoted to it? Is it worth trying, or is it easier to give up?

Learners are in charge of their learning. If they don't feel able to learn or don't want to learn, there will be no learning.

Therefore, our challenge is to help you, the learner, want to learn classroom assessment skills and *believe* that doing so will improve your life and the lives of your current or future students. In short, our challenge is to convince you that the payoff is worth the effort.

We want to turn you on to the possibility of your own success as a classroom assessor. Therefore, we don't just "talk the talk," we "walk the walk" by involving you in your own assessment, tracking your own growth as a classroom assessor, and communicating about your success as a classroom assessor. We want you involved in your own assessment in several ways: repeated uses of the "Classroom Assessment Confidence Questionnaire" in Appendix A, repeated tries at analyzing real classroom assessments for quality, repeated self-assessment using developmental levels, and growth portfolios.

We briefly describe each of these in the following subsections. More assistance is provided throughout the *Workbook*.

Classroom Assessment Confidence Questionnaire

You will use the "Classroom Assessment Confidence Questionnaire" in Appendix A at least twice during your study of classroom assessment— at the beginning and at the end. You also may elect to use it more frequently. The goal is for you to analyze and reflect on your changing confidence as a classroom assessor. We suggest that your responses to the "Confidence Questionnaire" be part of your learning portfolio. Please look through the "Confidence Questionnaire" now.

Learning Log

In Chapter 8 (p. 247) of the textbook, Rick states, "*Learning logs* ask students to keep ongoing written records of the following aspects of their studies:

- Achievement targets they have mastered
- Targets they have found useful and important
- Targets they are having difficulty mastering
- Learning experiences (instructional strategies) that worked particularly well for them
- Experiences that did not work for them
- Questions that have come up along the way that they want help with
- Ideas for important study topics or learning strategies that they might like to try in the future

"The goal in the case of learning logs is to have students reflect on, analyze, describe, and evaluate their learning experiences, successes, and challenges, writing about the conclusions they draw."

We will ask you to keep a learning log in which you record your responses to both

1. Structured questions—those that occur at the end of each textbook chapter and the "Times for Reflection" that occur throughout each chapter

2. Learning activities or other classroom events that lead to ideas, insights, and self-observation of growth on the learning targets we have for you (the "standards" described in Figure 2)

Of course, the learning log is optional. But, we recommend that you try this option if you (a) want to try out a learning log before asking your own students to do one, or (b) find that maintaining a log helps you to reflect on your increasing confidence and competence as a classroom assessor. Learning log material can make excellent growth portfolio entries.

A sample learning log format is provided in Appendix A, "Assessment Learning Log." Feel free, however, to use any other format that you have encountered and have found useful. (And, please send us a copy. We're always looking for good ideas!)

Growth Portfolio

The growth portfolio we are asking you to assemble is intended to:

- Show you, and perhaps your teammates, how much you have grown and changed as a classroom assessor during your learning time.

- Reveal to you, and others, compelling evidence of your increasing competence on the targets/standards depicted in Figure 2.

- Celebrate your success as a learner of classroom assessment.

- Try out this type of portfolio yourself before asking your students to do it.

You will keep two files—your working folder and your actual growth portfolio.

Your Working Folder

This is FULL of interesting stuff. You don't need to include all the following things—they just represent options.

1. Your self-assessment of confidence in the form of completed "Classroom Assessment Confidence Questionnaires" in Appendix A.

2. Sample assessments that you use in your classroom (tests, quizzes, essays tests, performance assessments, surveys) along with your analysis of quality. Over time you will revisit your selections and think about how your ability to analyze assessments for quality has deepened. To assist in this process we provide rubrics for quality assessments and sample assessments that have been critiqued for quality (see Appendix B). Analyzing samples might be difficult at the beginning, as the ideas have not yet been covered. So, don't get overly concerned about your ability to do this at the start. It will get easier with time. One of the goals is for you to notice how your ability changes with time.

3. Your self-ratings on the developmental levels in Appendix C. They represent another way to self-assess and track progress. Repeat them over time and see your own growth!

4. Unit-building activities throughout the *Workbook*—we offer you the opportunity to plan and devise assessments that fit into one of your own units of instruction.

5. Artifacts from other *Workbook* activities or journal/learning log entries that provide evidence of your increasing confidence and competence. These can include:

    - Your best work
    - Something you found challenging
    - Work that taught you something as a classroom assessor
    - Work that shows how you solved a classroom assessment challenge
    - Work that shows how you've gotten better at something
    - Work you just LOVE
    - Concept maps, drawings, letters to others

6. If you are teaching, recruit your students to help you! Explain to them the nature of what you're trying to learn and the portfolio process you'll go through. Students can help:

    - Tell you how your assessments are changing and their reaction to these changes
    - Debrief on things you are trying
    - Identify possible entries for your portfolio
    - Provide samples of their own work that will illustrate the impact of your growing assessment literacy on their learning

Be sure to include a cover sheet for each entry to help you remember why you placed an item into your working folder. We provide a sample cover sheet in Appendix A ("Sample Working Folder/Portfolio Cover Sheet"), but feel free to use any other format that you like. (And once again, please send a copy to us, as we are always looking for good ideas.)

Your Growth Portfolio

This is a small, special collection culled from your working folder. The goal of this portfolio is to help you track your progress in mastering classroom assessment ideas. At the end of each section of the textbook (after Chapters 4, 8, 11, and 15), you will choose at least two items (but not more than five) from your working file to go into your portfolio.

What you choose is up to you. One entry can demonstrate growth in more than one area. Here are some suggestions (**means that an option is recommended):

1. ***Confidence surveys*—completed at least at the beginning and end of your learning experience; but, you could complete the survey at the end of each section.

2. ***Analyzed assessment samples*—at least three, one at the beginning, one at the end of Part III, and one at the end of the book.

3. *Unit-building activities*—include samples of your own work that highlight your growth.

4. *Other demonstrations of learning* from your working folder.

Further Assistance

We provide additional structured assistance throughout. The following are examples:

- Activity Intro-I helps you get started with your portfolio.

- At the end of Part II of the textbook (which emphasizes rules of evidence in assessments) we will ask you to analyze the evidence in your portfolio to determine how accurate a picture it paints of your growth.

- At the end of Chapter 14 in the textbook (on portfolios) we will ask you to review your portfolio using the guidelines for quality outlined in the chapter.

- At the end of Part IV of the textbook, we will provide additional assistance with organizing your portfolio, doing a final reflection, writing a cover letter, and planning portfolio conferences.

Teaming Up to Learn About Assessment

We believe that adult learners can take advantage of the great lessons learned over the years regarding the power of collaborative learning. We frequently learn faster and better working together than we do alone. So consider learning teams as a way to share your professional development experience, or study groups if you are a student completing coursework.

Setting Up and Conducting Learning Teams

Learning Team Defined

A *learning team* is not simply a group of individuals who get together periodically to talk about what is happening. Nor is it a book club that gathers to discuss what an author said. Rather, it is a small group of professionals who agree to experiment with new ideas and meet regularly for a specific period of time to share a specific professional growth experience guided by specific goals or purposes.

In our case, the goal is to acquire classroom assessment competencies. Learning team meetings are times for sharing lessons learned in the classroom, not just those derived from reading a textbook; a time to share successes and discuss strategies that resulted in student learning, as well as to share difficulties, determine why they arose, and find solutions. In short, a learning team provides a forum for learning, planning, testing ideas, and reflecting together.

Why learning teams?—Professional development in classroom assessment must build a deep understanding of the difference between sound and unsound assessment and of how to use assessment as a teaching tool. Because of the complexity of what is to be learned, we all must conceive of professional development as more than a series of workshops. Rather, it must achieve the following:

- Provide for the infusion of new ideas
- Offer the opportunity for learners to experiment with those ideas
- Encourage the pooling of ideas and experience to solve assessment challenges
- Deliver benefits in student motivation and achievement quickly
- Be flexible enough to fit into diverse and busy schedules

Learning teams provide this kind of professional development because they rely on the powerful principles of collaborative learning. Learning teams also model the kind of learning environment that should exist in every classroom, wherein learners:

- Begin to learn with a sense of what they already know
- Learn at their own individual rates
- Feel comfortable to risk trying new ideas
- Monitor their success
- Maintain records of their improving competence and confidence
- Feel a sense of personal accomplishment as they grow

In short, learning teams honor the professionalism of educators.

Learning Team Composition

There are many ways to organize learning teams. Teams usually consist of three to six teachers or administrators or, ideally, both. With more than six people, it becomes more difficult to arrange meeting times and allow time for each member to explore their experiences with the others. The smaller the group, the more likely that each member will take responsibility for making the team succeed. Consider the following possible configurations. See if any of these fit your needs. If not, set up your own configuration.

Example 1—Begin with School District Leadership Teams. One method involves setting up a leadership study team comprised of a few key teachers and administrators from various parts of the organization. The advantages for members of a leadership team include the following:

- Firsthand experience of the learning team process, so they can lead others

- The opportunity for this initial team to design and conduct an ongoing evaluation of the subsequent professional development effort to discern its impact

- The chance for this group to formulate a plan and a schedule for supporting multiple learning teams throughout the district over time

To advance their assessment literacy, these first team members would proceed through the textbook, following plans provided later in this *Workbook*. As members complete this initial experience and begin to feel confident about the message conveyed in the textbook, each might then fan out and form a new learning team. Those participants might then do the same, and so on, building a professional development pyramid. As time passes, those not involved may see others managing assessment with renewed confidence and thus become motivated to join a team.

Example 2—Begin with Those Individuals Most Interested in More Than One School. Another way to organize might be to start three to five learning teams in different schools and merge them into a collective effort. Staffs in each building might form teams and later meet with other building teams in larger sessions—say when they had finished each of the four parts of *Student-Involved Classroom Assessment*. Special video or workshop activities might be planned for these large-group sessions.

Example 3—Within a Single Building. Groups might also be formed from among faculty members and administrators within one building, on the basis of grade level (within or across levels), or on the basis of academic discipline.

Example 4—Ad Hoc Committees. Learning teams might come into existence when an ad hoc committee is assembled to evaluate and consider revising a report card or when a curriculum-development team decides to deal with some underlying assessment issues. In these cases, participants might work together only for the period of time needed to complete their study. Also, the team might not complete the entire textbook, but only those sections that relate most directly to the issue at hand. (But, it has been our experience that once a team gets started, members want to explore the entire textbook.)

Study Groups in Assessment Courses

A common variation on the learning team theme is the "study group," in which members of a class agree to become partners to help each other master the material. Most often these groups form among friendship or acquaintance groups for purposes of increasing the efficiency and effectiveness of study. The objective is to spread the work over several shoulders and to tap each other's particular expertise or strengths for the good of the entire group.

The Nature of Team Work

For effective professional development in classroom assessment, we recommend spending

25%   of total learning time reading or gathering information about potentially useful new assessment ideas and strategies

50%   in experimentation with new ideas and in reflection on "what I've learned about students, teaching and assessment"

25%   in learning team meetings sharing lessons each member learned in their classrooms

Between Meetings. Between team meetings (where 75% of the learning time is spent), each member completes agreed-on assignments designed to advance the team's collective knowledge and skills in classroom assessment. These assignments are usually the same for all team members. For example, members might read and reflect on the same pieces of professional literature (like a specific chapter from *Student-Involved Classroom Assessment*) or try a specific assessment strategy (e.g., from the *Workbook*) and bring the lessons they have learned from that experience to share with the group.

Opening 5–10 minutes	• Reaffirm group norms (periodically as needed). • Review goals, agenda, and participant roles for the meeting.
Content/Ideas 80–100 minutes	• Briefly review the key ideas in the chapters you read between meetings. This can be open ended or can use the "Quick Check" or "Consolidate Understanding" *Workbook* activities chosen by the group during the planning part of the previous meeting (or chosen by the group leader between meetings). • Share experiences with the applications tried between meetings and/or the portfolio work done— "Apply Learning" or "Self-Reflect" *Workbook* activities, or other applications designed by the group. • View ATI videos ("Consolidate Understanding") as appropriate.
Planning for next time 10–20 minutes	• *Student-Involved Classroom Assessment* chapters to read between meetings (see Figures 4 and 5). • *Workbook* activities to try between sessions. • *Workbook* or other applications to try between meetings. • Portfolio or other self-reflection work to be done between meetings. • Goals and agenda for the next meeting. The group (or leader for the next meeting) can select *Workbook* activities or design its own activities.
Wrap-up 5–10 minutes	• Reflect on the meeting—Use the "Sample Team Meeting Log" or the "Learning Log" in Appendix A. • The recorder completes the minutes for the meeting using the "Sample Team Meeting Log" in Appendix A. • Select or assign roles for next time.

Figure 3
Sample Meeting Agenda

During Meetings. Meetings (the final 25% listed) are times to share successes and learnings and discuss strategies that worked, as well as to share difficulties, determine why they arose, and find solutions. During team meetings members could engage in several kinds of activities—opening, content/ideas, planning, and wrap-up. A sample general meeting agenda is shown in Figure 3. Figures 4 and 5 present detailed suggestions for the content of specific meetings.

Recruiting Participants

Those who wish to stimulate interest in participating in the learning team experience can do so in several ways. The simplest is to go to the ATI web page (www.assessmentinst.com) and download the document, "Learning Teams for Assessment Literacy." Copy it and share it with colleagues or classmates. Then you can meet with them to discuss their interest.

Or, you can download the document, "Assessment, Student Confidence, and School Success." This article will be of interest to you, but may be of even greater interest to those in positions of instructional leadership. It explores the importance of assessment literacy and the learning team method of getting there. Have instructional leaders read it together with "Learning Teams for Assessment Literacy," and then discuss their interest in joining forces to form a team.

Finally, those who have professional development background and experience can stimulate interest in learning teams by offering an overview workshop on the importance of high-quality classroom assessment using the ATI interactive video training package, *Imagine! Assessments That Energize Students* (see Figure 1). This introductory workshop will establish the need to be assessment literate. With some practice, any experienced trainer or staff development specialist can use this video package to present such a workshop.

Regardless of the method used it is important to remember that workshops, including video workshops, can introduce new ideas, but that change in practice requires sustained effort. Therefore, we recommend that if you conduct workshops to generate interest, you highlight the benefits of the learning team method of professional development as listed in the previous section, "Why Learning Teams?"

Additional incentives may be created for participation, such as the following:

- Release time or extended contract time for those who want to participate
- Graduate credit through an institution of higher education. Appendix E outlines a universal assessment course description for use in negotiating such credit.

The Assessment Training Institute also offers continuous programs of seminars nationwide on the development of assessment literacy. These are designed to help district teams return home ready to set up productive learning team–based professional development. Although it is not necessary for a district to participate in one of these to get started, many find it helpful. Contact us at 1-800-480-3060 at any time for further details about these sessions.

Commitments of Members/Operating Principles/Group Norms

Group norms are informal ground rules that a group agrees to follow in order to help it do its work. Norms cover such things as how members interact with each other, how business will be conducted, how decisions will be made, and how members are expected to behave. Any group that meets regularly needs to either identify its existing norms or develop norms that the group agrees will help its work.

Although group norms will be established by the group during the first team meeting, there are several operating principles that tend to increase the power of the experience. To maximize the value of the experience, teams should be mindful of the following details.

Rotate Leadership. From our experience, the team experience is enhanced if meeting leadership rotates among the members. Doing so spreads the time and energy commitment of leadership. Shared leadership makes everyone responsible for the success of the group. On the other hand, leadership is deeply embedded in some cultural contexts so rotation of responsibilities for components of teamwork, while holding overall leadership constant, may be more appropriate. The team can decide for itself if leadership is to rotate.

Do Your Homework! To make the professional development experience succeed, team members must complete the agreed-on assignments—readings, reflections, and applications. If they don't, the team concept is lost and the value of the meeting is greatly reduced. Team members must be able to count on each other's commitment to the project.

When You Meet. It is important to allow enough time for all members to report on their learning, experiences, and/or progress. A member who has had a special success or confronted a particularly troubling problem can provide a special focus for a meeting—but only if everyone has had time to report.

Track Your Growth. Adults, like students, are most likely to strive for excellence when they have the opportunity to see that their work is having positive results. For this reason, all members should track their individual improvement as classroom assessors in personal portfolios as described previously.

Working folders and growth portfolios can be shared at any time. However, the final team meeting should be devoted to sharing this evidence of participants' increased classroom assessment skill. For this sharing, members, in turn, present their portfolios and describe their improved assessment approaches. Note that in this case members are modeling sound practices to be used in the classroom, including the demonstration and celebration of learning that is an essential component of the unit-building activities in this *Workbook*.

Possible Group Roles. The goal of having a variety of roles for team members is to help meetings run efficiently and effectively. Roles can rotate between members, but should be formally assigned from one meeting to the next. Your group can choose which, if any, of these to assign to members.

1. *Leader/Facilitator.* The leader is responsible for the following:

    - Reminding members of the time, location, focus/purpose, agenda, and homework for the next meeting.

    - Choosing *Workbook* activities to do during the next meeting (unless the group determined them during the previous meeting) and gathering any materials needed.

    - Bringing the team meeting to order and reviewing norms and role assignments, as needed.

    - Encouraging participation, working to see that participants are comfortable, and monitoring adherence to group norms.

2. *Recorder.* This person pulls together the group work for a meeting. This might occur in the form of a team log (see Appendix A).

3. *Timekeeper.* The timekeeper helps the group stay on task and on timeline. He or she would keep track of the agenda, the time, and the progress the group is making.

4. *Clarifier.* The clarifier's role is to check for common understanding among team members. For example, the clarifier might pose such questions as, "Are we in agreement on that?"; "Is there a way to make the idea clearer?"; "Are we missing something here?"; "How else could we say that?"; "Is it likely that students will understand?"; and "What's still unclear?"

Learning Team Meeting Schedules and Formats

One strength of the learning team approach is its flexibility. Each team can devise its own schedule to meet the needs of its members. Some teams might want to start at once, others later. Some might want to go fast, others slow. So, realizing the realities of school life, we offer several possible schedules for working through the textbook and this *Workbook*.

The first two options, 6 and 11 meetings, both require between 50 and 75 hours of total professional development time. This includes meeting time, reading time, and practice time in the classroom. Obviously, other options will take more time. Regardless of how you set up your learning team experience, it's important to spread meetings out enough so members don't feel rushed. It takes time to learn, experiment, and grow. We recommend at least two to three weeks between meetings.

Six-Meeting Schedule

One option is to plan for fewer meetings with more work to complete between meetings. The basic six-meeting schedule is an example. The advantage of this schedule is that you have fewer meetings to weave into busy schedules. The drawback is that so much material is covered between and within sessions that it is more difficult to delve very deeply into any single topic. Each meeting uses the agenda in Figure 3. Figure 4 presents a suggested outline of how to proceed through all six team meetings.

Because of the restricted meeting time, we recommend combining textbook chapters that deal with parallel topics. In Figure 4, we've combined Chapters 1–4, 5–8, 9–11, and 12–15, essentially dividing the schedule into the four major parts of the textbook.

Eleven-Meeting Schedule

Another option is to plan more meetings with a narrower focus each time. The mid-range 11-meeting schedule does this. This plan allows you to delve more deeply into various assessment topics. The meeting format is the same as in the six-meeting option (see Figure 3), but with fewer chapters to cover between meetings. An outline of how to divide text chapters and proceed through all 11 meetings is shown in Figure 5. (Preservice note: This schedule fits a syllabus for a quarter-based college course.)

Seventeen-Meeting Schedule

The schedule that affords the greatest depth of coverage is the more lengthy 17-meeting format. This format allows you to take more advantage of the various types of activities in the *Workbook*, as well as the ATI interactive video presentations. Essentially, this schedule allows one meeting per chapter, plus the opening orientation meeting and a final meeting for the presentation of portfolios.

For all meetings use the basic plan in Figure 3 for the Opening, Content, Planning and Wrap-up portions of the meeting. Figure 4 adds specific details for each meeting.

MEETING 1 Use of Meeting Time	*Opening/Content.* See the "First Team Meeting" section of this Introduction (p. 28). *Planning.* The focus of planning will be **Chapters 1–4**—the relationship between assessment and student motivation and the nature of quality classroom assessment. Also plan for beginning your growth portfolio (Activity Intro-1). Consider watching the videos *Imagine!* (Activity 2-5) or *Creating Sound Classroom Assessments* (Activity End Part I-2) next time.
Assignments	1. Read and experiment with material presented in textbook **Chapters 1–4** as planned. 2. Start to collect materials in your working file and growth portfolio. See Activity Intro-1 (p. 32) and the "Growth Portfolio" section of this Introduction (p. 12).
MEETING 2 Use of Meeting Time	*Content.* The focus will be **Chapters 1–4** and **portfolio work** as planned last time. *Planning.* The focus of planning will be **Chapters 5–8**—an in-depth look at assessment methods. Also plan the **End of Part II** activities, including portfolio development (Activity End Part II-3). Consider watching the *Paper and Pencil Assessments* video (Activity 5-1) next time.
Assignments	1. Read and experiment with material presented in **Chapters 5–8** on specific assessment methods as planned. 2. Complete **End of Part II** *Workbook* activities, including portfolio development (Activity End Part II-3).
MEETING 3 Use of Meeting Time	*Content.* The focus will be Chapters 5–8 and portfolio work as planned last time. *Planning.* The focus of planning will be Chapters 9–11—applications to specific learning targets. Also plan the End of Part III activities, including portfolio development (Activity End Part III-2). Consider watching the *Assessing Reasoning* video (Activity 9-5) next time.
Assignments	1. Read and experiment with material presented in **Chapters 9–11** on applications to specific achievement targets. 2. Complete **End of Part III** *Workbook* activities, including portfolio development (Activity End Part III-2).

Figure 4
Sample Six-Meeting Learning Team Schedule

MEETING 4 Use of Meeting Time	*Content.* The focus will be **Chapters 9–11** and **portfolio work** as planned last time. *Planning.* The focus of planning will be **Chapters 12–15**—effective communication about achievement (including the beginning Part IV activities). Consider watching the videos *Report Card Grading* (Activity 13-2) or *Student-Involved Conferences* (Activity 15-1) next time.
Assignments	1. Read and experiment with material presented in **Chapters 12–15** on effective communication about student achievement as planned. 2. Collect evidence of important learnings or insights in your working folder.
MEETING 5 Use of Meeting Time	*Content.* The focus will be on **Chapters 12–15** as planned last time. *Planning.* The focus will be the **End of Part IV** activities and final portfolio work (Activity End Part IV-3).
Assignments	Complete **End of Part IV** activities including portfolio development (Activity End Part IV-3). Prepare for your portfolio celebration of learning (Activity End Part IV-3).
MEETING 6 Use of Meeting Time	*Content.* Present and discuss all team member's growth portfolios. Consider inviting guests and making it a celebration. Debrief the entire experience and consider further learning experiences (for suggestions, see Appendix E).

Figure 4
Continued

For all meetings use the basic plan in Figure 3 for the Opening, Content, Planning and Wrap-up portions of the meeting. Figure 5 adds specific details for each meeting.

MEETING 1	
Use of Meeting Time	*Opening/Content.* See the "First Team Meeting" section of this Introduction (p. 28). *Planning.* The focus of planning will be **Chapters 1 and 2**—the relationship between assessment and student motivation and the various users and uses of assessment information. Consider watching the *Imagine!* video (Activity 2-5) next time.
Assignments	1. Read and experiment with material presented in text **Chapters 1 and 2** as planned. 2. Start to collect materials in your working file and growth portfolio. See Activity Intro-1 (p. 32) and the "Growth Portfolio" section of this Introduction (p. 12).
MEETING 2	
Use of Meeting Time	*Content.* The focus will be **Chapters 1 and 2** as planned last time. *Planning.* The focus of planning will be **Chapters 3 and 4**—types of achievement targets and their alignment to various assessment methods including beginning of Part IV activities. Also plan the **End of Part I** activities, including portfolio development (Activity End Part I-4). Consider watching the *Creating Sound Classroom Assessments* video (Activity End Part I-2) next time.
Assignments	1. Read and experiment with material presented in **Chapters 3 and 4** as planned. 2. Complete **End of Part I** *Workbook* activities as planned.
MEETING 3	
Use of Meeting Time	*Content.* The focus will be **Chapters 3 and 4** and **End of Part I** activities as planned last time. *Planning.* The focus of planning will be **Chapters 5 and 6**—selected response and essay methods of assessment. Consider watching the *Paper and Pencil* video (Activity 5-1) next time.
Assignments	1. Read and experiment with material presented in **Chapters 5 and 6** as planned. 2. Collect evidence of important learnings or insights in your working folder.

Figure 5
Sample Eleven-Meeting Learning Team Schedule

MEETING 4	
Use of Meeting Time	*Content*. The focus will be **Chapters 5 and 6** as planned last time. *Planning*. The focus of planning will be **Chapters 7 and 8**—performance assessment and personal communication forms of assessment.
Assignments	1. Read and experiment with material in **Chapters 7 and 8** as planned. 2. Collect evidence of important learnings or insights in your working folder.
MEETING 5 Use of Meeting Time	*Content*. The focus will be **Chapters 7 and 8** as planned last time. *Planning*. The focus of planning will be the **End of Part II** *Workbook* activities, including portfolio development (Activity End Part II-3).
Assignments	1. Complete **End of Part II** activities, including portfolio development (Activity End Part II-3) as planned.
MEETING 6 Use of Meeting Time	*Content*. The focus will be **End of Part II** *Workbook* activities as planned last time. *Planning*. The focus of planning will be **Chapter 9**—assessing reasoning. Consider watching the *Reasoning* video (Activity 9-5) next time.
Assignments	1. Read and experiment with material presented in **Chapter 9** as planned. 2. Collect evidence of important learnings or insights in your working folder.
MEETING 7 Use of Meeting Time	*Content*. The focus will be **Chapter 9** as planned last time. *Planning*. The focus of planning will be **Chapters 10 and 11**—assessing skills, products and dispositions. Also plan for **End of Part III** *Workbook* activities, including portfolio development (Activity End Part III-2).
Assignments	1. Read and experiment with material presented in **Chapters 10 and 11** as planned. 2. Complete **End of Part III** activities, including portfolio development (Activity End Part III-2) as planned.

Figure 5
Continued

MEETING 8 Use of Meeting Time	*Content.* See Figure 3. The focus will be **Chapters 10 and 11** and **End of Part III** *Workbook* activities as planned last time. *Planning.* See Figure 3. The focus of planning will be **Chapters 12 and 13**—standardized testing and grading. Consider watching the *Grading* video (Activity 13-2) next time.
Assignments	1. Read and experiment with material presented in **Chapters 12 and 13** as planned. 2. Collect evidence of important learnings or insights in your working folder.
MEETING 9 Use of Meeting Time	*Content.* The focus will be **Chapters 12 and 13** as planned last time. *Planning.* The focus of planning will be **Chapters 14 and 15**—portfolios and student-involved conferences. Consider watching the *Student-Involved Conferences* video (Activity 15-1) next time.
Assignments	1. Read and experiment with material presented in **Chapters 14 and 15** as planned. 2. Collect evidence of important learnings or insights in your working folder.
MEETING 10 Use of Meeting Time	*Content.* The focus will be **Chapters 14 and 15** as planned last time. *Planning.* The focus of planning will be **End of Part IV** *Workbook* activities, including portfolio building and final celebration (Activity End Part IV-3).
Assignments	Complete **End of Part IV** activities, including portfolio development (Activity End Part IV-3). Cull through the working folder to assemble final growth portfolio and prepare for portfolio celebration of learning (Activity End Part IV-3).
MEETING 11 Use of Meeting Time	*Content.* Present and discuss all team member's growth portfolios. Consider inviting guests and making it a celebration. Debrief the entire experience and consider further learning experiences (for suggestions, see Appendix E).

Figure 5
Continued

All Schedules

All schedules call for confidence surveys to be completed at the beginning and end, the development of a growth portfolio that includes at least three sample assessments analyzed for quality with self-reflections on improvement, and a final meeting in which portfolios are shared and growth is celebrated. These form the foundations of your evaluation of progress.

Workbook activities can be woven into any of these schedules in two ways. First, learning teams can review the activities available for a given chapter and select some to be completed as part of their homework assignment between meetings in preparation for the discussion of that chapter. Or, the leader for a given team meeting can select an activity to be completed as part of the meeting agenda.

Evaluating Progress

Short-Term Evaluation of Each Session

The first sense of *progress* is merely how well the meetings are going. Do participants find them productive? Do they provide evidence to others that teachers are hard at work? To evaluate this type of progress we suggest the option of reflecting on the success of each team meeting at its end, and keeping a log, record, or minutes of team meetings. Logs, records, and minutes serve to document what was done, capture group insights, provide a reminder of previous decisions, record the learning growth of the group, provide evidence to others (if needed) that important work is being accomplished, and provide an opportunity to think about group functioning. A sample agenda, summary of activities, and evaluation of a meeting's success is given in Appendix A in the "Sample Team Meeting Log."

Long-Term Evaluation of Learning

In the ultimate sense, *progress* means "have folks learned?" This type of progress has already been discussed—learning logs, confidence surveys, and growth portfolios. It can be very instructive to pool these at the end of the experience to draw conclusions about where the team succeeded.

The First Team Meeting

The first meeting of a learning team is critically important and is the same regardless of the meeting schedule you decide on. After that, each team will follow its own plan.

Meeting Objectives

1. Finalize team meeting schedule, location, and other logistics.
2. Establish norms for group interaction (Activity Intro-2).
3. Develop a baseline for the team's classroom assessment competence and confidence.
4. Review assignments and plan for Meeting 2.

Agenda

We assume that all members of the group are ready to develop their assessment literacy—no one needs to be convinced. So work can begin in earnest.

Finalize Logistics (20 minutes). Members must agree on the time frame for the team experience, the schedule of events, and the types of learning activities that will take place.

- *Select a regular meeting day and time* and place it on everyone's calendar. Study teams usually meet once every two to three weeks for about two hours. You should set the dates and times for all meetings. If you have chosen an 11-meeting format, for example, you need to decide that you will meet every two to three weeks from November to May. Pick specific dates and times, and have everyone enter them on their own calendars.

- *Choose a meeting site* and make arrangements to secure it for the time needed. Possibilities include the teacher's lounge, classroom, library, conference room at the district office building, coffee shop, bookstore, and homes of individual members. If you decide to rotate the meeting location, make sure it is on everyone's calendar.

- *Agree on the general kinds of activities* to be conducted at each meeting. This will be some combination of (a) reflecting on the specific assignments from the previous meeting; (b) activities designed to consolidate understanding of material read; (c) planning applications; and/or (d) activities designed to prepare the team for the next topic to be covered. The *Workbook* contains activities of all these types.

  Specifically, you should decide if you will do the unit-building activity series. This involves planning assessments from beginning to end for individual teacher's instructional units. This is the ultimate application of the knowledge presented in the textbook, but it requires a chunk of team time. You should also decide whether you will use the video series that accompanies the textbook and this *Workbook* (see Figure 1). If so, you need to order videos early so that you have them on hand when you need them.

- *Agree on leadership responsibility* for planning and conducting each team meeting. Will meeting leadership be the responsibility of one person for all sessions or will it rotate? If it is to rotate, we recommend that assignments be made for all meetings at this first meeting.

- *Other roles.* Will you use the other roles outlined previously—recorder, timekeeper, and clarifier? Do you see the need for other roles? Will these rotate?

Establish Group Interaction Norms (30–45 minutes). After agreeing on a schedule of sites, dates, and times, your group needs to establish norms. The norms frame the behavioral guidelines that members will follow. Activity Intro-2 leads you through the steps to establish group norms.

Plan for Evaluation of Team and Individual Member Growth (20–25 minutes).

- (5 minutes) Discuss the use of meeting logs to document the progress of the group. Discuss how you will document individual learning—growth portfolio (recommended), learning logs (optional), confidence survey (recommended).

- (10 minutes) Complete the "Classroom Assessment Confidence Questionnaire" in Appendix A. When sharing results with other team members, consider the following questions: Where are we now in our confidence and competence as classroom assessors? With this baseline in place, are there additional ideas on how the team might track its own growth?

- (5–10 minutes) *Optional.* Develop a list of "team assets." Identify special background knowledge, or experiences of team members that might be used to strengthen the learning experience. What special resources might some members be able to contribute to benefit the entire team?

Finalize Plans for the Next Session (10–15 minutes).

1. Assign roles and responsibilities.
2. Plan homework:
   - Note the chapter or chapters to read (see suggested chapters in Figures 4 and 5).
   - Begin to collect material in your working folder in preparation for the development of your growth portfolio—see Activity Intro-1. (Additional detail is in the "Growth Portfolio" section of this introduction.)
   - Identify *Workbook* activities to be completed, if any, *before* the next meeting

3. Decide on *Workbook* activities that your team will complete during the next meeting. Or, you can assign this responsibility to the leader of the next meeting.

Reflect on This Meeting (5–10 minutes). What worked? Did you accomplish what you wanted? Do you need to add to or adjust group norms? You can use the "Sample Team Meeting Log" in Appendix A.

For Further Reading on Study Teams

Sue Francis, Stephanie Hirsh, and Elizabeth Rowland. 1994. "Improving school culture through study groups." *Journal of Staff Development* 15 (2): 12–15.

Heartland AEA 11 Schools. 1999. *Learning team activities*. Heartland AEA 11, 6500 Corporate Drive, Johnston, IA 50131 (tel. 515-270-9030).

Linda Munger. 1994. *Facilitation skills for effective teamwork*. Iowa City Community School District, 4471 91st St., Des Moines, IA 50322.

Carlene Murphy. 1992. Study groups foster schoolwide learning. *Educational Leadership*, November 71–74.

Carlene Murphy, Charlotte Danielson, and Agnes Crawford. 1996. Folder one—Learning through study groups. In *An ASCD professional inquiry kit: Performance assessment*, (pp. 1-4) edited by Judy Arter. ASCD, 1250 N. Pitt St., Alexandria, VA 22314 (tel. 703-549-9110).

Activity Intro-1   Where I Am Right Now

Recommended

Goals/Rationale

Do this activity before beginning your study of classroom assessment. The goal is to start with a baseline of current understanding of student-involved classroom assessment so that you can track your progress over time. This activity will also orient you to the topics to be examined during your study of assessment through a clear statement of the learning targets you are to attain.

> **Cross-Reference to *Student-Involved Classroom Assessment*, 3d ed.**
>
> The use of portfolios will be covered in Chapter 14.
>
> **Additional Materials Needed**
>
> WORKBOOK: Appendix A, "Classroom Assessment Confidence Questionnaire," "Sample Working Folder/Portfolio Cover Sheet," and "Assessment Principles"; Appendix B, "Classroom Assessment Quality Rubrics." OTHER: Large expandable file folder and small manila folder.
>
> **Time Required**
>
> Open, it's homework.

What to Do

1. *Recommended.* Answer the questions on the "Classroom Assessment Confidence Questionnaire" in Appendix A. This will take about 10 minutes. Remember, this is a baseline—it's okay to be honest, no one else will see this unless you want them to.

2. *Recommended.* Select an assessment (test, quiz, essay test, or performance assessment) that you have recently used or taken. This can be one that someone else developed or it can be one that you developed yourself. *If you are a current teacher, it must be one that you administered, scored, and recorded for use within the context of your teaching.*

    Using the "Classroom Assessment Quality Rubrics" provided in Appendix B, reflect on the quality of this assessment and write a brief analysis. What are its strengths? What things might you improve? Is it appropriate for all of your students? This might be difficult the first time you try it. But, that's okay, do the best you can. You'll get better at this over time— that's the goal of having a baseline.

3. *Optional.* Write or draw about your current understanding of why quality classroom assessment is essential and why there is so much emphasis on it right now. How essential is classroom assessment to the well-being of students?

4. *Optional.* Consider the "Assessment Principles" in Appendix A. These were crafted by a group of educators who were trying to reach consensus on their values with regard to assessment. We don't necessarily intend them to be accepted as is; rather, they are a springboard for you to articulate and consider your own values. Which principles affirm your own beliefs? Why? Are there any with which you disagree? Why? What concerns might you have about any of them?

   Remember, it's okay to say what you think—no one else will see your comments unless you want them to. Additionally, you won't hurt anyone's feelings by making supportive or questioning comments—this is anonymous.

5. *Recommended.* Complete a portfolio cover sheet (see Appendix A, "Sample Working Folder/Portfolio Cover Sheet") for each item above that you have chosen for your portfolio. Place these items in your manila folder. Label the folder in an appropriate fashion ("My Assessment Growth Portfolio" or anything else that is appealing to you). Place the thin (portfolio) folder into the large expandable (working) file folder. Keep it close by for easy access.

Honoring Diversity in Learning—Analyzing an Assessment for Quality

Do you think of things as a whole or do you more easily see the parts of a whole that contribute to its quality? Different types of thinking are valued in different cultures. Also, within the same culture, various of us gravitate naturally toward different thinking patterns.

If you are used to thinking of things as a whole, here's how to think analytically, in the manner suggested in "What to Do" item 2. Thinking analytically requires pulling apart the main dimensions or traits of a whole assessment that contribute to its overall quality. In other words, we're asking you to think of the assessment you choose to analyze not as a whole, but in terms of the extent to which it has clear targets, has clear users and uses, involves students, uses the best assessment method, samples achievement well, and avoids possible sources of bias and distortion.

If you do not normally think in these terms, begin by looking at the assessment as a whole—How good is it? Then list your reasons why— What does it do well? What could be improved? Finally, compare your reasons to the dimensions of quality listed above. It is likely that many of the strengths and areas for improvement you have listed reveal the traits (standards) of sound assessment.

Activity Intro-2

Establishing Group Norms in a Learning Team*

Optional

Goals/Rationale

Effective groups usually have a set of "norms" that outline behavioral expectations for participation—how members should act to ensure a climate that is safe and conducive to learning for all. These include such things as active listening, taking turns, commitment to doing homework, confidentiality, respecting all opinions, taking responsibility for one's own learning, beginning and ending on time, giving everyone the opportunity to share their experiences at each meeting, and being on time. This activity results in group norms for your learning team.

> **Cross-Reference to *Student-Involved Classroom Assessment*, 3d ed.**
>
> None.
>
> **Additional Materials Needed**
>
> Index cards or Post-It™ Notes, pens/pencils, chart pack paper, tape, self-adhesive colored dots.
>
> **Time Required**
>
> 30–45 minutes.

What to Do

1. (5 minutes) Review the rationale for developing group norms and give five index cards or Post-It™ Notes to each person in the group.

2. (5–10 minutes) Ask each person to reflect on behaviors they consider ideal for productive group interaction and work. Each conducive behavior or action should be written on a separate card or Post-It™ Note. If you need to prime the pump, think about these questions:

    a. How does a group of individuals become a team?

    b. What keeps team members working well together?

    c. How does a team function effectively?

*Adapted from Joan Richardson, "Norms put the golden rule into practice for groups," *Tools for Schools*, NSDC, (August/September 1999), 1–6; Carlene Murphy, Charlotte Danielson, and Agnes Crawford, "Folder one—Learning through study groups, in *An ASCD professional inquiry kit: Performance assessment*," (pp. 1-4) edited by Judy Arter (Alexandria, VA: ASCD, 1996); and Linda Munger, *Facilitation skills for effective teamwork* (Des Moines, IA: Iowa City Community School District, 1994).

3. (5–15 minutes) Every opportunity should be taken to ensure anonymity. This can be accomplished by gathering and shuffling cards or having everyone randomly place their Post-It™ Notes on a piece of chart paper. Discuss the ideas and group similar ones together.

4. (5 minutes) Summarize the norms that have been suggested onto a sheet of chart paper.

5. (5 minutes) Give five self-adhesive colored dots to each person. Members vote for ideas by placing a colored dot next to the idea. Dots can be allocated in any manner—for example, a separate dot for each idea or all five dots for one idea.

6. (5 minutes) Tally the dots. Make sure that the final list of group norms will be agreed to by everyone.

Notes:

PART I

Understanding the Classroom Assessment Challenge

A Story of Classroom Assessment Success

Big Ideas in This Chapter

This chapter answers the following guiding question:

What does it look like and how is learning enhanced when classroom assessment is working to its full productive potential to motivate student learning?

Rick begins the journey into classroom assessment with a scenario that casts the process in a very positive light. The story about Emily establishes the point that constructive classroom assessment environments are achievable. But, the chapter stresses that such environments can be achieved only if we all attain appropriate levels of assessment literacy. The purpose of this chapter is to motivate readers to care deeply about their classroom assessment responsibilities and to want to learn as much as they can about quality assessment.

The **General Principles** in this chapter are as follows:

1. The most powerful forms and applications of assessment take place day to day in the classroom. Classroom assessment affects students—for better or worse.

2. Classroom assessment reaches its full potential to help students learn only if teachers adhere to sound assessment

practices. Violate principles of sound assessment practice and students will be hurt. Sound assessment practice means that you:

a. Know and understand what it means to succeed academically in your classroom—what it looks like when your students are making adequate progress toward success. Further, it means that others in your field would agree with your definition of academic success.

b. Can transform your vision of success into assessment exercises and scoring schemes that provide dependable information about student success.

c. Understand how to use both assessment and its results to help students learn, to believe in themselves as learners, and to strive for academic success. Students are the key users of assessment information.

d. Understand and can apply principles of effective communication about student achievement.

Links to Subsequent Chapters

1.   This chapter is the first of two that discuss the users and uses of assessment information. The focus in this chapter is the critical importance of students as the key assessment users.

2.   This chapter also begins to build the argument for the importance of sound classroom assessment. Assessment affects students' lives. This theme is carried throughout the book.

Portfolio Reminder

We recommend that you develop a portfolio that tracks your growth as a learner about classroom assessment. It is important to keep material handy so that as you build your portfolio you will have items to add to it. Following are some suggestions:

1.   A learning log or journal, in which you record your responses to (a) the "Times for Reflection" that occur throughout Chapter 1, and (b) structured questions at the end of Chapter 1.

2.   Artifacts (worksheets, outlines, student work, etc.) that result from any of the practice activities undertaken in Chapter 1.

3.   Other artifacts from the classroom that lead to ideas about, insights about, or growth in classroom assessment.

Roadmap

Activity	Title	Activity Description	Time	Icons
1-1	*Inside the Black Box* Discussion	The impact of classroom assessment on student achievement. The need to involve students in assessment. *Cross-reference to Chapter 1:* General Principles 1 and 2.	30 min; rest is prework	CONSOLIDATE UNDERSTANDING
1-2	Pop Quiz	The impact of classroom assessment on motivation. *Cross-reference to Chapter 1:* General Principle 1.	20 min	QUICK CHECK
1-3	*Our Own Experiences with Assessment and Implications for Practice	This activity connects your own personal experiences with assessment to motivation and sound assessment practice. *Cross-reference to Chapter 1:* General Principles 1 and 2.	30 min	CONSOLIDATE UNDERSTANDING

*Recommended

Activity 1-1   *Inside the Black Box* Discussion

Optional

Keep these items in your working folder. As needed, use the "Working Folder/Portfolio Cover Sheet" in Appendix A to note the reasons you added an item.

Goals/Rationale

This article (see "Additional Materials Needed") presents the research about the dramatic impact of classroom assessment on student achievement. It also describes the changes in classroom assessment that need to occur in order to realize this impact. Among the changes are improved quality and student involvement.

> **Cross-Reference to *Student-Involved Classroom Assessment*, 3d ed.**
>
> General Principles 1 and 2: High-quality classroom assessment is essential for students' well-being.
>
> **Additional Materials Needed**
>
> *Inside the Black Box: Raising Standards Through Classroom Assessment* by P. Black and D. Wiliam, *Phi Delta Kappan, 80* (October 1998), 139–148, or from Kappan's Website at www.pdkintl.org/kappan/kbla9810.htm.
>
> **Time Required**
>
> 30 minutes; rest is prework.

What to Do

Part A: Preparation/Prework

As you read the article, make note of the following points:

1. What is the evidence of the impact of improved classroom assessment on student achievement?

2. What student-involvement methods are mentioned in the paper that can result in these achievement gains?

3. What other changes in classroom assessment need to happen to realize these achievement gains?

4. Will these changes work exactly the same for all students, or might the cultural or linguistic background of certain students affect the way they involve themselves? What might be different?

Part B: Do with Colleagues

(30 minutes) In the team meeting, do the following:

1. Summarize everyone's notes on the four questions above and the impact this information has had on your beliefs about classroom assessment.

2. List five specific examples of how the information in this article reinforces the information in Chapter 1.

3. Discuss which methods of student involvement are most appropriate in your setting.

4. Who else needs to know about the results summarized in the article? How will you let them know?

Pop Quiz   Activity 1-2

Optional

Goals/Rationale

We've all seen productive and counterproductive things happen with respect to assessment in the classroom. This activity brings it down to specific cases that make motivation (or lack of it) real.

> **Cross-Reference to *Student-Involved Classroom Assessment*, 3d ed.**
>
> General Principle 1: The most important assessments are those done in the classroom.
>
> **Additional Materials Needed**
>
> None.
>
> **Time Required**
>
> 20 minutes.

What to Do

1. (10 minutes) Read each of the scenarios in the worksheet, "Classroom Assessment Scenarios—Motivational or Not?," and decide if the likely outcome for the student(s) will be positive motivation and belief in their ability to learn or limiting motivation and decreased belief in their ability to learn. Circle "thumbs up" or "thumbs down" as appropriate. If you can't be sure of the motivational effects, circle (?). Write down your reasons.

> **Honoring Diversity**
>
> Might some students react in ways you do not expect? Who might they be? What might motivate students in other cultures?

2.   (10 minutes) Discuss your answers with a partner, if available, and add your own similar experiences.

Classroom Assessment Scenarios—Motivational or Not?

Scenario	Motivational Effect	Why?
Alan is having his students score each other's quizzes and then call out the scores so he can plot them on the board.	👎 👍 ?	
Students in Eileen's class are discussing samples of anonymous science lab notes to decide which are great examples, which have some good points, and which don't tell the story of the lab at all well. They're gradually developing criteria for their own lab "learning logs."	👎 👍 ?	
Catherine has just received a grade on a report she wrote for social studies. She got a B. There were no other comments.	👎 👍 ?	
Students in Henry's basic writing class are there because they have failed to meet the state's writing competency requirements. Henry tells students that the year will consist of teaching them to write. Competence at the end will be all that matters.	👎 👍 ?	
Jeremy's teacher tells him that his test scores have been so dismal so far that no matter what he does from then on he will fail the class.	👎 👍 ?	
Pat's latest story is being read aloud for the class to critique. Like each of her classmates, she's been asked to take notes during this "peer assessment" so that she can revise her work later.	👎 👍 ?	

Our Own Experiences with Assessment and Implications for Practice

Activity 1-3

Recommended

Goals/Rationale

This activity allows you to draw on your own experience with assessment to (a) examine the points in the book about the effect of classroom assessment on motivation, and (b) draw inferences for sound classroom assessment practice. Participants usually recreate the standards for quality assessment described in the chapter. This experience tends to make the principles of sound assessment more memorable.

> **Cross-Reference to *Student-Involved Classroom Assessment*, 3d ed.**
>
> General Principles 1 and 2: High-quality classroom assessment is essential for students' well-being.
>
> **Additional Materials Needed**
>
> Chart paper and pens.
>
> **Time Required**
>
> 30 minutes.

What to Do

1. Prepare a sheet of chart paper to look like item 2 on the "Our Own Experiences" worksheet.

2. (5 minutes) Individually complete the worksheet titled "Our Own Experiences with Assessment and Implications for Practice." To help prime the pump, consider the following questions:

    a. Think of your own experiences being assessed. What emotions do you recall? How about when your teacher reminded you to tell your parents it was report card time again? How about when your teacher came in with a surprise quiz? How about the morning of your college admissions test or the GRE?

    b. Do you recall any teacher who used the assessment process in a way that caused you to want to succeed? How did you feel? What did that teacher do to make assessment a positive experience?

   c. Do you recall a class in which an assessment was a negative experience? What were your feelings? What were the characteristics of the experience that caused it to be so negative?

3.   (5 minutes) Share your experiences with a partner (or with the group, if it is small).

4.   (15 minutes) Combine the thoughts of everyone onto the chart paper you prepared for item 1.

   a. How do your lists of what happens to students when classroom assessment is done "well" or "poorly" compare to the information in Chapter 1?

   b. How does your list of the characteristics of assessment "done well" compare to Rick's statement of the nature of sound classroom assessment as stated in the chapter?

- In your experience, has assessment "done well" included a clear idea of "what it means to succeed academically in the classroom—what it looks like when students are making adequate progress toward success"?

- In your experience, has assessment "done well" included the "transformation of the vision of success into assessment exercises and scoring schemes that provide dependable information about student success? This includes having a clear idea of what is to be assessed, knowing how the results will be used and who will use them, matching targets and uses to assessment methods, sampling well, and avoiding factors that might bias or distort our judgment of student competence"?

- In your experience, has assessment "done well" included "using both the assessment process and its results to help students learn, to believe in themselves as learners, and to strive for academic success"? In your experience has it included "involving students in their own assessment"?

- In your experience, has assessment "done well" included "applying the principles of effective communication about student achievement"?

   c. What actions might you take in the classroom based on the characteristics you listed for assessments "done poorly" and "done well"?

5. (5 minutes) You have probably had more positive experiences with assessment than have many students. After all, you presumably wouldn't be where you are now if you weren't good at tests. How might a student with mostly negative test-taking experiences answer the preceding questions?

Our Own Experiences with Assessment and Implications for Practice

1. Share with a partner:

    One GOOD experience you've had being assessed. What made it good?

    One BAD experience you've had being assessed. What made it bad?

2. With others in your group, answer the following questions:

What happens to students when classroom assessment is done well?	What does "done well" look like?
What happens to students when classroom assessment is done poorly?	What does "done poorly" look like?

Notes:

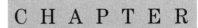

The Role of Assessment in Student Success

Big Ideas in This Chapter

This chapter answers the following guiding question:

What contributions can and should assessment—both large-scale and classroom—make to the process of helping students succeed in school?

The **General Principles** in this chapter are as follows:

1. Assessments serve many purposes in schooling; that is, they inform a variety of important users and uses, from policy makers to students and parents. All these users are important and deserve information suited to their information needs. While large-scale assessments can meet the needs of policy makers, they can't meet the needs of teachers, students and parents. Implications:

    a. We need a balanced view of assessment, one that values and supports excellence in both large-scale and class-room assessment.

    b. Use determines design. The assessment designs most useful for large-scale assessment probably won't be those most useful for classroom assessment.

    c.   There are different uses for classroom assessment that go far beyond grading. These uses might require different designs and features.

2.   Students, teachers, and parents make decisions based on classroom assessment information. In the order of priorities, students are the most important users, followed by their teachers, and then their parents. Classroom assessments need to be of high quality to meet the information needs of all three groups.

3.   To understand why students are the most important users of assessment information, one must carefully examine and come to understand the relationship between assessment and student motivation. As the result of this relationship, classroom assessments have to be designed to involve students and to have a positive impact on them.

Links to Previous Chapters

This is the second of two chapters on the users and uses of assessment information. While the previous chapter built the case for student involvement and the impact of improved classroom assessment on student achievement, this chapter takes a broader view. It begins by listing all the users and uses of assessment, resulting in the need for balance in assessment.

Having established the need for balance, the chapter proceeds to describe in detail why students are the primary users—the link between assessment, student motivation, and school success.

Links to Subsequent Chapters

Assessment affects students' lives. This theme is carried throughout and informs the remainder of the book.

Portfolio Reminder

As you work through Chapter 2, you might generate material that you can use to track your increasing confidence in and knowledge about classroom assessment. Follow the suggestions laid out in Chapter 1 for such entries.

Roadmap

Activity	Title	Activity Description	Time	Icons
2-1	*Balance in Assessment	The need for both large-scale and classroom assessment. *Cross-reference to Chapter 2: General Principles 1 and 2.*	20-30 min	CONSOLIDATE UNDERSTANDING
2-2	Interview Others on Their Uses of Assessment	Draw conclusions about current classroom uses of assessment information. *Cross-reference to Chapter 2: General Principle 1.*	25-40 min; rest is home-work	APPLY LEARNING
2-3	Student Assessment Questionnaire	How do your students use the results of assessments? *Cross-reference to Chapter 2: General Principles 2 and 3.*	15-20 min; rest is home-work	APPLY LEARNING
2-4	What Went Wrong? –Case Discussion	What in the chapter provides insights on the triggers for the student actions depicted in the cases? *Cross-reference to Chapter 2: General Principles 2 and 3.*	20-30 min	CONSOLIDATE UNDERSTANDING
2-5	*Imagine! Assessments That Energize Students*—Video Discussion	The *Imagine! Assessments That Energize Students* video leads you through the ideas linking assessment, student motivation, and school success. *Cross-reference to Chapter 2: General Principles 2 and 3.*	90 min	CONSOLIDATE UNDERSTANDING
2-6	Analyze Sample Assessments for Clear Users and Uses	What does it look like in actual classroom assessments when users and uses are clearly specified? *Cross-reference to Chapter 2: General Principle 1.*	50-90 min	CONSOLIDATE UNDERSTANDING

*Recommended

Activity 2-1   Balance in Assessment

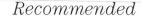

Recommended

Goals/Rationale

There can be two distinct reactions to the idea of balance in assessment. First, there might not be acceptance of the idea that classroom assessment is important. Second, there is a natural tendency for some educators to consider standardized testing as a waste of time and harmful to students. Our challenge is not to eliminate large-scale assessment but to learn how to use such assessments well and in balance with classroom assessments to help students prosper. The problem is not with the assessments themselves, but with the way the results are used. Each can help students learn if used properly. This activity helps learners think through these issues.

> **Cross-Reference to *Student-Involved Classroom Assessment*, 3d ed.**
>
> General Principles 1 and 2: There are different users and uses for assessment, but students are the most important users.
>
> **Additional Materials Needed**
>
> None.
>
> **Time Required**
>
> 20–30 minutes.

What to Do

1. (5-10 minutes) Use the worksheet, "Standard 2: Users and Uses," to individually list the various users of assessment information. Then list what decisions each user makes on the basis of that information.

2. (5 minutes) Check whether each user/use on the list depends mostly on large-scale or classroom assessment information.

3. (10–15 minutes) Think through or discuss the implications. **Don't look at the following list until you've generated your own ideas!** Some possible conclusions:

    a. Large-scale standardized tests do have an important function. They serve the information needs of some educators. Whose needs would not be met without standardized tests?

b. Classroom assessment is essential to the well-being of students. Many very important decisions are made on the basis of these data. What would happen if classroom assessments were not of high quality?

c. Classroom assessment uses go far beyond grading.

d. Students are important consumers and users of assessment information. We have to know what we're doing to minimize negative effects and maximize positive effects.

e. Both large-scale and classroom assessments are important for the well-being of students.

Standard 2: Users and Uses

USERS and USES—Who uses assessment information about students? What do they use it for?		Which LEVEL of ASSESSMENT does each user depend mostly on?	
User	Decisions Each User Might Make	Large-scale (L)	Classroom (C)

Conclusions about classroom assessment:

Activity 2-2   Interview Others on Their Uses of Assessment

Optional

Goals/Rationale

How people use assessment and think it should be used reveals their (sometimes contradictory) underlying beliefs about assessment itself, about the role they see for assessment in student learning, and the likelihood that they will or will not use assessment results to guide their own, their students', and others' actions. This activity involves using personal communication—interviews—to create a picture of the multiple uses of assessment in your setting, and sets the stage for discussion about common goals for assessment. You will also have the opportunity to practice the kinds of questioning that opens and encourages important conversations about assessment uses.

> **Cross-Reference to *Student-Involved Classroom Assessment*, 3d ed.**
>
> General Principle 1: There are many users and uses of assessment information.
>
> **Additional Materials Needed**
>
> None.
>
> **Time Required**
>
> 25–40 minutes; rest is homework.

What to Do

Part A: Preparation

1. (5–10 minutes) Read the worksheet, "Preparing to Interview: Coaching for Learning," for information about how to question others in a way that opens and encourages conversation rather than cutting it off. For purposes of this activity the terms *interviewing* and *coaching* are used synonymously.

2. (5-10 minutes) Think about your purposes for conducting interviews and who you will interview. What do you want to know about who uses assessment information and for what purposes? How will *you* use the information? For those in schools, you might interview a peer or someone else with whom you're comfortable. For those without access to a K-12 classroom, interview a professor in one of your classes, a classmate who is currently teaching, or one of your previous teachers. Brainstorm a list of possible questions to ask.

3. (10 minutes) If you are working in a group, use the following procedure to refine your brainstormed list of questions. Using the worksheet, "Turning Conversations About Assessment On or Off: It's Your Choice," practice interviewing with a partner or set up a "fishbowl" in which a pair takes the roles of interviewer and interviewee while the rest of the team notes the reactions of each to practice questions. Discuss as a group which questions are "openers" that encourage more conversation, which are "closers" that shut down the interview before it can really get started, and why.

4. (5-10 minutes) Revisit the brainstormed list of interview questions. Are there some that you can improve or refine? Some that should be removed? Are there other questions that would be helpful? If you're part of a team, will you all ask the same questions?

Part B: Homework

1. Set a time and comfortable place for your interview and decide how you will record the results of the interview.

2. After the interview, consider what you learned about how assessment information is used. Think about:

    a. The primary way your interviewee uses assessment information.

    b. Your thoughts and reactions—What agrees with your perceptions? What were you surprised by?

    c. Implications for your own practice.

Multicultural Considerations

In some cultures, questioning without a larger context is simply not done. Asking questions that you (the questioner) know the answers to is also not common in some cultures. In the classroom, for example, some students are from cultures that define a good student as one who listens and observes carefully and quietly. The common American practice of public teacher questioning of students and the expectation that individual students will reply publicly before others is a very new and often difficult experience for students from outside our primary culture.

Because your purpose is to get honest and accurate ideas about the ways that others use assessment data, you may want to consider what key information your interviewee needs to feel comfortable before the interview begins. To help bridge different cultural communication patterns, you might want to do the following: Explain that the interview is part of your own learning about assessment. Be sure that your partner knows how the interview information will and will not be used. Give your interviewee the opportunity to ask you about the interview, why you're involved in deepening your assessment literacy, and make sure it's clear that you are not trying to judge her assessment practices.

Preparing to Interview: Coaching for Learning

A brief word about coaching for learning

Throughout this book there will be opportunities to learn from others—from classmates, fellow teachers, professors, your learning team and, where possible, from K-12 students. One of the most powerful ways to encourage learning is through coaching—working together with another to deepen the learning and practice of each. Based on the work of Art Costa and others, the term *coaching* describes a process that focuses on the following:

1. Mutual benefit

2. Using open questions to begin and expand substantive conversations

3. Reflecting and describing what has been observed as an "extra set of eyes and ears" in the classroom

4. Prompting reflective thinking and problem solving

5. Using insights from coaching reflections to take action to improve learning

The effects of coaching questions

In this activity, as you work with and interview others about their uses of assessment, consider the power of your questions to either open and expand the conversation or to close your interviewee's mouth, ears, and eyes. The questions you ask can create defensiveness and block learning when they reveal that you've already judged and found the interviewee's assessment practices wanting. Coaches are not judges; they ask questions that encourage the interviewee to thoughtfully consider and make explicit their uses of assessment and then engage in follow-up conversations that reveal the interviewee's thinking about his goals for assessment, the assessment practices in use, and their impact on student learning.

Good coaching is more than tactfulness

If you decide to interview someone whose uses of assessment may need some rethinking or major adjustment, remember that your purpose is twofold—to gain insights into the assessment beliefs and practices of your interviewee, and to cause that person to more closely examine her current uses of assessment. Remind yourself too, that the person who is doing the most work (in this case thinking and reflecting) is the one who is learning the most.

Some possible ground rules

1. Choose questions that OPEN conversations, such as, "I'd like you to tell me about some of the uses you make of assessment information in your classroom."

2. If asked to make a judgment about your interviewee's uses of assessment, turn the question back to him with a question such as, "What do you think?" "Are there some things you're thinking of doing differently?" OR *describe* what you know of the person's practice (without evaluative terms) and then turn the question back.

3. Follow up responses that don't give you a very clear picture of assessment uses with a probe such as, "Can you tell me more about _____?"

4. Prompt your interviewee to consider the impact of her specific uses of assessment on student motivation and learning.

5. Encourage your interviewee to talk about how students are involved in assessment.

6. Invite your coaching partner to summarize current uses and thoughts about future uses of assessment.

7. Close with thanks and a description of what you've learned; invite the interviewee's comments and reactions as well.

Turning Conversations About Assessment On or Off: It's Your Choice

The questions below include samples of both "opening" questions and those that stop or "close" the responses of an interviewee. Which is which?

1. Why aren't you using other forms of assessment?

2. What kinds of assessment are you using in your classroom? What information do you gain from each?

3. What does assessment do for students in your class?

4. How does assessment contribute to student learning in your class?

5. Don't you realize that multiple-choice tests are completely inappropriate for some kinds of learning targets?

6. Have you noticed how many students are turned off by the assessments you use?

7. How can you include early work in your grades when more recent work really shows what your students have mastered?

8. What data are most useful to you as you decide on next steps in instruction? Why?

9. What's wrong with your assessments?

10. I've noticed that some of the assessments are biased against minority students. What comments do you have about that?

11. Are there students who seem to have great difficulty with assessments in this class? Why do you think they're struggling?

12. Are you comfortable involving students in developing assessments? Are there benefits you see in this practice?

13. Why do you use assessment as a behavior management tool?

14. How do you use information from standardized tests?

15. Who do you consider the most important users of assessment information? Why?

Characteristics of questions that open and encourage conversations:

Characteristics of questions that shut off or close conversations:

Student Assessment Questionnaire

Activity 2-3

Optional

Goals/Rationale

One of the primary premises of Rick's book is that we can profitably involve students in assessment. This activity gives you the chance to ask them directly the uses they make of assessment results and what they think about the assessments they are taking.

> **Cross-Reference to *Student-Involved Classroom Assessment*, 3d ed.**
>
> General Principles 2 and 3: Students are important users of assessment information.
>
> **Additional Materials Needed**
>
> None.
>
> **Time Required**
>
> 15–20 minutes; rest is homework.

What to Do

Part A: Preparation

1. (5 minutes) Examine the worksheet, "Assessment Questionnaire (Middle and High School)," to familiarize yourself with its contents.

2. (10–15 minutes) Decide how you will use the questionnaire to gather insights from students about the assessments they encounter in your class. Options:

    a. As an action research startup questionnaire that you give to all students (anonymously).

    b. To choose several students to interview in more depth. You might, for example select students who have done very well on past assessments and others who may see themselves as constant "losers" in the assessment process.

    c. As individual questions that are discussed by student groups and reported anonymously for the group by students.

    d. As food for thought when creating your own questionnaire to use with students.

Part B: Try with Students

Prepare students for the questionnaire by letting them know that you're interested in their experiences with assessment and how they use information from assessments to make decisions about learning. You'd also like to know how assessment has affected them because you want to re-examine your own uses of assessment data. This is their chance to help you see assessment from their point of view. Have students respond, then analyze the results, discuss, and reflect on what you've learned about how students use current assessments.

Assessment Questionnaire
(Middle and High School)

A. General Questions

1. Why are you taking this test? (Check all that apply.)

   ❏ I don't have a clue.

   ❏ For a grade.

   ❏ My teacher requires it.

   ❏ To show how I compare with other students.

   ❏ To show what I've learned.

   ❏ Other: _____

2. Who's the test information for?

3. How will *you* use information from your test?

B. Assessment Preferences

1. If you had a choice about how you'd show all the facts you know about a topic, which kind of assessment would you choose? Why?

   ❏ Multiple-choice test

   ❏ True/False

   ❏ Matching

   ❏ Short answer/fill-in

   ❏ An essay about the topic

   ❏ An oral presentation

   ❏ A chart, poster, drawing, mural, model that I explain

   ❏ A demonstration

   ❏ An oral exam

   ❏ Other: _____

   Why?

2. If you had a choice about how you'd show what you can do, which kind of assessment would you choose? Why?

    ❏   Multiple-choice test
    ❏   True/false
    ❏   Matching
    ❏   Short answer/fill-in
    ❏   An essay about the topic
    ❏   An oral presentation
    ❏   A chart, poster, drawing, mural, model that I explain
    ❏   A demonstration
    ❏   An oral exam
    ❏   Other: _____

    Why?

3. If you had a choice between solving problems that the teacher creates or making up problems that you see in life around you (that you also solve), which would you choose? Why?

C. **What do you do with the assessment information you get from . . . ?**

    1. The district's annual standardized test report (ITBS, SAT9, CTBS, etc.)

        ❏   Nothing
        ❏   Hide it/burn it
        ❏   See where I am in relation to a national average
        ❏   Look for hints about my strengths and weaknesses
        ❏   Choose courses I can do well in
        ❏   Decide if I should try for a selective college
        ❏   Other: _____

    My answer depends on:

2.   Multiple-choice, true/false, matching or short answer tests
    you take in class

  ❏   Decide what to study

  ❏   Nothing

  ❏   Decided on courses to take

  ❏   Decide if it's worth studying

  ❏   Think about what I need to do to pass/get a higher grade

  ❏   Other: _____

My answer depends on:

3.   A performance assessment such as:

Product	**Performance**
Report	*Presentation*
Chart	*Demonstration*
Display	*Debate*
Artwork	*Role play*

  ❏   Decide if it belongs in my portfolio

  ❏   Keep it to study from

  ❏   Edit/revise/add to it for a better grade/higher score

  ❏   Use it to check whether my work is getting closer to
       standard

  ❏   Think about what I need to do to pass/get a higher grade

  ❏   Nothing

  ❏   Other: _____

My answer depends on:

**If I were in charge, the main purpose of assessment
would be . . .**

Activity 2-4   What Went Wrong?—Case Discussion

Optional

Goals/Rationale

This activity gives you the opportunity to practice solving real-life problems based on what you've learned in this chapter.

> **Cross-Reference to *Student-Involved Classroom Assessment*, 3d ed.**
>
> General Principles 2 and 3: Students are the most important users of assessment information; the motivational implications of assessment.
>
> **Additional Materials Needed**
> None.
>
> **Time Required**
> 20–30 minutes.

What to Do

1. (10–15 minutes) Choose and read one of the two cases on the "Case Studies" worksheet: "Maryland Boy Fakes His Own Disappearance" or "The Disappearing Motivation."

2. (10–15 minutes) Think about or discuss the following:

    a. What in the chapter provides insights on triggers for the student actions depicted? How might the classroom assessment, record-keeping, and communication processes be contributing to the situation?

    b. What could be done about it?

    c. What similar situations do you know about?

Case Studies

Md. Boy Fakes His Own Disappearance[1]

11-Year-Old Says He Feared Punishment for Bad Report Card

The ransom note, handwritten in the script of a child, provided the first clue about the possible kidnapper. "I got Keith. You need $400 by 5:30," it said.

But Prince George's County police wouldn't figure out the kidnapper's identity until 10:45 pm Wednesday, seven hours after the note was found, when the 11-year-old Landover boy returned home and later confessed that he had faked his own disappearance.

The boy told police he staged the hoax because he feared the punishment he would receive for bringing home a bad report card, police spokesman Royce Holloway said.

"We're certainly glad that the incident turned out the way it did," Holloway said. "Sometimes when young minds think in the wrong direction, they do the wrong thing."

It was 3:44 pm Wednesday when the boy's stepfather called police to report what he believed at the time was a kidnapping.

The parents became concerned when the boy did not return home as expected by 2:30 pm.

The note, written on a piece of notebook paper, had been left on the front door. Obviously written by a child, the note contained no specific instructions. That made police suspicious, Holloway said, but officers immediately began investigating the disappearance as a "critical missing person." The FBI was also contacted.

For the next several hours, officers canvassed the apartment complex on Landover Road and the surrounding neighborhood. They talked to neighbors, who reported seeing the boy get off the bus, Holloway said. Later that evening, the boy was spotted walking through the apartment complex.

Police escorted him home, then to police headquarters, where he confessed, Holloway said. The boy had spent most of the evening at a friend's house.

"It shows that we take these things seriously," Holloway said.

No charges have been filed in the incident.

[1]Lisa Frazier, Washington *Post*, 22 November 1997, p. G-3. Reprinted by permission.

The Disappearing Motivation

A Mom tells her story:

"When Mario first started school, he was so cute and enthusiastic. He couldn't wait to get to class each day. He seemed to think so much of his teachers. He did very well academically, too. So did his friends from the neighborhood.

"But about fifth and sixth grade, this began to change. I can remember other moms beginning to ask the same thing: 'What happened? What changed?' At about 11 or 12 years old, our kids began to care less and less about school. Some parents attribute it to adolescence. They lose interest in academic things, what with hormones, girls, and all. But I don't buy that totally. Others think it's the teachers in those grades. But Mario's teachers seem to have been terrific. I think there must be more to it. Still other parents attribute the problem to the peer group. It's just not 'cool' to care about school. But I don't know. Mario has always been pretty independent. I just can't figure it out. We even took him to the doctor for a physical exam to see if he's okay. He is.

"The interesting thing is that the transition was slow: less homework to do or less time devoted to doing homework, more frequent expressions of frustration with his teachers, a growing sense of boredom with the whole enterprise. No teacher ever complained about Mario. But, you know, he just seemed to give up on himself. He began to think it was futile—he just couldn't do it. His grades slid gradually over a few years. He still isn't failing exactly, but his grades are low. And he's negative about school!

"At teacher conferences, they dismiss the problem. 'He's just going through a phase,' they say. 'He'll get past it and his grades will return to the top. He's such a smart boy.'

"When I ask them how they plan to motivate him in positive ways, they have no reply. All they say is, 'When he realizes what it's going to take to get into college, he'll straighten up.' But it may be too late by then. He'll be so far behind.

"I'm at my wits end. What should I do?"

Activity 2-5 *Imagine! Assessments That Energize Students*—Video Discussion

Optional

Goals/Rationale

Have an alternative learning style? Want another approach to thinking about the content of this chapter? The Assessment Training Institute video, *Imagine! Assessments That Energize Students*, takes you step by step through the ideas associated with assessment, student motivation, and school success. The video comes complete with a facilitator's guide that helps you work through key issues.

> **Cross-Reference to *Student-Involved Classroom Assessment*, 3d ed.**
>
> General Principles 2 and 3: Students are the most important users of assessment information; the motivational implications of assessment.
>
> **Additional Materials Needed**
>
> VIDEO: *Imagine! Assessments That Energize Students*, available from the Assessment Training Institute, 800-480-3060.
>
> **Time Required**
>
> 90 minutes.

What to Do

Follow the steps that are clearly laid out in the facilitator's guide.

Analyze Sample Assessments for Clear Users and Uses

Activity 2-6

Optional

Goals/Rationale

In some classroom assessments it is very clear who the users and uses are intended to be. But, in other assessments it is not clear at all why the teacher wants to collect the information. You might be interested to see if you can detect the users and uses in some real classroom assessments, and then think about the implications for your own practice.

> **Cross-Reference to *Student-Involved Classroom Assessment*, 3d ed.**
>
> Guiding Principle 1: What are the uses of classroom assessments?
>
> **Additional Materials Needed**
>
> WORKBOOK: Appendix B, Sample rubrics 2a, 2b, and 2c; "Assessment Sample 4: Exhibition of Mastery."
>
> **Time Required**
>
> 50–90 minutes.

What to Do

1. (10 minutes) Read through the rubrics, "Standard 2a—Why: Clear and Appropriate Users and Uses," "Standard 2b—Student Involvement," and "Standard 2c—Communicates Effectively to Users and Uses" (*Workbook* Appendix B). These

rubrics describe the types of things to look for in an assessment to determine (a) how clear the uses are (rubric 2a), (b) the extent and nature of student involvement (rubric 2b), and (c) how the author has planned for communicating results (rubric 2c).

2.   (5–10 minutes) Do you agree—do the rubrics cover those things that truly describe assessment quality with respect to clear and appropriate users and uses? What would you add?

3.   (10-15 minutes) Look at "Sample Assessment 4, Exhibition of Mastery" in *Workbook* Appendix B. Can you find any statements of users and uses? Using the rubrics, try to put "scores" on the assessment for the trait of "users/uses" by matching the assessment to the statements under each level of the rubrics.

(*Hints:* Did you notice that, although there is an allusion to the purpose of the assessment—"exit outcomes" and "final exhibition"—the author makes no real statement of how the results will be used and who will use them? Will this result in a grade? A judgment of overall mastery? Do students have to "pass" this assessment in order to move on?

Did you also notice that there is no student involvement and no acknowledgement that student involvement might be a desirable thing, especially with so complex a "final exhibition"?

Did you note that the author has not considered communication at all? There is a rubric, but it is not clear how it is to be used.)

---

4.   (10–30 minutes) Look at the other assessments in Appendix B. What do you notice about them with respect to clear users and uses? (Writeups of each assessment are also included in Appendix B, but don't peek ahead.)

5.   (10 minutes) Think about other assessments you've seen or used. In what percentage is it clear who the users and what the uses are? What users and uses are usually specified?

6.   (5–15 minutes) Think about or discuss the questions:

   a. Does <u>every</u> assessment have to involve students or does there just need to be a pattern of involving students over time?

   b. Does <u>every</u> assessment have to plan for good communication or does there just need to be a pattern of good communication over time?

   c. Does <u>every</u> assessment have to be clear on users and uses or does there just need to be a pattern of clarity over time?

   d. What are the implications for the assessments you use in your own classroom? What might you do differently?

Defining Achievement Targets

Big Ideas in This Chapter

This chapter answers the following guiding question:

What kinds of achievement targets must teachers assess in the classroom?

The **General Principles** in this chapter are as follows:

1. If our goals are accurate assessment and academic success for students, then teachers must clearly and completely define the achievement targets that students are to hit.

2. Those achievement targets must center on the truly important proficiencies students are to master—they must represent the core of a discipline and reflect the best thinking in the field.

3. Those achievement targets can be categorized in ways that help us understand how to assess them accurately—knowledge/ understanding, reasoning, skills, products, and dispositions.

This chapter serves three functions. First, it lays a foundation for the definition of quality assessment that permeates the rest of the book. Quality assessments arise out of clear and appropriate achievement targets. It's impossible to develop assessments, share a clear vision of success with students, and plan instruction if student learning targets are not crystal clear.

Second, various kinds of learning targets (knowledge, reasoning, skills, products, and dispositions) are defined. These definitions are simple to understand and provide a functional way to frame the classroom assessment challenge.

Third, and perhaps most importantly, Chapter 3 is intended to motivate readers to care deeply about the clarity and appropriateness of their own visions of academic success for their students.

Links to Previous Chapters

Chapters 1 and 2 presented the first standard for quality assessment—clear and appropriate users and uses. This chapter presents the second standard—clear and appropriate targets of learning and instruction. (Please find these standards in Figure 2 in the *Workbook* Introduction.)

Chapters 1 and 2 established students as primary users of assessment materials and information. This implies that learning targets need to be clear to them, too. In fact, making achievement targets crystal clear to students is a basic premise of student-involved classroom assessment.

Links to Subsequent Chapters

Five types of student outcomes are discussed in this chapter—knowledge/understanding, reasoning, skills, products, and dispositions. This chapter provides an overview. Each type of learning target will be covered separately in Chapters 9–11. This classification scheme for learning targets will also be used to match targets to assessment methods in Chapter 4.

Portfolio Reminder

Remember to keep worksheets, products, and other artifacts from these activities in your working folder to be ready for possible later use in your portfolio.

Roadmap

Activity	Title	Activity Description	Time	Icons
3-1	What's Worth Assessing?—Case Discussion	Targets need to be both clear and appropriate. This activity looks at targets that might not be worth the time to assess. *Cross-reference to Chapter 3:* General Principle 2.	20–30 min	QUICK CHECK
3-2	What's Creative Problem Solving?—Case Discussion	Targets need to be both clear and appropriate. This activity looks at the "clear" part of the equation. *Cross-reference to Chapter 3:* General Principle 1.	20-30 min	QUICK CHECK
3-3	*What's in a Content Standard?	Practice in clearly stating the targets embedded in content standards. *Cross-reference to Chapter 3:* General Principles 1, 2, and 3	40-60 min	CONSOLIDATE UNDERSTANDING
3-4	*Is It Worth Our Time and Effort to Have Clear Targets?	Is it worth the time and effort to have clear targets? *Cross-reference to Chapter 3:* General Principle 1.	15-20 min	CONSOLIDATE UNDERSTANDING
3-5	Inviting Students Into the Target	Making targets clear to students. *Cross-reference to Chapter 3:* General Principle 1.	30-45 min; rest is homework	APPLY LEARNING
3-6	Write a Letter	Practice making targets clear to parents or instructors. *Cross-reference to Chapter 3:* General Principles 1, 2, and 3.	15–30 min; rest is homework	APPLY LEARNING
3-7	Analyze Sample Assessments for Clear and Appropriate Targets	What does it look like in actual classroom assessments when targets are clearly specified and appropriate? *Cross-reference to Chapter 3:* General Principles 1 and 2.	45-70 min	CONSOLIDATE UNDERSTANDING
3-8	Unit-Building Activity, Assignment 1—You Build Assessment into One of Your Instructional Units	The ultimate application—develop clear targets for one of your units. *Cross-reference to Chapter 3:* General Principles 1, 2, and 3.	15–30 min; rest is homework	APPLY LEARNING

*Recommended

Activity 3-1   What's Worth Assessing?—Case Discussion

Optional

Goals/Rationale

Learning targets for students must be both clear and appropriate. This case study addresses the "appropriate" side of the equation. We always need to ask ourselves, "Is this target worth the assessment time devoted to it?"

> **Cross-Reference to *Student-Involved Classroom Assessment*, 3d ed.**
> General Principle 2: What's a target? What's worth assessing?
>
> **Additional Materials Needed**
> None.
>
> **Time Required**
> 20–30 minutes.

What to Do

1. (5 minutes) Read the case study, "What's Worth Assessing?"

2. (5 minutes) Individually think through the following questions:

    a. Are there curriculum questions that need to be raised before the review and critique is completed? If so, what are they?

    b. What advice would you give as a member of the "critical friends" review team? How would you change the sample items?

    c. Can you think of an instance—as a student, parent, or teacher—when you took a test that included items you felt weren't worth learning or assessing? How did you react?

    d. In your own situation, how are decisions made about what's worth learning, teaching and assessing? Who has a say? In what ways are students involved?

3. (5 minutes) If you are working in a group, discuss your responses to questions 2a–d.

4. (5–15 minutes) *Optional.* Examine a selected response assessment you've used recently. Is "importance of learning targets" one of the criteria you used to decide what to assess?

What's Worth Assessing?—Case

An assessment study group of middle school social studies teachers from Pacific Islands drafted selected response test questions—multiple-choice, true/false, matching, and short answer. Design teams of teachers, principals, and specialists posted their work and then began a "critical friends" review and critique in which each team reviewed the work of the others, writing commendations and suggestions for improvement, noting where quality guidelines were violated, and posing questions for the authors.

One set of questions was developed around Pacific Island government symbolic seals. Each seal contains images of the island state, its environment, cultural values, people, history, and unique features. Colors and design elements add meaning.

First and second drafts of questions were posted to enable reviewers to note improvements. The multiple-choice team was proud of its work, pleased that the list of commendations next to its questions grew longer as the review continued.

Toward the end of the critical friends session, one design team stood before the multiple-choice drafts for the Island seals. While the group felt that guidelines for designing sound multiple-choice items were followed, one of the teachers quietly raised a different concern. Pointing to Question 1, ("How many items are there in our national seal?"), he asked, "Is this worth assessing? It doesn't seem important enough to be worth testing. Maybe importance should be one of our criteria for quality test questions."

Another teacher argued that knowing the symbols and their meaning was really important, while a third suggested that one of the symbols, a star with 24 points, was important because the four largest points represent each of the regional centers and the other points indicate how many atolls (chains of low sandy islands) are part of the nation. The first teacher responded with another question: "Is it important to know how many points there are or to know what each point represents? What do we really want our children to know about the symbols on our seals? What's worth knowing? What's the role of symbols in our sense of nationhood?"

Activity 3-2

What's Creative Problem Solving?— Case Discussion

Optional

Goals/Rationale

Learning targets for students must be both clear and appropriate. This activity addresses the "clear" side of the equation. Just because a target is stated doesn't imply that everyone agrees on what it means. For example, we can all agree that we want students to be good writers. Would we agree on what good writers know and can do? The same applies to an even greater extent in the current example.

> **Cross-Reference to *Student-Involved Classroom Assessment*, 3d ed.**
>
> General Principle 1: Targets need to be clear.
>
> **Additional Materials Needed**
> None.
>
> **Time Required**
> 20–30 minutes.

What to Do

1.   (5 minutes) Read the case study, "What in the World is Creative Problem Solving?"

2.   (5 minutes) Individually think through the following questions:

   a.   What are the sources of frustration in this case?

   b.   What would you recommend to this group? How might they more clearly define the learning target they are trying to assess?

   c.   In general, how can we deal with something that is greatly valued but vague? How can we make it clearer?

   d.   Can you think of an instance—as a student, parent, or teacher—when targets weren't clear? How did you react?

3.   (5 minutes) If you are working in a group, discuss your responses to questions 2a–d. Concentrate on question 2c.

4.   (5–15 minutes) *Optional.* Examine some of your own content standards or course goals. Are any of them vague? What might you do to make them clearer?

What in the World is Creative Problem Solving?—Case

Early in a district's move toward creating a student-centered school, parents, community, and teachers crafted a vision for the future of their children. One of the key elements of that vision was developing learners who are creative problem solvers. The words "creative problem solving" evoked smiles of satisfaction and were used throughout the following months to draft a proposal for restructuring the curriculum, instruction, and assessment.

The next fall, teachers met to begin developing curricular units, implementing hands-on and cooperative learning strategies, and identifying assessments that would provide insights into student growth. "Creative problem solving" was selected as the starting point. A classroom assessment specialist arrived to work with teachers and asked the question, "What does creative problem solving look like?" Thus began a multi-year effort to define this learning target.

In an early meeting, teachers agreed that this part of the vision was not limited to mathematics. They challenged each other to think broadly about the kinds of problems that children encounter throughout their day. Early brainstorming resulted in some of the following descriptors:

- Students can apply what they know in a new way.

- Students can state the problem as a question.

- Students can identify the key information in the problem.

- Students can plan and successfully carry out a process for solving a problem.

- Students can describe what they did and why.

While some uncertainties remained, it was time to try things out. Almost immediately there were additional concerns:

- Does creative problem solving involve applying what is known in a new way?

- What are "problems"? Is everything that kids learn for the first time a problem?

- Is it creative problem solving when the student comes up with a process or solution that is "new" for her but not necessarily unique? Does *creative* have to mean *unique*?

- Does every response to a problem have to be creative?

- Is it possible to have a solution that is elegant in its simplicity but is not creative?

- What is "creative" for very young learners?

A kindergarten teacher summed up her frustration: "It feels like I have to reshape the whole curriculum into problems, but I still don't know what we're looking for." A fourth-grade teacher said, "I don't want this to become a set of steps that students memorize; that misses the point." Everyone had labeled a target but couldn't define—let alone assess—it.

Activity 3-3

What's in a Content Standard?

Recommended

Goals/Rationale

The most effective way to become comfortable with achievement targets is to practice defining them. This activity not only provides practice, but it also addresses another common concern—how to merge local content standards into assessment and instruction.

> **Cross-Reference to *Student-Involved Classroom Assessment*, 3d ed.**
>
> General Principles 1, 2, and 3: Clear and appropriate targets are essential.
>
> **Additional Materials Needed**
> None.
>
> **Time Required**
> 40–60 minutes.

What to Do

1.   (5–10 minutes) Select an everyday skill from your experience, like driving a car, and brainstorm the following:

     a.   What one must know/understand to do this task.

     b.   What kinds of reasoning might be brought to bear to do this task.

     c.   What skills must be used to succeed.

     Or, center your thinking on a product, such as a completed income tax form, a fishing rod, or a piece of clothing. What are the knowledge/understanding, reasoning, and skill prerequisites for this product? Be creative.

2.   (5–10 minutes) Now turn to a school-related product such as a term paper, a science fair exhibit, or a piece of art. What are the knowledge, reasoning, and skills required to perform well in developing this product? List them.

3. (5 minutes) This is the type of productive thinking you can apply to all content standards. For example, read the worksheet, "What's in a Content Standard?" First, individually try to match each standard on the right to the type of learning target it embodies (on the left).

4. (5 minutes) If you are working in a group compare the matches made by various members. Did everyone agree? Did you find that different people matched things up differently? Why or why not?

5. (10 minutes) Now try "unpacking" each of the content standards. What knowledge or understanding would be required for a student to be successful on each? What reasoning would students need to employ? What skills would be necessary? What products must be developed? Which content standards are just plain vague? In other words, which content standards could you match to different types of targets depending on your interpretation?

6. (10–20 minutes) Think about or discuss the following points:

    a. Will all teachers interpret all content standards the same? If they don't, what are the instructional implications? What are the assessment implications? What might be the nature of competence demonstrated by the students of different teachers? Can we hold students responsible for achieving competence if teachers have different definitions of the target?

    b. The reason that some matches are different might be that some content standards are just plain vague—you need to clarify what is meant before you can design instruction or assessment. What are some strategies for clarifying targets?

    c. The reason that other matches are different is that some targets are BIG and COMPLEX and you look at different, relevant aspects of the target. In this case, you need to analyze the knowledge/understanding, reasoning, skills, and products aspects of the standard before you can design instruction and assessment. In other words, you need to "unpack" the complex ones.

    d. In your own context, is there a need to better divide up responsibility for helping students progress along the path to competence on content standards like these? If we want to take students from beginning to competent as they proceed through school, how do we create an integrated curriculum across grade levels that is efficient—a "continuous progress curriculum"? What strategies could we use to apportion responsibility across grade levels?

e. Do you agree with the statement, "The teachers who are most able to develop and use quality assessments are those who know and understand their own target responsibilities and see how their targets arise from what has come before and lead to what is to follow"? Why or why not?

What's in a Content Standard?

Match each content standard on the right to the type of target on the left.

Target Type	Sample Content Standards
a. **Knowledge & Understanding** b. **Reasoning** c. **Skills** d. **Products**	1. **Reading**—The student understands the meaning of what is read. Specifically, the student will comprehend important ideas and details. 2. **Writing**—The student writes clearly and effectively. Specifically, the student will use style appropriate to the audience and purpose; use voice, word choice, sentence fluency for intended style and audience. 3. **Communication**—The student communicates ideas clearly and effectively. Specifically, the student will develop content and ideas; develop a topic or theme; organize thoughts around a clear beginning, middle and end; use transitional sentences and phrases to connect related ideas; speak coherently and compellingly. 4. **Mathematics**—The student uses mathematical reasoning. Specifically, the student will analyze information from a variety of sources; use models, know facts, patterns, and relationships to validate thinking. 5. **Science**—The student understands and uses scientific concepts and principles. Specifically, the student will recognize the components, structures, and organization of systems and the interconnections within and among them. 6. **History**—The student applies the methods of social science investigation to investigate, compare, and contrast interpretations of historical events. Specifically, the student will analyze historical information; evaluate different interpretations of major events in state, U.S., and world history. 7. **Geography**—The student understands the complex physical and human characteristics of places and regions. Specifically, the student will identify the characteristics that define the Pacific Northwest and the Pacific Rim as regions. 8. **Civics**—The student analyzes the purposes and organization of governments and laws. Specifically, the student will compare and contrast democracies with other forms of government.

Is it Worth Our Time and Effort to Have Clear Targets?

Activity 3-4

Recommended

Goals/Rationale

We believe that clear targets are nonnegotiable. However, you might not agree. This activity gives you a chance to raise your doubts and concerns and come up with solutions to barriers. If you still have doubts and concerns after this activity, file them in your working folder to revisit later.

> **Cross-Reference to *Student-Involved Classroom Assessment*, 3d ed.**
>
> General Principle 1: Is it worth our time to have clear targets.
>
> **Additional Materials Needed**
>
> Chart paper and pens.
>
> **Time Required**
>
> 15–20 minutes.

What to Do

1. Prepare a piece of chart paper (for groups) or regular paper (if working alone) that has the following column headings: "Pluses/Benefits," "Minuses/Barriers," and "Possible Solutions to Barriers."

2. (5 minutes) Individually jot down your ideas on the pluses/benefits and minuses/barriers of taking the time and energy required to be clear about our achievement expectations for students. These ideas can come from the chapter, but they can also come from individual experience. Then, for each minus/barrier jot down your ideas for solutions.

3. (5 minutes) If you're working in a group, make a synthesized list of ideas on the chart paper. If more than one person has listed a particular point or idea put check marks next to it—one for each person making the point.

4. (5–10 minutes) Think about or discuss the following:

   a. Which way does the scale tip for each individual and for the group as a whole?

b. One of the major barriers to articulating visions of success for students is finding time to do it. Was this a major consideration for you? If articulating clear and appropriate learning targets for students is important, how might you address the barrier of time? Is there district work to be done here? Who should do it? Is there a role for you?

| Activity 3-5 | # Inviting Students into the Target |

Optional

Goals/Rationale

One of the primary premises of Rick's book is that we can profitably involve students in assessment. One way to do this is to ensure that students have a clear vision of the targets they are supposed to hit. This activity gives you a chance to practice restating targets in student-friendly (kid) language and then actually determining the extent to which students understand what you mean. This activity also promotes consideration of the extent to which targets are equally clear to all students or whether there might be some targets that are unclear to students from diverse backgrounds.

> **Cross-Reference to *Student-Involved Classroom Assessment*, 3d ed.**
>
> General Principle 1: Making targets clear to students.
>
> **Additional Materials Needed**
>
> Index cards and curriculum or standards documents that define learning targets in your setting.
>
> **Time Required**
>
> 30–45 minutes; rest is homework.

What to Do

Part A: Preparation/Do with Colleagues

1. (5 minutes) Look at the sample targets listed below and decide which will be clear to students as written and which might need some "refinement" to make it more student-friendly (clear).

    a. Carry out scientific investigations of an environmental issue in your community/locale.

    b. Use information about personal interests and academic strengths and weaknesses to set personal goals using a variety of decision making strategies.

    c. Communicate effectively for a variety of purposes and audiences.

    d. Understand the organizational structures of government.

    e. Conduct historical studies using the tools and methods of historians to reconstruct the past. This includes developing a historical question, gathering information about the question, interpreting information from a variety of sources, and comparing and contrasting different accounts about past events, people, places, or situations.

2. (10-15 minutes) Review the worksheet, "Clarifying Targets— Options with Examples," to select a process for clarifying the target statements that are likely to be unclear to students. Individuals may select individual targets to refine and then review with the entire team.

3. (10–15 minutes) If you're working in a group, compare your refinements to others' and discuss which will provide the clearest target to your students. If appropriate, make additional improvements. Consider the following questions:

    a. Are you sure the key words you've used have the same meaning for students who are English-language learners? Could your key words have more than one interpretation? Might there be similar words in their language that have quite different meanings?

    b. Is it clear what actions students will take to demonstrate their achievement? Have you carefully selected action words or phrases that make explicit what students will do?

    c. Have you made sure that the target statement is not a kind of straightjacket that requires every student to respond in exactly the same way, or have you made clear WHAT needs to be in their work, but *not* exactly HOW they must get there? ("Read a wide RANGE of texts including fiction and nonfiction, informational texts for work in other subject areas, functional/"how-to" texts, and multiple genres and authors for a minimum of 25 books per year" rather than "Read *Where the Wild Things Are, Harry Potter and the Sorcerer's Stone, Time for Kids* magazine, and *How to Set up an Aquarium*"). This encourages students to draw on knowledge, experiences, and strengths of their heritage while reaching for common targets. This is an essential component of learning targets that honor student diversity.

4. (5–10 minutes) *Optional.* Consider the learning targets in your classroom and whether there are some that need to be clarified for you and for your students. Clarify and refine these targets using the techniques in the "Worksheet Clarifying Targets—Options with Examples." Discuss the *appropriateness* of your refined targets for students of various ages and grade levels. Are the targets right for students at all ages or more appropriate for a particular set of grades? Are they appropriate at all? Do they focus on essential learning? Are they important enough to spend teaching, learning, and assessment time pursuing? Are some students more likely than others to misunderstand the target?

Part B: Try with Students

1. Select three to four student-friendly learning targets to show to students.

2. Place each target on a separate index card. For a large class, make duplicate cards.

3. Prepare students for their role in the activity by letting them know that you're asking them to help you make sure it's crystal clear what they and other students will be expected to do to reach specific learning targets.

4. Pass out one or two targets to each student group. Ask groups to list or describe on the card what they would do to show that they've mastered this target. If time is available, have students pass their work to another group whose job is to see if they agree with the description of what it takes to achieve the target and, if not, to revise for clarity.

5. Analyze student responses to see how clear the learning targets were to students. Think about the following questions and be prepared to discuss your responses with your colleagues.

    a. Does this target communicate clearly with your students?

    b. How closely do their ideas about achieving the target match with your own?

    c. Are there any targets that students have misunderstood?

    d. Are there language or cultural barriers present in your targets that are revealed by student descriptions? What action is needed to clarify these targets for students?

    e. What parts of the target are problematic?

    f. How else could the target be presented?

6.   *Optional.* Create target cards or worksheets for an upcoming unit and use them to introduce your vision of the targets to students.

Clarifying Targets—Options with Examples

Option 1: Identify the key elements of the target

Target	Key Elements
Read a range of texts (literary, informational, and func- tional) for a variety of purposes.	**Range**—all kinds of texts, genres, authors **Literary texts**—fictional texts from a variety of genres: novels, classics, short stories, mysteries, science fiction, poems, etc. **Informational texts**—nonfiction texts from textbooks, essays, newspapers, brochures, magazines, research reports, encyclopedias, etc. **Functional texts**—how-to manuals, recipes, schedules, patterns, instruction sheets for products, directions on a computer program, etc. **Purposes**—enjoyment, job preparation, research, passing exams, etc.

Option 2: Turn the target statement into one or more "I can" statements

Target	Key Elements
Read a range of texts (literary, informational, and func- tional) for a variety of purposes.	**I can show that I read a range of texts, which means that . . .** I can read lots of different kinds of books, stories, and poems that come from an author's imagination (literary) and I read different authors. I can read books and articles that are factual/nonfiction, like newspaper articles, a magazine article of someone's life, a history book, a report, etc. I can read things that help me get information about a topic, like a science chapter on blood circulation. I can read and follow directions that tell me how to do something. Some of what I read I read for fun. I can also read to find answers, or to learn about a place, person, or thing, and I can find out how to do something.

Activity 3-6   Write a Letter

Optional

Goals/Rationale

In this activity you write a letter to an instructor (preservice) or a parent (inservice) describing what the targets are (or what you think they are) for a subject or course. This provides practice in making targets clear to various audiences. In inservice settings it also helps to build sound working relationships with parents. In preservice settings it can also raise the consciousness of instructors on the need to make their targets clear to their students—you.

> **Cross-Reference to *Student-Involved Classroom Assessment*, 3d ed.**
>
> General Principles 1, 2, and 3: Clear and appropriate targets are essential.
>
> **Additional Materials Needed**
>
> None.
>
> **Time Required**
>
> 15–30 minutes; rest is homework.

What to Do—Preservice

1. Think about a class you are taking. What are the knowledge/ understanding, reasoning, skills, products, and dispositional outcomes for this course? Did the instructor make them clear or do you have to infer them?

    Even if the instructor listed them, are they really clear? For example, if the instructor wants to build skills in problem solving, is it clear what it will look like when you are successful? If it is, what did the instructor do to make the targets clear—definitions, samples of acceptable work, illustrative test questions, references to daily life, rubrics? If the targets are not clear, what do you wish the instructor had done to help you understand what it will take to succeed?

    (How did we, the authors of the textbook and *Workbook*, try to make our learning targets in assessment clear—definitions, rubrics, samples of work?)

2. Draft a letter to the instructor in this class that describes your current understanding of the various kinds of learning targets. Ask the instructor if your interpretation is correct. Be sure to tell the instructor why you are asking—it is part of a course

on assessment. Consider the tone (voice) that you should use in your letter. (See the text box for assistance with tone.)

3. Try the letter out on the instructor in your assessment course or on another student. Is your analysis sound? Is the tone conducive to a productive dialogue or will it turn off the recipient?

4. Revise your letter as necessary and try it out. What was the result?

What to Do—Inservice

Part A: Preparation/Do with Colleagues

(15–30 minutes) Think about or discuss the following:

- What learning targets in your course or grade level might be useful to carefully define for parents? Pick one or two. Consider those targets that are most important, are most misunderstood, and/or are hardest to define.

- How might you describe these learning targets to parents so that they are crystal clear? How will you help parents see that these are worthy and important targets? Is it enough just to list the target, or do you need more? What is the role of Rick's five types of learning targets in helping to make your target(s) clear? What is the role of definitions, samples of student work, illustrative test questions, references to daily life, and rubrics in making your target(s) clear? (How did we, the authors of the textbook and *Workbook*, try to make our learning outcomes in assessment clear through definitions, rubrics, and samples of work?)

- What tone (voice) should be used in a letter to parents defining targets? (See the textbox for assistance with tone.)

Part B: Homework

1. Write the letter and show it to a colleague. Ask the colleague to explain the target back to you. Did he get what you intended? Does he agree with your definition? Does he believe the tone (voice) of the letter is appropriate—will it lead to a constructive dialogue or put the parent off?

2. Ask students to help, if you feel comfortable doing so. How would they explain this learning target to their parents?

3. Show the letter to a friendly parent and get their reaction. Is it clear? Is it persuasive? Is the tone (voice) inviting? Can the parent accurately describe the target back to you? What would you change for next time?

> **"Tone (voice) of a letter to a parent or instructor"**
>
> What is the role of tone (voice) in writing? What types of voices are available to you—sarcastic, supportive, funny, inquisitive, bemused, sincere, "we're all in this together," formal, informal, "help me out here," "here's where you're wrong," "look, I may not know what I'm talking about, but," "do I have it right?" etc.? What voice does Rick use in his textbook? What voice do we use in the *Workbook*?
>
> What tone or voice would be most appropriate in your letter to a parent or instructor? How do you get the tone you want? Consider: vocabulary, sentence length, person (first, second, or third), and the content of the first sentence.
>
> What should the first sentence say to (a) intrigue the reader; (b) make the reader want to consider your ideas, and (c) not insult the reader, but get him or her on your side?

Activity 3-7

Analyze Sample Assessments for Clear and Appropriate Targets

Optional

Goals/Rationale

In some assessments the author is very clear on the targets to be assessed. In many other assessments the targets are not clear at all. This activity gives you the chance to evaluate the clarity and appropriateness of the targets being assessed in some real classroom assessments, and then think about the implications for your own practice.

Cross-Reference to *Student-Involved Classroom Assessment*, 3d ed.

General Principles 1 and 2: Clear and appropriate learning targets are essential.

Additional Materials Needed

WORKBOOK: Appendix B, "Standard 1—What: Clear and Appropriate Learning Targets," "Assessment Sample 1: Reading Rate."

Time Required

45–70 minutes.

What to Do

1. (10 minutes) Read through the rubric, "Standard 1—What: Clear and Appropriate Learning Targets" in *Workbook* Appendix B. This rubric describes the types of things to look for in an assessment to determine the clarity and appropriateness of the learning targets being assessed. Do you agree? Does the rubric cover those things that truly describe clear and appropriate targets?

2. (10 minutes) Look at "Sample Assessment 1, Reading Rate" in *Workbook* Appendix B. Use the rubric to decide the extent to which the target being assessed is clear and appropriate. Try to put a "score" on the assessment by matching the assessment to the statements under each level of the rubric. Then look at the footnotes here to see what we think.[1,2]

3. (10–30 minutes) Look at the other assessments in Appendix B. What do you notice about them with respect to clear and appropriate learning targets?

---

[1]Yes, the target is clear—reading rate. The formula for calculating reading rate is clearly implied, and a target reading rate is clearly stated.

[2]We are uncertain as to the target's appropriateness. Is reading rate the only thing being assessed, or is it just one part of a more comprehensive assessment of reading? Is the formula used to calculate rate widely accepted as the best? Is the target rate widely accepted?

4. (10 minutes) Think about other assessments you've seen or used. In what percentage are the targets clear and appropriate?

5. (5–10 minutes) Think about or discuss: (a) Does every single assessment have to have clear targets or does there just need to be a pattern of having clear targets sometimes? (b) What are the implications for the assessments you use in your own classroom? What are you thinking about doing differently?

Unit-Building Activity, Assignment 1— You Build Assessment into One of Your Instructional Units

Activity 3-8

Optional

Goals/Rationale

The ultimate application of all the ideas in Rick's book is day-to-day life in the classroom. This includes unit building. In fact, planning assessments as an integral part of building units is what we recommend. But, to be able to do that, you need practice. The unit-building sequence of activities allows you this practice—at the end of many chapters you'll have an opportunity to apply the concepts to your developing unit. Activity 3-8 is the first step in the unit-building sequence—setting the targets for learning.

Be advised in advance that this is a sizable project that will command a good deal of time to complete well. But also be aware that the time will be well spent.

> **Cross-Reference to *Student-Involved Classroom Assessment*, 3d ed.**
>
> General Principles 1, 2, and 3: Clear and appropriate learning targets are essential.
>
> **Additional Materials Needed**
>
> An instructional unit on which you'd like to work.
>
> **Time Required**
>
> 15–30 minutes; rest is homework.

What to Do

Part A: Preparation/Do With Colleagues

(15-30 minutes) Review the steps in Part B and clarify questions.

Part B: Homework

1. Select a unit on which you'd like to work. As you think about the instructional unit you might use, realize that ultimately you are going to be asked to identify its important achievement targets, devise an assessment plan for it, design and develop the actual assessments, devise systems for communicating with students about assessment results and, if feasible, carry out your assessment plan. As you select your focal unit, think about the following:

    a. The best option is to focus this project on a previously developed unit for which you already have clearly framed goals, objectives, and instructional plans. In this way, you can concentrate your efforts on the assessment work to be done. However, you also can develop the unit of instruction from scratch (for example, an idea for a unit based on standards), or choose a unit developed by someone else—found on an education website, borrowed from a colleague, or included in a course textbook.

    b. The unit should include at least several days or even weeks of instruction, covering a good deal of material. If possible, strive for a unit that includes all four types of

achievement: knowledge/understanding, reasoning, skills, and products. This will extend you into all dimensions of assessment, providing broad practice.

   c. If you are currently a teacher, it might be prudent to select a unit you teach regularly or plan to teach in the future.

2. Using the content from Chapter 3 of the textbook, take a first pass at identifying the important achievement targets of your unit.

   a. What is the important knowledge students are to understand? Differentiate that content you expect students to learn outright from content you expect them to be able to retrieve later if they need it. Think about the knowledge that is central to the discipline.

   b. Reflect on the patterns of reasoning you want your students to acquire. Be careful here. Rick does not discuss patterns of reasoning in detail until Chapter 9. So, this represents only a beginning.

   c. Identify any skill or product development targets. What things do you want students to be able to do? What kinds of products do you want them to create? Again, give yourself room here; detail about skill and product targets doesn't occur until Chapters 7 and 10.

   d. Finally, what dispositions do you hope your students will acquire?

3. Try to connect your draft targets to local or state content standards. To do this, you might need to "unpack" your local content standards as described in Activity 3-3, "What's in a Content Standard?" Remember this is just a beginning. You may want to continue thinking about these questions as you progress through the textbook.

   a. What is the major content standard(s) that will be addressed through your unit?

   b. Are there any other aspects of the content standards that could profitably be added to your draft list of targets?

   c. Are there any draft targets that might be modified to be a better match to content standards?

   d. Does your unit match enough content standards to make it worthwhile? Might you need to modify your unit (targets, content, and instruction) to make it a better match?

Notes:

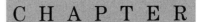

Understanding Our Assessment Alternatives

Big Ideas in This Chapter

This chapter answers the following guiding question:

What is the best assessment method?

The **General Principles** in this chapter are as follows:

1. We have a variety of assessment methods to choose from for any particular classroom assessment situation. (This plays out in the chapter as a discussion of the types of assessment methods.)

2. The method of choice in any particular classroom assessment context is a function of the desired achievement target and the purpose for the assessment; that is, there is no universally best method. (This plays out in the chapter as matching methods to targets and purposes, or "Target-Method Match.")

3. Once we select a method we must understand how to use it correctly. (Translation: there are rules of evidence for each method; we need to sample well and avoid sources of bias and distortion; we need to avoid common problems when writing assessment questions and tasks. Adhere to these rules

of evidence and we can use all methods productively. Violate the rules and put students at risk. Our assessment challenge is how to use each method well.)

4.   There are barriers to changing assessment practice, but these can be overcome.

Links to Previous Chapters

- Chapters 1, 2, and 3 presented the first two standards for quality assessment—clear and appropriate users and uses and clear and appropriate learning targets (see Figure 2 in the *Workbook* Introduction). This chapter presents the third, fourth, and fifth standards—target-method match, sampling, and eliminating potential sources of bias and distortion. (Find these in *Workbook* Figure 2.)

- Both the nature of the targets we want to assess (Chapter 3) and the purposes for which we use assessment (Chapters 1 and 2) have implications for which method of assessment to choose. Assessments are designed with targets and users/uses in mind.

- This chapter is again about balance. Whereas in Chapters 1 and 2 Rick discussed balancing standardized tests and classroom assessment, this chapter is about balancing assessment methods. No assessment method is inherently better than another; it's how we use them that matters. Keep thinking: balance, balance, balance . . .

- Chapter 4 introduces assessment methods—selected response, essay, performance assessment, and personal communication. These methods are crossed with the target types presented in Chapter 3—there are better and worse ways to assess each type of target.

- Chapter 4 also describes potential barriers you might face with respect to improving classroom assessment. Such barriers were also discussed somewhat in Activity 1-3, "Our Own Experiences with Assessment and Implications for Practice."

Links to Subsequent Chapters

- Chapter 4 provides an overview of assessment methods and how they cross with targets. Each method has its own chapter later—Chapters 5–8. Later chapters include additional detail on sampling, potential sources of bias and distortion, and student involvement.

- Chapter 4 continues to frame the classroom assessment challenge. The rest of the book offers guidance in meeting that challenge. The idea is to proceed in small steps to keep from being overwhelmed.

Portfolio Reminder

Once again, we remind you that it is important to keep potential portfolio material handy. Note suggestions in Chapter 1.

Roadmap

Activity	Title	Activity Description	Time	Icons
4-1	How Purpose Affects Method	Purpose affects method. *Cross-reference to Chapter 4: General Principle 2.*	20–30 min	CONSOLIDATE UNDERSTANDING
4-2	What's the Learning Here?— Case Discussion	Illustrates why performance assessment might not be the best choice for knowledge targets. *Cross-reference to Chapter 4: General Principles 1 and 2.*	20 min	QUICK CHECK
4-3	*What Questions Do You Have About Matching Targets to Methods	Target-method match. *Cross-reference to Chapter 4: General Principles 1 and 2.*	30-40 min; rest is homework	CONSOLIDATE UNDERSTANDING
4-4	Analyze Sample Assessments for Target-Method Match	Target-method match. *Cross-reference to Chapter 4: General Principles 1 and 2.*	35–60 min; rest is homework	CONSOLIDATE UNDERSTANDING
4-5	Unit-Building Activity, Assignment 2—Making Your Matches	The ultimate application—target-method match for one of your units. *Cross-reference to Chapter 4: General Principles 1, 2, and 3.*	15–30 min; rest is homework	APPLY LEARNING
4-6	Solutions to Barriers—Video Discussion	What are the barriers to better classroom assessment? *Cross-reference to Chapter 4: General Principle 4.*	30-35 min	CONSOLIDATE UNDERSTANDING

*Recommended

How Purpose Affects Method   Activity 4-1

Optional

Goals/Rationale

Chapter 4 emphasizes *target*-method match. It only deals briefly with *purpose*-method match. This activity gives you the opportunity to explore *purpose*-method match in a little more detail.

> **Cross-Reference to *Student-Involved Classroom Assessment*, 3d ed.**
>
> General Principle 2: Purpose-method match.
>
> **Additional Materials Needed**
> None.
>
> **Time Required**
> 20–30 minutes.

What to Do

1.   (5 minutes) Read the worksheet, "Purpose-Method Match."

2.   (5 minutes) In Chapters 1 and 2, we considered various uses for classroom assessment—monitoring student progress, grading, evaluating the effectiveness of instruction, reporting to parents, involving students, getting a "quick picture" of the status of a group, and so on. Choose two of these (or other classroom purposes for assessment) and play out the design implications of these purposes using the attached worksheet, "How Purpose Affects Method."

     You may discover that two purposes can have exactly the same design. You may find, however, that purpose affects design to a large degree.

3.   (10–20 minutes) If you are working in a group, discuss your responses to questions 3a–c.

     a.   What differences did you find from your comparison in item 2 above?

     b.   What questions do you have about methods and assessment design that still need to be answered before you can fully do this activity?

     c.   What insights did you gain? What implications does this activity have for classroom practice? What implications does it have for what you might do next week?

Purpose-Method Match

It's probably obvious that an assessment good for one purpose—say, providing detailed diagnosis of a student's strengths and needs—is not necessarily best for other purposes, such as student self-assessment.

Consider the assessment design implications of various uses of information from large-scale and classroom assessments. For example:

1. A single multiple-choice or short answer multiplication test may be perfectly acceptable to determine whether third graders have learned their multiplication facts before moving on, but would not be appropriate for making a decision about the overall impact of the third-grade mathematics program. The latter use would require a sample of questions that covers the whole curriculum, and large-scale administration to many third-grade classrooms.

2. A large-scale assessment designed to see overall how students are doing on a set of skills might look different from a classroom assessment designed to identify the learning needs of individual students. In the first case, developers might split up a large number of test questions among examinees—not all students answer all questions. This decreases testing time. Results amongst all students would then be combined to make overall estimates of student status. Thus, it would be impossible to generate complete information for individual students even if you wanted to.

3. A large-scale assessment designed to select students for a special program might look different from a classroom assessment designed to see if instruction has been effective. Selection requires only the ability to rank order students—assessments can be short and sweet. An assessment designed to see if instruction has been effective needs to sample thoroughly what students are supposed to have learned.

Here's a classroom assessment example: Consider two common classroom uses for assessment information—tracking student progress and student involvement. For the former, you might use a scoring rubric that is simple, and understandable only to the teacher. For the latter, you need a scoring rubric that is student friendly—one that clearly describes the features of quality in terms students can understand.

How Purpose Affects Method

Choose two purposes for classroom assessment. Write these purposes in the space provided. Then describe how these purposes might affect the various design choices listed on the left.

Point of Difference	Classroom Purpose 1:	Classroom Purpose 2:
Assessment method—selected response, essay, etc.		
Content/breadth of sampling/number of questions		
Scoring procedures and materials		
Who scores/role of assessor		
Plan for feedback		
Other		

Activity 4-2

What's the Learning Here?—Case Discussion

Optional

Goals/Rationale

As Rick points out in this chapter, an essential reason for using selected response and essay formats is to check for understanding of information before seeing the extent to which students can apply this knowledge and understanding.

One pitfall for good assessment is to assume that "authentic" performance assessments are always better than selected response questions. To see why this is a pitfall, consider the following scenario: A student fails to perform well on an authentic performance assessment. Why? Was it because the student was not able to apply her knowledge and reasoning skills to the task at hand, or was it because the student didn't have the knowledge or reasoning skills to begin with? On the surface, we don't know. It is a mistake to rely solely on a complex assessment method to get information about student achievement.

This activity presents you with samples of students' actual unsuccessful responses to performance assessment tasks. Can you tell why they did not succeed? What other form of assessment could help you determine why they failed to do well?

> **Cross-Reference to *Student-Involved Classroom Assessment*, 3d ed.**
>
> General Principles 1 and 2: All forms of assessment are needed.
>
> **Additional Materials Needed**
> None.
>
> **Time Required**
> 20 minutes.

What to Do

1. (10 minutes) Read the worksheet, "Sample Student Response to Complex Tasks." Individually look at each sample. How successful was the student at responding to the task? To the extent that the student was not successful, can you tell why? What other forms of assessment would help you determine why?

2. (10 minutes) Think about or discuss the implications of the following questions:

   a. Can you always tell from a performance assessment what went wrong if a student is not successful?

   b. What is the role of selected response and essay questions in determining prerequisites for complex tasks?

   c. Might you ever want to conduct a performance assessment without assessing prerequisite knowledge and skills first?

Sample Student Response to Complex Tasks— Case

Student Sample 1: Grade 8 Mathematics[1]

You are in charge of setting up a room for an awards banquet at your school. A total of 122 people will attend the banquet. The school has tables that seat either 8 or 10 people. No empty seats are allowed. How many of each size table will you need to make sure everyone has a seat? Show all your work and explain in words how you arrived at your answer.

Student response:

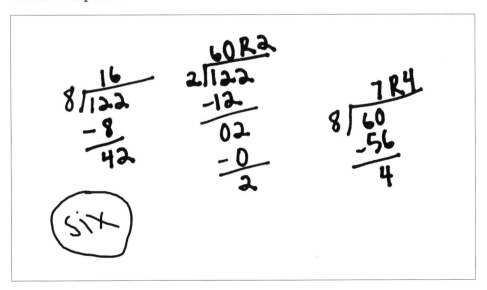

Student Sample 2: Grade 4 Writing in Response to Reading[2]

Write a personal response to "Since Hanna Moved Away" on the lines below. Your response might include answers to the questions below, but you do not need to answer all of them.

What has happened in this poem? Who is Hanna? What feelings do you have as you read this poem? What images does the speaker use to create these feelings? Which images do you like the best? Do you like this poem? Tell why or why not.

HANNA MOVE AWAY i THINK
THE POEM WAS PRETTY STUPID
AND BORING. THIS DID NOT CREAT
ANYTHING iN MY MIND NO i DO
NOT LIKE THE POEM AT ALL.

Activity 4-3

What Questions Do You Have About Matching Targets to Methods?

Recommended

Goals/Rationale

The heart of Chapter 4 is the manner in which targets match up to assessment methods. Although there is a lot of agreement on the types of learning targets and how they match to methods, Rick's Table 4.1 (textbook p.93) should not be taken as "the only truth in the universe." Once again, it is a convenience to help us think about how targets and methods match up.

As you read the chapter you may have found that you either disagreed with some of Rick's matches or had questions about them. This activity gives you the opportunity to think about and discuss these questions with others so that either your questions get answered, or at least you are clear about what questions you need answered.

[2]From Northwest Regional Educational Laboratory, *Improving Classroom Assessment: A Toolkit for Professional Developers*, Sample B.3, p. 1, Portland, OR: Author, 1998.

Cross-Reference to *Student-Involved Classroom Assessment*, 3d ed.

General Principles 1 and 2: Target-method match.

Additional Materials Needed

TEXTBOOK: Table 4.1, "Links Between Achievement Targets and Assessment Methods." OTHER: Chart paper and pens.

Time Required

30-40 minutes; rest is prework.

What to Do

Part A: Preparation/Prework

1. Before your next team or course meeting, consider the following questions:

    a. Do you wish to know more about any of the assessment methods before you feel confident in choosing the best method for given targets and uses? Which? Why? What are your questions?

    b. Do you agree with Rick's matching table (Table 4.1)? Why or why not? Did you find anything confusing? What are your questions? If you have questions about why performance assessment is not recommended for assessing knowledge targets, try Activity 4-2 to explore the reasons.

    c. Try to think of specific learning targets for each cell in the table noted as being a strong match.

2. If working in a group, the leader or instructor should post three pieces of chart paper—one for each prework question in item 1. On the third piece of chart paper actually make a target-by-method grid.

Part B: Do with Colleagues

1. (5 minutes) As folks come in, ask them to write their questions on the chart paper. They should put a check mark next to any question they have that someone else has already entered. They should write their targets on Post-It™ notes and put them into the grid. (Post-It™ notes allow people to move targets around if they are unsure of the cell.)

2. (10–15 minutes) The group should help each other answer the questions. Begin with the questions having the most marks. Note, for later consideration, those questions no one has an answer to yet. Consider placing both answered and unanswered questions in your working folder.

3. (10 minutes) Consider the sample targets participants have placed in the grid. Does anyone want to move theirs to another cell? Are there any disagreements? Would "unpacking" any of the listed targets (as done in Activity 3-3, "What's in a Content Standard?") help determine which methods to use?

4. (5–10 minutes) Think about or discuss how the information from textbook Chapter 4 and this activity will affect what you will do in your classroom next week.

Activity 4-4

Analyze Sample Assessments for Target-Method Match

Optional

Goals/Rationale

In some assessments the author of the assessment matches targets to methods very well. But, in other assessments the author seems not to have considered the need to match targets to methods. Sometimes the problem is that the targets are not clear to begin with—authors will have trouble picking a good assessment method if they are not clear on what targets to assess. This activity gives you practice in evaluating target-method match in some real classroom assessments, and then invites you to think about your own practice.

> **Cross-Reference to *Student-Involved Classroom Assessment*, 3d ed.**
>
> General Principles 1 and 2: Target-method match.
>
> **Additional Materials Needed**
>
> WORKBOOK: Appendix B, sample rubrics and assessments.
>
> **Time Required**
>
> 35–60 minutes; rest is homework.

What to Do

Part A: Do With Colleagues

1. (10 minutes) Read through the rubric, "Standard 3—How: Target-Method Match" in *Workbook* Appendix B. This rubric describes the types of things to look for in an assessment to determine how well the author matched methods to targets. Do you agree? Does the rubric cover those things that truly describe clear and appropriate targets?

2. (10 minutes) Look at Sample Assessment 6: Interview in *Workbook* Appendix B. Are the targets being assessed clear? (Remember, it will be difficult to evaluate target-method match if the targets aren't clear.)[1] Using the rubric, try to put a "score" on the assessment for the trait of "target-method match" by matching the assessment to the statements under each level of the rubric.[2]

3. (10–30 minutes) Look at the other assessments in Appendix B. Find a strong and weak example of target-method match. (Writeups of each assessment are also included in Appendix B, but don't peek ahead.)

4. (5–10 minutes) Think about or discuss the following questions:

   a. Does every assessment have to have methods consciously matched to targets or does there just have to be a general pattern of target-method match?

   b. What are the implications for the assessments you use in your own classroom? What are you thinking about doing differently?

Part B: Homework—Inservice

Analyze your last four assessments for target-method match. Did you use a variety of methods? Why or why not? Might you want to revise any of these assessments the next time you use them? How might you use the information in Chapter 4 next week in your classroom?

Part B: Homework—Preservice

Analyze the last four assessments you took. Did the instructor(s) use a variety of methods? Why or why not? Did the methods match well to the learning targets the instructor set for the course? Why or why not? What are the implications for how you'll conduct assessments when you become a teacher?

---

[1] Answer—Yes, more or less. Although the statements of targets are scattered, they may be readily inferred. The teacher is assessing student skills in filling out a job application, writing an application letter, and doing a job interview.

[2] Although you have to make some inferences, it appears that target-method match is good on this assessment. The author states that the assessment's purpose is to "simulate as closely as possible the job application and interview process." This means that the assessment is not only performance based, but set in as realistic a context as possible by having real business people review real application materials and conduct a mock interview. The only thing more realistic would be to participate in an actual job interview. You may have had some questions regarding the assessment of prerequisite skills. What might these prerequisite skills be, and how might you assess them? In any case, performance assessment is the best way to assess the skills stated.

Activity 4-5

Unit-Building Activity, Assignment 2—Making Your Matches

Optional

Goals/Rationale

This is the second in a series of direct applications for day-to-day life in the classroom—the continuing development or refinement of a unit based on the ideas and strategies you are encountering in *Student-Involved Classroom Assessment*. This part of the unit building process centers on using the targets identified in Assignment 1 to create a general framework for building assessments.

> **Cross-Reference to *Student-Involved Classroom Assessment*, 3d ed.**
>
> General Principles 1, 2, and 3: Target-method match.
>
> **Additional Materials Needed**
>
> The unit on which you are working.
>
> **Time Required**
>
> 15–30 minutes; rest is homework.

What to Do

Part A: Do with Colleagues

(15-30 minutes) Review and clarify the steps below as needed.

Part B: Homework

You will be devising a very general assessment plan for your unit. This plan will detail the sequence of your important assessment events— what you plan to assess, when you will assess it as the unit unfolds, and how you will assess it. This is just the first pass at the plan; you will have time later to refine it.

1. Reflect on your knowledge, reasoning, skills, and product targets. In what order do you expect students to practice and/ or master these targets? When do you plan to check on their progress toward or mastery of this material? When will you need information to help plan subsequent instruction? You might develop a preliminary calendar of instruction and assessment events. As part of this plan carefully note purposes for each assessment. To plan instruction? To involve students? To grade?

2. What assessment methods would you employ in this plan? Add this to your calendar.

Solutions to Barriers—Video Discussion

Activity 4-6

Optional

Goals/Rationale

Several years ago, we began to recognize that we were designing and presenting engaging, productive workshops and courses on classroom assessment, but participants didn't use the information to change practice even though they left wanting to. As we began to investigate, we uncovered a crisis in confidence. Our classroom assessment ideas appeared risky. What if students failed to hit the targets? Who would get blamed? What if failure was due to factors beyond the control of teachers, and they were blamed anyway? Better, given the risk, to remain vague about targets and couch assessments in gradebook terminology so that no one could figure out who really learned what. For some, this is a safer place.

In addition, we found that teachers lacked the time to assess well, faced immense community pressures to continue with old practices regardless of their quality, and simply didn't learn enough about how to assess effectively and efficiently based on the limited coverage available in a workshop. Quality classroom assessment will remain beyond reach as long as these issues remain unaddressed. This activity allows you to directly consider these barriers.

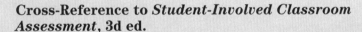

Cross-Reference to *Student-Involved Classroom Assessment*, 3d ed.

General Principle 4: Barriers to assessing well.

Additional Materials Needed

VIDEO: *Creating Sound Classroom Assessments*, available from the Assessment Training Institute, 800-480-3060. OTHER: Chart paper and pens.

Time Required

30-35 minutes.

What to Do

1. (5 minutes) Use a chart pack (for a group) or regular sheet of paper (if you are working alone) with two columns: "Barriers" and "Possible Solutions to Barriers." Using this sheet, brainstorm the barriers to improving classroom assessment (or, recall the barriers mentioned in Chapter 4).

2. (10 minutes) Watch the video segment on barriers. (It's toward the end of the video. The facilitator's guide will help you find it.) While you watch the video, listen for Rick's solutions to these barriers. Jot down solutions on your "Barriers/Solutions" sheet.

3. (10 minutes) If you're working in a group, synthesize your solutions on the chart paper.

4. (5–10 minutes) Come up with other solutions. Discuss the following:

    a. Which of these barriers are most applicable to you? To your school or district?

    b. Which solutions to barriers might work for you? For your school or district? What might you try?

End Part I

Activities

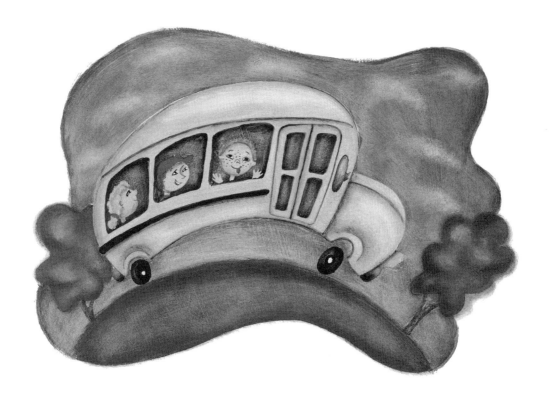

Roadmap

Activity	Title	Activity Description	Time	Icons
PI-1	What Does It Mean to "Set High Standards"?—Case Discussion	Help solve a real-life dilemma using your current understanding of assessment quality. *Cross-reference to textbook:* Uses learning from Chapters 1–4.	30 min	CONSOLIDATE UNDERSTANDING
PI-2	Creating Quality Classroom Assessments—Video Discussion	A video presentation of standards for quality assessment. *Cross-reference to textbook:* Uses learning from Chapters 1–4.	60–120 min	CONSOLIDATE UNDERSTANDING
PI-3	*Show What You Know	Show what you currently understand about high quality, student-involved classroom assessment. *Cross-reference to textbook:* Reflect on learning from Chapters 1–4.	Homework	SELF-REFLECT
PI-4	*Portfolio Building	Select items for your growth portfolio. *Cross-reference to textbook:* Reflect on learning from Chapters 1–4.	Homework	SELF-REFLECT

*Recommended

Portfolio Building

The activities in this section are intended to consolidate understanding of all the material in Part I of the textbook. This is your chance to reflect on what you've learned so far and convert this self-reflection and assessment into portfolio entries.

What Does It Mean to "Set High Standards"?—Case Discussion

Activity PI-1

Optional

Goals/Rationale

This case study presents a real-life dilemma for you to solve using your current learning from textbook Chapters 1–4.

> **Cross-Reference to *Student-Involved Classroom Assessment*, 3d ed.**
>
> Chapters 1–4.
>
> **Additional Materials Needed**
>
> None.
>
> **Time Required**
>
> 20-30 minutes.

What to Do

1. (10 minutes) Read the case study, "My Whole Fourth-Grade Class Cried." Individually think about the assessment quality issues raised by this case. Could differences in visions of users and uses have contributed to this situation? Could differences in definitions of targets have contributed to this situation? (For example, does "higher standards" mean different things to different people?) Could inadequate match between targets and methods have contributed to this situation?

2. (10–20 minutes) If you are working in a group, discuss your responses to questions 2a–d.

    a. What assessment quality issues/problems could underlie the situation described?

    b. What are the implications for student motivation of not being clear about what we mean by "higher standards"?

    c. What might the test developers have done to avoid the situation depicted?

    d. Have you ever encountered a similar situation? If it happens again, what will you do differently?

My Whole Fourth-Grade Class Cried—Case

As president of the X Mathematics Council (XMC), a professional organization of 10,000 mathematics educators, I am writing you to express our grave concern over legislation affecting the teaching and learning in K–12 schools throughout the State of X. This legislation mandated the development and implementation of a new standards-based, statewide assessment. Norm-referenced Test Y was selected to be the assessment. Because Y is a nationally normed test and did not match our state standards, an augmented assessment was necessary—the Z. XMC is requesting that you either move to suspend the administration of the current testing program (Y and Z) or call for a legislative inquiry into this newly implemented testing system.

The National Council of Teachers of Mathematics, with a membership of 110,000 educators, recently held its annual conference in our state. Over 18,000 educators from throughout the nation attended. Our state's Y and Z exams were a hot topic of conversation among all participants. Comments I heard included the following:

- "My whole fourth-grade class cried, the Y and Z were so hard." The truth is this comment came from a number of teachers at different grade levels.

- "The test strategy seems to be, 'If the students have trouble with the topic in seventh grade, let's teach it to them in fourth grade!'"

- "The eleventh grade Z test was only partially reasonable for my honors/precalculus students. For the majority of juniors, the test was practically impossible and students just guessed!"

- One troubling remark came from the parent of a mathematically gifted student who wanted to become a mathematician. After taking the Z, the student is questioning this career choice.

Teachers reported that Z test items surpassed the boundaries of reasonable difficulty, emphasizing too many obscure topics and procedures, material that teachers would not consider meeting the standards' criteria of "what every student should know." It is not that the Z items called for extensive reasoning and problem-solving ability, but that they asked students to recall arcane procedures and exotic factoids.

The Y is a nationally norm-referenced test that does not match our standards because X's state standards were benchmarked at least one year above grade level. (Third graders are now expected to do fourth-grade work. This is true throughout the system.) An example of this problem is that one text recommended for approval in X is identified as a grade 5/4 textbook. Across the nation this textbook is in use by either fifth graders or advanced fourth graders. That's what the designation "5/4" means. Yet the panel approved this "5/4" textbook for use at grade 3 in X state because of the difficulty of the Y and Z standards and tests! Such developmentally inappropriate material will be a detriment to student learning.

Mathematics educators and students need your help. The Y and Z hold students to unreasonable expectations. These expectations will surely cause the next generation to be even more math phobic than our generation. A more reasonable, educationally sound approach is needed! You and your fellow legislators are the only ones who can stop this destructive action.

Creating Quality Classroom Assessments—Video Discussion

Optional

Activity PI-2

Goals/Rationale

The *Creating Sound Classroom Assessment*s video takes you step by step through the ideas associated with the five standards of quality assessment—clear and appropriate users and uses, clear and appropriate learning targets, target-method match, sampling, and potential sources of bias and distortion. It also explores barriers to better classroom assessment. The video comes complete with a facilitator's guide that helps you work through key ideas.

> **Cross-Reference to *Student-Involved Classroom Assessment*, 3d ed.**
>
> Chapters 1–4.
>
> **Additional Materials Needed**
>
> VIDEO: *Creating Sound Classroom Assessments*, available from the Assessment Training Institute, 800-480-3060.
>
> **Time Required**
>
> 60 minutes to view the video without doing the embedded activities. At least two hours if all the activities in the video are completed.

What to Do

Acquire the video and follow the steps clearly laid out in the trainer's guide.

Activity PI-3   Show What You Know

SELF-REFLECT

Recommended

Goals/Rationale

Periodically we encourage you to stop and reflect on your increasing confidence and competence as a classroom assessor. The reasons are twofold. First, we believe that self-reflection, self-assessment, and tracking one's own progress toward expertise—in short, learner involvement in assessment—can increase learning and motivate learners. Second, we're giving you an opportunity to try this out and see for yourself how it works, in case you want to try it with your own students. You can experience firsthand both the resistance to and the benefits of doing this kind of activity.

One aspect of self-reflection is to ask learners to "show what they know"—explain and articulate what they are learning and how it connects to other things in their lives. This activity proposes several ideas for doing this—ideas that might appeal to different learning styles. Any of the "show what you know" activities can be considered prime potential portfolio material.

Cross-Reference to *Student-Involved Classroom Assessment*, 3d ed.

Chapters 1–4.

Additional Materials Needed

None.

Time Required

Open, it's homework.

What to Do

1. *Recommended.* Make a list of assessments that do and don't meet standards of quality as outlined in Chapters 1–4. Briefly describe your rationale for including each on the list.

2. *Optional.* Write a letter to a colleague, student, parent, or instructor that answers the question: "What is quality classroom assessment and why should we care?"

3. *Optional.* Choose one or more of your most significant insights from the first four chapters. Explain it (them) in a journal-like article.

4.   *Optional.* Draw a concept map to show your current understanding of how the following ideas link:

Student-involved classroom assessment	Knowledge/Understanding targets
Clear and appropriate learning targets	Reasoning targets
Clear and appropriate users and uses	Skills targets
Selecting the proper method— target-method match	Products targets
Communicating clearly about results	Dispositional targets

5.   *Optional.* Draw pictures or make posters of your current understanding of the items in number 4.

6.   *Optional.* Outline the major learnings in Part I of *Student-Involved Classroom Assessment*, 3d ed. Include a statement of which of these might need to be considered for future assessment planning in your building or district. Include a list of questions that you might need to ask before you can determine future assessment planning in your district or building. Consider the barriers you might face in pursuing these areas that need improvement.

7.   *Optional.* Prepare a half-day workshop agenda for others that would (a) motivate participants to want to learn more about quality classroom assessment, and (b) help participants understand the nature of quality classroom assessment.

Activity PI-4   Portfolio Building

Recommended

Goals/Rationale

At the beginning of your study of classroom assessment you selected an assessment for your portfolio and critiqued it using the rubrics in *Workbook* Appendix B (see Activity Intro-1). Here's where you get to make additional choices from your working folder to put into your growth portfolio. Remember, the goal here is to reflect on and self-assess your growth on the following learning targets:

1. Standard 1—Clear and appropriate learning targets
2. Standard 2a—Clear and appropriate users and uses
3. Standard 2b—Sound communication about assessment
4. Standard 2c—Student involvement in assessment
5. Standard 3—Choosing the most appropriate assessment method
6. Standard 4—Sampling
7. Standard 5—Eliminating sources of bias and distortion

> **Cross-Reference to *Student-Involved Classroom Assessment*, 3d ed.**
>
> Chapters 1–4.
>
> **Additional Materials Needed**
>
> WORKBOOK: Appendix A, "Classroom Assessment Confidence Questionnaire," "Assessment Principles," and "Sample Working Folder/Portfolio Cover Sheet"; Appendix B, "Classroom Assessment Quality Rubrics"; Appendix C, "Self-Assessment Developmental Levels."
>
> **Time Required**
>
> Open, it's homework.

What to Do

Items 1 and 2 are recommended. The rest are optional. *Be sure to include a cover sheet* (such as that in Appendix A) with each portfolio entry that describes the date of production, the date entered in the portfolio, and what this entry shows about your increasing confidence and competence as a classroom assessor.

1. *Recommended.* At the beginning of study you selected an assessment to put in your portfolio (see Activity Intro-1). Take another look at it. Amend your commentary on its quality. (Do not remove your original commentary because it's useful to see how one's commentaries evolve over time.) Use the

rubrics in Appendix B to help direct your commentary. Do you notice any difference in the content and depth of your original commentary and your amended commentary?

2. *Recommended.* Select a new assessment (test, quiz, essay test, or performance assessment) that you have recently used or taken. This can be one that someone else developed or it can be one that you developed yourself. *If you are a current teacher, it must be one that you administered, scored, and recorded for use within the context of your teaching.* Using the rubrics in Appendix B, reflect on the quality of this assessment and write a brief analysis. What are its strengths? What things might be improved?

3. *Optional.* Self-assess using the developmental levels in Appendix C. There is a developmental levels for each of the five standards of quality assessment.

4. *Optional.* Write a statement of what you are doing differently in the classroom as the result of what you've learned so far.

5. *Optional.* complete the "Classroom Assessment Confidence Questionnaire" in Appendix A again.

6. *Optional.* What questions from your learning log or previous activities can you now answer? What new questions do you have?

7. *Optional.* Reread the document, "Assessment Principles" in Appendix A. Now, which principles affirm your own beliefs? Why? Are there any with which you disagree either in part or in whole? Why? What concerns might you have about any of them?

8. *Optional.* Add other artifacts from your working folder to your portfolio to demonstrate increasing competence and confidence in the knowledge, reasoning, skills, and products associated with sound classroom assessment.

Notes:

PART II

Understanding Assessment Methods

Selected Response Assessment: Flexible and Efficient

Big Ideas in This Chapter

This chapter answers the following guiding question:

When and how do I use selected response assessment most effectively?

The **General Principles** addressed in this chapter are as follows:

1. Selected response assessments align well with knowledge and understanding targets, as well as with some patterns of reasoning.

2. They can be efficiently developed in three steps: blueprinting, focusing, and item writing.

3. This method can fall prey to avoidable sources of bias that can distort results if users are not careful.

4. By involving our students in selected response assessment development and use, we can set them up for confident, energetic, and successful learning.

Yes, multiple-choice, true/false, and matching are still valued! They are efficient and can be used to assess a range of targets. This first chapter on assessment methods deals with the strengths, weaknesses, and successful uses of the traditional selected response mode of assessment. Selected response formats require students to choose answers from a provided list rather than having to come up with an answer themselves. (Many assessment professionals also include "fill in the blank" in this category because of the simple nature of the recall that this method requires and because fill-in questions usually only have one [or a few] correct answers. Fill-in is closer to selected response than to constructed response methods.)

Links to Previous Chapters

This is the first of four chapters that expand on the assessment methods first introduced in textbook Chapter 4. This chapter covers the "selected response" column of textbook Figure 4.2, "A Plan for Matching Assessment Methods with Achievement Targets," more fully by:

- Detailing how to develop selected response assessments.

- Expanding on the notion of student involvement. Specifically, how does one involve students with selected response assessments?

- Going deeper into target-method match for selected response assessment methods.

- Delving into a topic only briefly described in Chapter 4: reliability and validity issues—sampling and potential sources of bias and distortion in selected response assessments.

Links to Subsequent Chapters

- As noted above, this is the first of four chapters that focus on specific assessment methods. Chapters 6–8 deal respectively with essay, performance assessment, and personal communication.

- Resigning selected-response assessments well requires some understanding of patterns of reasoning—which is not covered thoroughly until Chapter 9. As a result, some of the *Workbook* practice activities have been simplified if they require more extensive knowledge of reasoning patterns than is presented in Chapter 5.

Portfolio and Learning Log Reminder

Once again, we remind you that it is important to keep potential portfolio material handy. Look at suggestions from the previous chapters. We highly recommend that you keep a learning log to record your questions as they come up during the reading of these next four chapters. This will help you monitor your own comprehension and increase your understanding of the topics.

Roadmap

Activity	Title	Activity Description	Time	Icons
5-1	*Common Sense Paper and Pencil Assessments*—Video Discussion	Target-method match, developing high-quality selected response questions, and student involvement. *Cross-reference to Chapter 5:* General Principles 1, 2, 3, and 4.	1–2 hours	CONSOLIDATE UNDERSTANDING
5-2	*Write Propositions and Test Questions	Writing test items from a blueprint using propositions. *Cross-reference to Chapter 5:* General Principles 2 and 3.	10–15 min; rest is homework	CONSOLIDATE UNDERSTANDING
5-3	Test of Franzipanics	Writing high quality test items. *Cross-reference to Chapter 5:* General Principle 3.	15-20 min	QUICK CHECK
5-4	Setting up a Tropical Fish Tank—Case Discussion	Writing high-quality test items. *Cross-reference to Chapter 5:* General Principles 2 and 3.	45-70 min	CONSOLIDATE UNDERSTANDING
5-5	*Item Sleuth	Sources of bias/distortion. *Cross-reference to Chapter 5:* General Principle 3.	15–30 min; rest is prework	APPLY LEARNING
5-6	Unit-Building Activity, Assignment 3—Selected Response Questions	The ultimate application—developing selected response questions for one of your units. *Cross-reference to Chapter 5:* General Principles 1, 2, and 3.	30–40 min; rest is prework	APPLY LEARNING
5-7	Try This with Students	How to involve students with selected response test items. *Cross-reference to Chapter 5:* General Principle 4.	5–15 min; rest is prework	APPLY LEARNING

*Recommended

Activity 5-1

Common Sense Paper and Pencil Assessments—Video Discussion

Optional

Goals/Rationale

The *Common Sense Paper and Pencil Assessments* video takes you step by step through the ideas associated with developing and using selected response assessment formats. It comes complete with a facilitator's guide that helps you work through key issues.

> **Cross-Reference to *Student-Involved Classroom Assessment*, 3d ed.**
>
> General Principles 1, 2, 3, and 4: Target-method match, developing high-quality selected response questions, and student involvement.
>
> **Additional Materials Needed**
>
> VIDEO: *Common Sense Paper and Pencil Assessments*, available from the Assessment Training Institute, 800-480-3060.
>
> **Time Required**
>
> 60 minutes to view the video without doing the embedded activities. At least two hours if all the activities in the video are completed.

What to Do

Acquire the video and follow the steps clearly laid out in the facilitator's guide.

Activity 5-2

Write Propositions and Test Items

Recommended

Goals/Rationale

This activity is intended to provide practice in transforming important learnings stated as propositions into test items. When you develop a test first as a list of propositions, you can gauge the appropriateness of the coverage by asking if the propositions really capture what is important in the material. When that coverage is appropriate, then test items fall out naturally. By stating important learnings as propositions, you can center on clear and appropriate knowledge and reasoning targets—the focus of Chapter 3.

Cross-Reference to *Student-Involved Classroom Assessment*, 3d ed.

General Principles 2 and 3: Writing high quality test items from a blueprint using propositions.

Additional Materials Needed

None.

Time Required

10–15 minutes; rest is homework.

What to Do

Part A: Practice

1. (5 minutes) Study the worksheet, "Transforming Propositions into Test Items." Note that the transformation is quite literal in every case.

2. (5–10 minutes) Transform into test items each of the subsequent examples of propositions given on the worksheet.

Part B: Apply to Your Own Classroom

Based on the material you teach or plan to teach, formulate propositions that capture learnings that will be important for your students to master. Then transform them into selected response test questions.

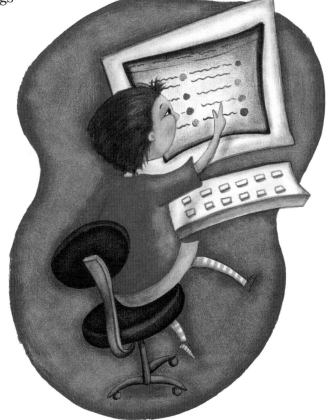

Transforming Propositions Into Test Items— Examples

Proposition

Three causes for the rapid decline of the numbers of Pacific salmon are destruction of river spawning habitat, overfishing by commercial interests, and weakened genetics due to hatchery reproduction.

True True/False: One reason for declining numbers of Pacific salmon is destruction of spawning habitat.

False True/False: One reason for declining numbers of Pacific salmon is the failure to fund more hatchery breeding.

Fill in: What are the reasons for declining numbers of Pacific salmon?

Multiple Choice: Which of the following is a reason for decline numbers of Pacific salmon?

a. Too many fish spawning in the same beds

b. Destruction of river spawning habitat

c. Overfishing by sport anglers

d. Failure to fund more hatchery breeding

More Review

To review another example, return to textbook Chapter 5 to the section on propositions (p. 135-136) and study the transformations of the proposition on government.

Now It's Your Turn

Transform into test items the following propositions, from differing grade levels and content areas:

- Automobiles and factories are the major causes of air pollution in cities.

- The water cycle depends on evaporation and condensation.

- In the United States, we have a bicameral legislature.

- Our free market economy system is based on the law of supply and demand.

Test of Franzipanics

Activity 5-3

Optional

Goals/Rationale

When selected response questions are flawed, the test-taker can get questions correct without knowing anything. This is illustrated in the worksheet, "Test of Franzipanics." Even though the test is nonsensical, it is still possible to get all the questions correct by knowing some of the pitfalls in item construction.

> **Cross-Reference to *Student-Involved Classroom Assessment*, 3d ed.**
>
> General Principle 3: Sources of bias and distortion in selected response questions.
>
> **Additional Materials Needed**
>
> None.
>
> **Time Required**
>
> 15-20 minutes.

What to Do

1. (5 minutes) Take the "Test of Franzipanics" on the attached worksheet. Note your rationale for choosing each answer.

2. (5 minutes) If you are working in a group, compile the "right" answers and what gave away the answer.

3. (5–10 minutes) Think about or discuss characteristics of high-quality test items—What should you avoid doing? What should you be sure and do? Consider compiling this list for everyone.

Test of Franzipanics[1]

Directions: Circle the correct answer for each question.

1.　The purpose of the cluss in furmpaling is to remove
　　a.　cluss-prags
　　b.　tremalis
　　c.　cloughs
　　d.　plumots

2.　Trassig is true when
　　a.　lusp trasses the vom
　　b.　the viskal flans, if the viskal is donwil or zortil
　　c.　the belgo frulls
　　d.　dissles lisk easily

3.　The sigla frequently overfesks the trelsum because
　　a.　all siglas are mellious
　　b.　siglas are always votial
　　c.　the trelsum is usually tarious
　　d.　no trelsa are feskable

4.　The fribbled breg will minter best with an
　　a.　derst
　　b.　morst
　　c.　sorter
　　d.　ignu

5.　Among the reasons for tristal doss are
　　a.　the sabs foped and the foths tinzed
　　b.　the kredges roted with the orots
　　c.　few rakobs were accepted in sluth
　　d.　most of the polats were thonced

6.　Which of the following (is, are) always present when trossels are being gruven?
　　a.　rint and vost
　　b.　sot and plone
　　c.　shum and vost
　　d.　vost

7.　The mintering function of the ignu is most effectively carried out in connection with
　　a.　a raxma tol
　　b.　the groshing stantol
　　c.　the fribbled breg
　　d.　a frally sush

8.
　　a.
　　b.
　　c.
　　d.

[1]Here are the answers, but don't peek until you get done. 1 = a (the word "cluss" is repeated); 2 = b (it's the longest); 3 = c ("usually" is more often correct than "all" "always" and "no"); 4 = d ("an" in the stem implies the answer will begin with a vowel); 5 = a ("are" implies more than one reason); 6 = b ("vost" is in all the others); 7 = c (the answer to 4 gives this one away); 8 = d (the pattern of responses go a, b, c, d).

Setting up a Tropical Fish Tank—Case Discussion

Activity 5-4

Optional

Goals/Rationale

A good strategy for helping novice test developers become comfortable is to provide them with sample "flawed" tests. This activity gives you this opportunity.

> **Cross-Reference to *Student-Involved Classroom Assessment*, 3d ed.**
>
> General Principles 2 and 3: Developing high-quality selected response questions.
>
> **Additional Materials Needed**
>
> WORKBOOK: Appendix B, "Assessment Sample 3: Fish Tank."
> TEXTBOOK: Figure 5.3, "Test Item Quality Checklist."
>
> **Time Required**
>
> 45-70 minutes.

What to Do

1.   (10-15 minutes) You will be reading about a lesson for grades 5-8 on how to set up an aquarium. The lesson has two parts. In part one the students read an information sheet and then observe the instructor actually setting up a new tank. In part two students work in small groups to actually set up a tank using the directions provided by the instructor. "Setting up a Tropical Fish Tank" (*Workbook* Appendix B) includes the information sheet, a set of test specifications to guide the development of a test, and the test the instructor developed to assess learning. (Students can view the information sheet as they take the test.)

     Read "Setting up a Tropical Fish Tank.". Is it clear what targets the teacher is addressing with this lesson? What's most important for this unit: Remembering facts? Drawing inferences? Making judgments? Something else? Are these important enough targets to devote this amount of testing time? Discuss your opinions with your colleagues, if you are working in a group.

2.   (5–10 minutes) The teacher has also developed a blueprint (test specifications) for a test on this unit. Does the blueprint offer a good testing plan, given the content of the lesson? Why

or why not? Discuss your opinion with your colleagues, if you are working in a group.

3. (10-15 minutes) For now assume that everyone agrees that the lesson targets are important enough to assess and that the blueprint is okay as is. This may not be so, but the purpose of the next part of this activity is to see whether the creator of this blueprint did in fact write a test to match it. You will need to do the following:

    a. Determine the types of thinking skills actually called for by the test questions.

    b. Match the actual breakdown to the breakdown in the blueprint.

    c. Answer this question: Did the instructor choose the best method to assess each target? If the answer is no, what might be done differently?

4. (20-30 minutes) Regardless of the correctness of the methods chosen, are the questions well written? Look at one or more questions. What are possible problems? Use textbook Figure 5.3, "Test Item Quality Checklist," as needed.

Activity 5-5 — Item Sleuth

Recommended

Goals/Rationale

The best way to learn about writing quality items is to look at flawed items and fix them. In this task, you become an "item sleuth" to find and fix selected response test items.

> **Cross-Reference to *Student-Involved Classroom Assessment*, 3d ed.**
>
> General Principle 3: Avoiding possible sources of biased distortion in selected response test items.
>
> **Additional Materials Needed**
>
> Team members will need to find their own flawed questions.
>
> **Time Required**
>
> 15–30 minutes; rest is prework.

Part A: Preparation/Prework

Individual team or class members should find at least three flawed selected response test questions from tests they have recently given or taken. Note the nature of the flaw and rewrite the question to fix the flaw.

Part B: Do with Colleagues

(15-30 minutes) Share items with each other. Can anyone find additional flaws in any of the questions? Can anyone rewrite any question in other ways?

Unit-Building Activity, Assignment 3— Selected Response Questions

Optional

Activity 5-6

Goals/Rationale

This is the third in a series of direct applications to day-to-day life in the classroom. This unit-building activity centers on the role of selected response questions in the unit you are developing.

> **Cross-Reference to *Student-Involved Classroom Assessment*, 3d ed.**
>
> General Principles 1, 2, and 3: Developing high-quality selected response questions.
>
> **Additional Materials Needed**
>
> Your draft unit plan so far.
>
> **Time Required**
>
> 30–40 minutes; rest is prework.

What to Do

Part A: Preparation/Prework

Zero in on one or more knowledge and understanding targets in your draft unit that would be appropriate for selected response assessment. Attend also to the prerequisite knowledge and reasoning skills implied by your skills and product targets.

1. Develop a test blueprint (table of specifications) for the selected response component(s) of the target(s) that you have identified.

2. Find the key propositions for each cell in your table and construct test questions for your propositions. Be sure to follow the guidelines for high-quality questions in Chapter 5.

Part B: Do with Colleagues

1. (10–15 minutes) Act as a "critical friend" for a partner and ask questions about the test blueprint, propositions, or high-quality selected response questions. (Reminder: This is a first run; there's no expectation of perfection. There will be opportunities later to refine your initial work.)

2. (15 minutes) Work together to repair any questions that violate one or more guidelines.

3. (5–10 minutes) Have a whole-team discussion about selected response assessment. Draw on the group to strengthen your understanding of this method.

Activity 5-7

Try This with Students

Optional

Goals/Rationale

There are ways to involve students in all types of assessment. Chapter 5 provides examples for selected response methods. In this activity you'll choose something you want to try with students, try it out and report back.

> **Cross-Reference to *Student-Involved Classroom Assessment*, 3d ed.**
>
> General Principle 4: Student involvement.
>
> **Additional Materials Needed**
>
> You may need extra materials depending on the application you choose.
>
> **Time Required**
>
> 5–15 minutes; rest is prework.

What to Do

Part A: Preparation/Prework

Choose one of the ideas in the worksheet, "Ideas for Student Involvement—Selected Response Formats," and try it with students. Make notes on what you did and how it worked. Would you try it again? Why or why not? What might you do differently next time?

Part B: Do with Colleagues

(5–15 minutes) Share your activities and results with other members of your team or class.

Ideas for Student Involvement—Selected Response Formats*

1. Develop a table of test specifications for a final unit test before teaching the unit. Share a copy of that plan with every student. Review it carefully at the beginning of the unit and explain your expectations at that time. Now students and teacher share the same vision.

2. Involve students in devising the test plan, or involve them from time to time in checking back to the blueprint (1) to see together—as partners—if you might need to make adjustments in the test plan and/or (2) to chart your progress together.

3. Involve students in writing practice test items. You can use these items in the following ways:

    a. Have students work in pairs to answer each other's items. (If quality is an issue, collect the items and redistribute the best ones for pair practice.)

    b. Assign teams of two or three students responsibility for writing a few items for one cell of a test blueprint. Then have teams exchange and answer each other's items.

    c. Use one or two student-generated items on the actual test, if they are good enough.

       Think of the benefits: the students will have to evaluate the importance of the various elements of content, and they will have to become proficient in using the kinds of thinking and problem solving valued in your classroom. Developing sample test items provides high-fidelity practice in doing these things.

4. As a variation on this theme, provide unlabeled test items and have students practice (1) placing them in the proper cell of the test blueprint, and (2) answering them.

5. As another variation, have students evaluate the quality of the tests that came with the textbook—do they match your plan developed for instruction?

*Based on textbook Figure 5.5, "Ideas for Student Involvement."

6.   Have students use the test blueprint to predict how they are going to do on each part of the test before they take it. Then have them analyze how they did, part by part, after taking it. If the first test is for practice, such an analysis will provide valuable information to help them plan their preparation for the real thing.

7.   Have students work in teams, with each team responsible for finding ways to help everyone in class score high in one cell, row, or column of a table of specifications or on one learning objective.

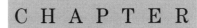

Essay Assessment: Subjective and Powerful

Big Ideas in This Chapter

> This chapter answers the following guiding question:
>
> *When and how do I use essay assessment most effectively?*

1. Essay assessment aligns well with knowledge and understanding targets, as well as with various patterns of reasoning.

2. Assessments can be effectively developed in three steps: assessment planning, exercise development, and preparation to score student responses.

3. This method can fall prey to avoidable sources of bias that can distort results if users are not careful.

4. By involving our students in essay assessment development and use, we can set them up for energetic and successful learning.

Teachers need to know the strengths, weaknesses, and keys to successful use of the essay assessment format, especially in these times of increasingly complex achievement targets. When teachers understand the scoring process for essays and can manage it, they can turn essay assessment into a surprisingly efficient method.

Textbook Chapter 6 points out that the power of the essay stretches far beyond its perceived capacity to provide data on student achievement when we make students partners in assessment design and development.

Links to Previous Chapters

This is the second of four chapters that expand on the assessment methods first introduced in textbook Chapter 4. Chapter 5 looked at selected response assessments, the current chapter considers essay assessments, and the next two deal with performance assessment and personal communication.

This chapter covers the "essay" column of textbook Figure 4.2, "A Plan for Matching Assessment Methods with Achievement Targets," more fully by:

- Detailing how to develop essay assessments.

- Expanding on the notion of student involvement. Specifically, how does one involve students with essay assessments?

- Going deeper into target-method match for essay assessment methods.

- Delving into a topic only briefly described in Chapter 4: reliability and validity issues—sampling and potential sources of bias and distortion in essay assessments.

Links to Subsequent Chapters

- Essay assessment, and the next two chapters on performance assessment and personal communication, are alike in that these forms of assessment all require a concrete means to judge the quality of student responses—performance criteria.

- As with selected response assessments, designing essay assessments well requires some understanding of patterns of reasoning—which is not covered thoroughly until Chapter 9. Therefore, some of the activities in Chapter 6 will be simplified.

Portfolio Reminder

Once again, we remind you that it is important to keep potential portfolio material handy. See the suggestions in previous chapters.

Roadmap

Activity	Title	Activity Description	Time	Icons
6-1	Accounting for More—Case Discussion	Avoiding subjectiveness in scoring essays. *Cross-reference to Chapter 6:* General Principle 3.	10–20 min	QUICK CHECK
6-2	*When to Use Essay	Clarifies target-method match for essay assessment. *Cross-reference to Chapter 6:* General Principle 1.	15–30 min	CONSOLIDATE UNDERSTANDING
6-3	*Practice Analyzing Essay Questions	Provides practice in analyzing essay questions for quality. *Cross-reference to Chapter 6:* General Principles 2 and 3.	30–45 min; rest is homework	CONSOLIDATE UNDERSTANDING
6-4	Assessing Conceptual Understanding	Practice in scoring essay questions in mathematics for conceptual understanding—both you and your students. *Cross-reference to Chapter 6:* General Principles 2, 3, and 4.	40-75 min; rest is homework	APPLY LEARNING CONSOLIDATE UNDERSTANDING
6-5	Unit-Building Activity, Assignment 4—Essay Assessment	Continued work on your own unit, choosing when to use essays and developing high-quality essays. *Cross-reference to Chapter 6:* General Principles 1, 2, and 3.	45–60 min; rest is homework	APPLY LEARNING

*Recommended

Activity 6-1   Accounting for More

Optional

Goals/Rationale

This activity is good for "activating prior knowledge" about essay exams by bringing up a situation familiar to all teachers—consistent scoring. The activity also brings up many of the topics in Chapter 6— target-method match, scoring, and designing novel essay questions to assess reasoning.

> **Cross-Reference to *Student-Involved Classroom Assessment*, 3d ed.**
>
> General Principle 3: Avoiding sources of bias/distortion.
>
> **Additional Materials Needed**
> None.
>
> **Time Required**
> 10–20 minutes.

What to Do

1. (5–10 minutes) Read the worksheet, "Accounting for More." Think about the following questions as you read:

    a. Is it fair to place one student higher on a continuum of achievement when there was nothing in the prompt that suggested more than one solution would be rewarded?

    b. What implications does this have for the way the essay question is worded?

    c. What is the relationship between essay question wording and criteria for scoring responses?

    d. Is it clear what is really being assessed here? Recall of facts? Ability to reason? Ability to apply knowledge to a new situation? Is it possible to make recommendations about this particular essay question and scoring mechanism without clearly knowing the learning target(s) being assessed?

    e. What strategies could be used to ensure that students understand the criteria for strong responses?

2. (5–10 minutes) Think about, or if working in a group, discuss the following questions:

a. Did you ever encounter a similar situation? What are the underlying issues?

b. What advice would you give this group of middle school teachers? Why?

c. As the result of this activity are there any questions you can answer now that you couldn't before?

Accounting For More—Case

You're part of a group of middle school teachers scoring student responses to an essay. The scoring guide uses a continuum that combines numeric scores (1–5) and descriptive words (Exemplary, Proficient, Developing, etc.). One of the criteria that you are scoring is the correctness of the answer.

There isn't much of a description for this criterion and at first that doesn't seem to be a problem. As one of the teachers at your table jokes, how can there be degrees of correctness to a correct answer? Then the group arrives at the following essay item:

Prompt: A farmer lost his entire crop. Why might this have happened?

Response 1: Drought

Response 2: Floods and heavy rains destroyed them.
Unsuitable soil/land, so the crop died.
Drought destroyed them.
The birds ate all the seeds.
Was demolished for business construction.
He didn't take proper care of his crops.
Went bankrupt, unable to look after his crop.
Unsuitable environment for growing his crops.

It seems fairly obvious that the second response is a much fuller and more complete answer. Then one teacher raises the question of whether the exercise communicated clearly to students that multiple reasons were required for an exemplary answer. He asks the group to think about the student who provided the first response. "How would we respond if the student points out that she answered the question and that the answer is correct? I know that some of my students would think it was really unfair to demand more than the task prompts, especially at their age, when they are incredibly sensitive about fairness."

Another teacher argues that you must be honest about the quality of the answers. "The first student's answer is okay but not sufficient to be scored exemplary. It isn't even a complete sentence. Any student would know that such a minimal answer is not going to get a high score."

The first teacher disagrees. "I don't think that the prompt is clear about what would constitute an exemplary answer. If we want students to produce quality work, we need to include enough detail in the question itself to help them understand what quality work looks like."

A third teacher calls the group back to the criteria. "Our criteria for judging quality aren't fully developed yet. This is an example of what happens when we only have sketchy criteria—we can all interpret the criteria differently, and so can students."

Activity 6-2

When to Use Essay

Recommended

Goals/Rationale

Essay questions can be used to assess knowledge, understanding, and reasoning learning targets. This activity is designed to solidify understanding of those targets best assessed with essay formats.

> **Cross-Reference to *Student-Involved Classroom Assessment*, 3d ed.**
>
> Guiding Principle 1: Target-method match; essay should be used to assess knowledge and understanding targets.
>
> **Additional Materials Needed**
> None.
>
> **Time Required**
> 15–30 minutes.

What to Do

1. (5-10 minutes) Think about the following questions:

   a. What is the definition of *essay assessment*? What is an *essay*?

   b. What learning targets are best measured with essay questions?

   c. What questions do you have about either the definition or the way it matches to targets?

2. (5–10 minutes) Sometimes the relationship between essay and performance assessment is confusing. When does an essay become a performance assessment? Is an open-ended math problem an essay or a performance assessment? Is a writing assessment an essay or a performance assessment?

Look at the diagram below, "Venn Diagram: Essay versus Performance Assessment." This figure represents Rick's view of the relationship between essay and performance assessment. Think about or discuss how your current understanding matches this. Do you disagree with the figure at any point? Where?

3. (5–10 minutes) Think about, or if you are working in a group, discuss the following proposition: There is no truth in the assertion that essay exams and performance assessments only overlap when assessing writing. These labels are merely conceptual conveniences to assist us to order our thinking. Which is more important: (a) having a good idea of the assessment options and how targets match to methods in general, or (b) splitting hairs on what is or is not an essay or a performance assessment?

Venn Diagram: Essay versus Performance Assessment

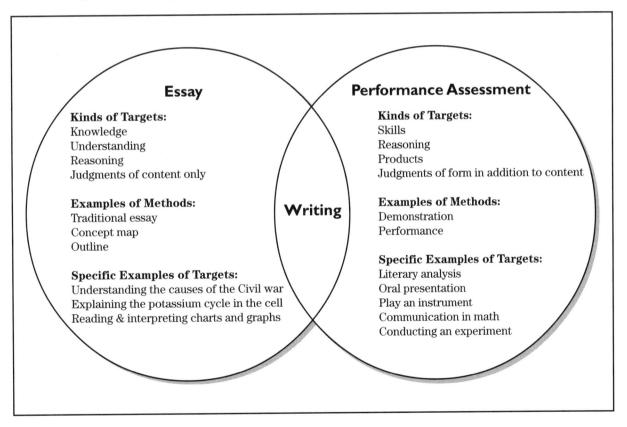

Activity 6-3   Practice Analyzing Essay Questions

Recommended

Goals/Rationale

One of the best ways to become familiar with characteristics of quality essay questions is to analyze samples for quality. This activity provides sample essay questions and then invites you to become essay assessment sleuths to find and fix other essay questions with which you are familiar.

> **Cross-Reference to *Student-Involved Classroom Assessment*, 3d ed.**
>
> General Principles 2 and 3: How to write high-quality essay test items.
>
> **Additional Materials Needed**
> None.
>
> **Time Required**
> 30–45 minutes; rest is homework.

What to Do

Part A: Preparation/Do with Colleagues

1. (5 minutes) If you are working in a group, make sure everyone understands the following assignment: Use the worksheet, "Quality Guidelines for Essays," to evaluate for quality each item in the worksheet, "Sample Essay Questions." Brainstorm other factors besides those in the worksheet "Quality Guidelines for Essays" that can cause a score to misrepresent real student achievement.

2. (10–15 minutes) Individually critique the items on the worksheet, "Sample Essay Questions."

3. (10–15 minutes) Think about or discuss with each other what you noted about the quality of the essay questions.

4. (5–10 minutes) Think about or discuss insights about essay questions and the implications of this activity for what you might be doing in your classroom next week.

Part B: Homework

Find additional essay questions that you use or have experienced and critique them for quality. Be ready at the next team meeting to report on what you have found.

Quality Guidelines for Essays

The following guidelines summarize the information from textbook Figures 6.2, 6.4, and 6.5 and relate it back to *Workbook* Figure 2, "Five Standards of Quality Assessment."

1. **Quality Assessment Standard 1—Clear and appropriate learning targets.** Are the targets to be assessed clear?

2. **Quality Assessment Standard 3—Target-Method Match.** Is essay assessment the appropriate method to use?

3. **Quality Assessment Standard 4—Sampling.** Do the exercises adequately sample the material? Do all students get the same exercises (ability to choose can bias results)?

4. **Quality Assessment Standard 5—Avoiding Sources of Bias and Distortion.**

   - *Task Clarity.* Do exercises call for brief, focused responses? Is the target knowledge clear? Is the thinking to be done clear? Is the essay question written at the lowest possible reading level—will all students understand what they are to do?

   - *Criteria Clarity.* Would qualified experts in the field agree with the definition of a quality response? Are the criteria clear—would the elements in the scoring plan be obvious to good students (without giving away the answer)? Do the criteria match the exercise?

   - *Student Considerations.* Will respondents' level of writing proficiency in English be adequate to show you what they know and can do? Is there anything in the question that might put a group of students at a disadvantage regardless of their knowledge level?

   - *Scoring Considerations.* Will the number of students to be evaluated be such that the raters can adequately assess each response? Is there an adequate amount of person time available to read and evaluate responses? Have all scorers been adequately trained to consistently score the essays—will there be a high level of rater agreement?

	Essay 1	Essay 2	Essay 3	Essay 4
Clear Targets?				
Appropriate Method?				
Adequate Sampling?				
Task Clarity?				
Criteria Clarity?				
Student Considerations?				
Scoring Considerations?				

Sample Essay Questions

Essay 1: Label the Graph.[1] This question is intended for grades 3–12. It is one of six exercises using different content to assess problem solving in mathematics. Results are used to track individual student progress toward mastery of state content standards. The scoring criteria have four traits, each scored separately by trained raters—conceptual understanding, mathematical procedures, strategic reasoning, and communication in mathematics. Students may or may not see the criteria depending on the teacher.

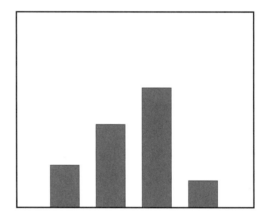

1. What might this be the graph of? Put titles and numbers on the graph to show what you mean.

2. Write down everything you know from your graph.

Essay 2: Assembly Line. Intended for grade 6. No scoring mechanism, uses, or targets are described.

"Describe the effect of the development of the assembly line on American society."

Essay 3: Day and Night.[2] The authors provide examples of several different types of assessment tasks in science—short response to assess knowledge, extended response (essay) to assess conceptual understanding, and performance assessments to assess "science knowledge in context," integration of knowledge, practical skills, and reporting skills. The authors use all the sample questions as examples to illustrate methods and when to use them; they specifically state "the assessment tasks provided . . . are not exhaustive, but exemplary. . . ." The sample questions are not meant to be a complete test of any targets.

---

[1]Used in several assessments, for example the Oregon state mathematics assessment in 1996.

[2]Australian Council for Educational Research Ltd., *Exemplary Assessment Materials—Science*, 1996, p. 15. Available from The Board of Studies, 15 Pelham St., Carlton, Victoria 3053.

The following task is intended for grade 2 to assess science understanding.

"Everyone knows about day and night. Write what you think makes day and night. [Four primary lines are given for the response.] Draw a picture to show what you think. (5"x5" box given for response.)"

The scoring criteria are shown in the following table. Students don't see the criteria.

Score	Label	Description	Examples
2	Scientific Conception	The response indicates that the Earth turns so that the same face is not always facing the Sun.	"The Earth turns every 24 hours and for 12 hours we are facing the Sun."
1	Opposite Sides	The response indicates that the Moon and Sun are on different sides of the Earth and the Earth rotates facing one and then the other. There is no implication that the Sun moves.	"In the day we face the Sun and in the night we turn to face the Moon."
0	Sun Moves	The response indicates that the Sun moves to cause night and day (possibly across the sky).	"The Sun moves and makes way for the Moon."

Additional Notes: Some responses may have mixed the elements of the last two categories. If so, give the score for the lower response. An indication that the Sun moves should take precedence in determining the lower category.

Essay 4: Emerson Quiz.[3] This quiz is intended for grades 10–12 to assess mastery of content knowledge (knowledge of Emerson) and reasoning in literature. Results will be used as 10 percent of the final grade in a literature class. Two of the ten similar essay questions are provided below. Students get 1 point for their answer and 1 point for their rationale.

"Read each of the statements below and put a check if Emerson would most likely complete the activity or put an X if he would disagree or not do the listed activity. For each answer, write your rationale. Include a statement from Emerson's work to support your check or X. Be sure to quote the statement directly and give the page number in parentheses. Use the introduction to Emerson, *Nature*, and 'Self-Reliance.'

2. _____ look to the past for guidance.
5. _____ join a popular civic organization.

[3]From Thomas Mavor, 1999, Brother Martin High School, 4401 Elysian Fields Ave., New Orleans, LA 70122.

Activity 6-4   Assessing Conceptual Understanding

Optional

Goals/Rationale

This activity gives users a chance to include students as partners in essay assessment scoring. This makes the connection between assessment and instruction/student involvement more real. By seeing how students might become involved in essay assessment, you might be more likely to use the essay format.

> **Cross-Reference to *Student-Involved Classroom Assessment*, 3d ed.**
>
> General Principles 2, 3, and 4: Developing high-quality essays and involving students.
>
> **Additional Materials Needed**
>
> TEXTBOOK: Figure 6.4, "Guidelines for Essay Scoring," Figure 6.6, "Ideas for Student-Involved Assessment."
>
> **Time Required**
>
> 40-75 minutes; rest is homework.

What to Do

Part A: Preparation/Do with Colleagues

1. (10–15 minutes) Read the worksheet, "General Conceptual Understanding Rubric." This rubric was developed to assist a high school physical education staff assess student health and fitness plans. However, it might be adaptable to assess the conceptual understanding of any topic. Think about or discuss the following questions:

   a. Would experts (you included) agree that the features in the rubric really are indicators of sound conceptual understanding? Are the indicators clear? Are there other important indicators? If you used this rubric would you *really* be assessing conceptual understanding?

   b. Could you use this rubric to assess conceptual understanding of *any* topic? Why or why not?

   c. Not all scoring mechanisms for essays have to be this complicated. Some can be simple, like the one in Activity 6-3, "Practice Analyzing Essay Questions," Sample 3. Simple scoring mechanisms might be best when using essay questions to assess knowledge, and more complicated rubrics are best when using them to assess conceptual understanding and reasoning. Do you agree? Why or why not?

2. (15–30 minutes) Practice using this rubric to score the samples of student work on the worksheet, "Sample Grade 4 Student Responses." Follow the guidelines in textbook Figure 6.4, "Guidelines for Essay Scoring," as you score—check the rubric against a few real responses to see if you must make any last-minute adjustments; refer to the rubric frequently when scoring; check your scores with those of others.

3. (10-15 minutes) If you are working in a group, debrief with others. Consider the following questions: What are the advantages of using a rubric when assessing essay responses? Could you use this rubric in your classroom? Would it make assessment easier or harder? Would it make communication to students about performance easier or harder? This is a rubric that can be used to assess conceptual understanding of any topic; might there be specific indicators of quality you could add for specific topics? For example?

4. (5–15 minutes) If you plan to try this activity with students, think about, or if you are working in a group, discuss the following questions:

   a. Could students score these essays using the rubric provided? What would students learn from doing this—what learning targets would this activity assist students to hit? Would the instructional time required to have students do this be worth the learning that occurs?

   b. In what grade levels could you use the rubric provided? Would you have to modify the rubric for student use in other grade levels? If so, how?

   c. Beginning at what grade level could students actually read the sample student responses well enough to assess their quality? What might you do at earlier grade levels to have students practice using criteria to score conceptual understanding?

    d. If you were to try scoring in the classroom with your students, how would you introduce the activity to them? What would you do first? Second? How would you tie this activity to the learning targets you want students to hit? How would you tie it together so that students understand what they will learn from practicing scoring?

Part B: Try with Students

The use of essay scoring criteria to help students understand the nature of quality is a hallmark of student involvement in assessment. Specifically, textbook Figure 6.6 states:

- "Have students play a role in developing the scoring criteria for some sample exercises."

- "Bring students into the actual scoring process."

Do the work required to modify the rubric or student responses so that your students can use them productively. (Get students to help!) Plan how you're going to do this activity in your classroom. Carry out your plan. Be prepared to share what happened.

General Conceptual Understanding Rubric

Conceptual understanding is the extent to which students understand the content they are to learn.

High: A high score in conceptual understanding means that the student shows an accurate and extensive understanding of the topic. This can be shown in many ways, including the following:

- Uses terminology correctly and precisely.

- Selects precisely the pieces of information required to make a point (no more, no less).

- Uses examples and counterexamples correctly and appropriately.

- Has few errors in information.

- Makes connections to other, related topics.

- Demonstrates which distinctions are important to make.

- Identifies and addresses key concepts.

- Sustains a relevant focus throughout the work.

- Makes relevant use of a diagram or graph; knows when such things will aid understanding.

- Explanations are concise and to the point.

Medium: A medium score in conceptual understanding means that the student presents some important information, but there is a sense that the student is only about halfway home in terms of understanding. Medium performance is indicated by the following:

- Reasonably clear ideas, but the reader needs to make some guesses as to what the student meant.

- Even though a general point is made, the student hasn't fine-tuned the topic.

- Some parts of the work seem repetitive.

- The balance in the work seems off.

- Some vocabulary is used well, some is not.

- Some examples and graphics are appropriate, some aren't.

- Sometimes the student seems to know which concepts and points are most important and telling; other times not.

- Information seems to be based on retelling rather than the student making his or her own connections.

- The focus tends to shift.

Low: A low score in conceptual understanding indicates that the student is still searching for the connections that will make the content meaningful. Weak performance is indicated by the following:

- Ideas are extremely limited or hard to understand, even when the reader tries to draw inferences based on what is there.

- The text may be repetitious or may read like a collection of disconnected, random thoughts.

- Information is inaccurate.

- Terminology is used incorrectly.

- There is little sense of which information is most important.

- Visual displays, when used, are not helpful or unrelated to any points the student is trying to make.

Sample Grade 4 Student Responses

Health:[4] "Explain why people should not tease, bully, or threaten each other. What are some ways of coping or dealing POSITIVELY with anger or frustration?"

Student response 1: People should not tease, bully, or threaten because they can get in trouble, and they can make friends. You could deal with it like just walk away or take deep breaths and ignore them or try controling yourself.

Student response 2: People should not tease, bully, or threaten because it hurts feelings or makes someone scared or even could pshically hurt someone let alone feelings. The way of coping or dealing with anger or frustration you could take deep breaths, don't do it in a rush, think about what your angry or frustrated about and try to solve it, punch a pillow or kick your bed to get it out, try to get busy to take your mind off of it. Scream in your pillow. Talk to the person that did or said something to make you angry or talk to a friend about it.

Student response 3: People should not bully or tease people because it could hurt them in two ways physically or hurt their feelings. If you or someone else is being bothered you first politely ask them to stop if they don't walk away, if they follow you and keep bothering you then go to the teacher.

Student response 4: People should not tease because the person that your teaseing will feel very sad and they mite tease you later. People should not bully because it could hert the other person their bullying. People shouldn't threaten other people because the person that is being threatened may go and tell his/her parent. When I am angry with somewon instead of punching a person I punch my pillow. When I get fresterated I break a pencil instead of ripping up my homework.

Student response 5: People should not tease, bully, or threaten each other. It can hurt people's feelings and make them feel bad. Think about how it would make you feel. Also, some people might get really mad and hurt other people. If you get angry or frustration you can count to 10, you can go hit a stick on the ground or punch a pillow, you can talk to the other person about it (but don't be angry), you can tell an adult, or you can go away.

Social Studies:[5] "Pretend you were a farmer living in Maine 200 years ago. Write a diary entry telling what life was like at that time."

Student response 1: Dear Diary—Today I got up when the sun came up and went out to feed the animals and milk the goats. We go to bed when it gets dark and get up when it gets lite to save candles. I fixed the wheel on our wagen because it broke going over some cobblestones in town. The roads are either very bumpy or very muddy. We ate cheese, bread, milk, and soup made with onions. The winter has been long so we're just about out of apples we saved from last fall. We had a lot of snow last night and made sleds out of barrel pieces. I need to trade some of the skins I trapped for flowr we'r just about out. Our nearest nabors are about a mile away. We have to walk everywhere we go or ride a horse or wagen. We play games and fix things at night.

Student response 2: Dear Diary—I just got done collecting egges from the hens. Mama said she will make raisin muffins! With the eggs I collected. Papa is milking the goat along with the cow. Ma is inside baking, and Marrianne is knitting mittens and hats this winter for the family. I donot have much time before I have to get back to work. So I will only tell you good news. Pa said he will teach me to milk the cow and train the colts.

Student response 3: Dear Diary, this is what I did today on the farm. Fist I wock up and hiched up the ox and they helped me hal wood to start a fier then I milked my cows with my two hands into a bukut then I picked the corn of the stoks and then I harvest the pumpkens and pea pods with my hands. Then I made some butter by stiring milk from the cows. In the winter I'm going to have to get ice blocks from the pond. I also made a big vat of maple surup by draining the sap into a bucek.

Student response 4: Dear Dierey, Working in the feaild shure is hard work but piking the stuf will be even harer. The women do a good job cooking with those veggies.

Student response 5: Dear Dairy, Today sales were good. I traded cow meat for a nice racoon hat and some hay and some chicken for a nice warm furr jacket. I went to the baker and trade 2 dozen eggs for some bread. It was very hot and dry today. Now you won't belive me but some pelole came in and traded some nice bufflow skin for 2 lbs of cow meet and 1 lbs of chicken. Today my wife had to mend my trousers. People were going down to the stream and filling buckuts of water because theres going to be a drout. Well go to go see you soon.

---

[4]From *Maine Educational Assessment, Performance Level Guide, Elementary, 1994–95,* Maine Department of Education, pp. 58–60. Used with permission. The original samples were scored on a scale of 1 to 4 = novice, basic, advanced, or distinguished. We have substituted a rubric different from the one originally used with these samples. Original scores: health 1 (novice), 2 (distinguished), 3 (advanced), 4 (basic), 5 (new sample—no score).

[5]From the same source, pp. 44–46. Used with permission. Original scores: social studies 1 (new—no score), 2 (basic), 3 (advanced), 4 (novice), 5 (distinguished).

Activity 6-5 Unit-Building Activity, Assignment 4— Essay Assessment

Optional

Goals/Rationale

This is the fourth in a series of direct applications to day-to-day life in the classroom. This unit-building activity centers around the role of essay questions in the unit you are assembling.

Cross-Reference to *Student-Involved Classroom Assessment*, 3d ed.

General Principles 1, 2 and 3: Choosing when to use essay and developing high-quality test items.

Additional Materials Needed

WORKBOOK: Activity 6-3 Worksheet, "Quality Guidelines for Essays." OTHER: Your own draft unit.

Time Required

45–60 minutes; rest is homework.

What to Do

Part A: Do with Colleagues

(15-20 minutes) Go over the homework steps and discuss them as needed.

Part B: Homework

1. Review your draft unit plan and identify complex structures of content and patterns of reasoning you regard as important.

2. Draft a table of specifications, find key elements for each cell in your table, and construct directions and criteria for essay questions that assess these key elements. Activity 6-4, "Assessing Conceptual Understanding," might help in this regard. It provides general criteria for conceptual understanding. It also provides the opportunity to think about when you need to use simple versus complicated scoring methods.

3. Review your essays using the worksheet, "Quality Guidelines for Essays," from Activity 6-3, "Practice Analyzing Essay Questions."

Part C: Do with Colleagues

(30–40 minutes) As needed, pair up with colleagues to review your essay questions using the "critical friends" method first described in Activity 5-6, "Unit-Building Activity, Assignment 3—Selected Response Questions."

Performance Assessment: Rich with Possibilities

Big Ideas in This Chapter

This chapter answers the following guiding question:

When and how do I use performance assessment most effectively?

The **General Principles** addressed in this chapter are as follows:

1. Performance assessments permit us to rely on professional judgment to gather evidence of student reasoning proficiency, performance skills, and product development capabilities.

2. They can be effectively developed in two steps: defining performance (through performance criteria, checklists, rubrics, and other scoring guides) and developing performance tasks or exercises.

3. This method can fall prey to avoidable sources of bias that can distort results if users are not careful.

4. By involving students in performance assessment development and use, we can set them up for energetic and successful learning.

Performance assessment has gotten lots of attention in recent years, but it is not new. Performance assessment is assessment based on observation and judgment, done frequently in the classroom. So, the goal is to take an essentially subjective form of assessment and make it as objective as possible so that it is more credible and useful.

Links to Previous Chapters

This is the third of four chapters that expand on the assessment methods first introduced in textbook Chapter 4. Like essay assessment, performance assessment involves extended constructed responses to tasks and exercises. Therefore, like essay assessment, performance assessments require structured ways to score or evaluate student responses—performance criteria, checklists, rubrics, and so on.

This chapter covers the "performance assessment" column of textbook Figure 4.2, "A Plan for Matching Assessment Methods with Achievement Targets," more fully by:

- Detailing how to develop performance assessments.

- Expanding on the notion of student involvement. Specifically, how does one involve students with performance assessments?

- Going deeper into target-method match for performance assessments.

- Delving into a topic only briefly mentioned in Chapter 4— sampling and potential sources of bias and distortion in performance assessments.

Links to Subsequent Chapters

There are three keys to helping you understand performance assessment—examples, examples, and more examples! The textbook and *Workbook* are full of them. But, some are not presented until Part III of the textbook. Chapter 7 is devoted to learning the basic design structure of performance assessment, using simple examples. More depth and richness will be added in Chapter 10.

Portfolio and Learning Log Reminder

Once again, we remind you that it is important to keep potential portfolio material handy.

Roadmap

Activity	Title	Activity Description	Time	Icons
7-1	*Achievement Targets for Performance Assessment	Which targets are worth the time and effort of a performance assessment? *Cross-reference to Chapter 7: General Principle 1.*	15–30 min	CONSOLIDATE UNDERSTANDING
7-2	A Term Paper Assignment— Case Discussion	Performance assessment, and issues of teacher work load, student motivation and quality. *Cross-reference to Chapter 7: General Principles 1 and 4.*	15–20 min	QUICK CHECK
7-3	Help Your Students Understand Performance Criteria	The pizza analogy for teaching criteria to students. *Cross-reference to Chapter 7: General Principles 1 and 4.*	25–30 min; rest is homework	APPLY LEARNING
7-4	*Sort Student Work	Practice developing performance criteria. *Cross-reference to Chapter 7: General Principles 2 and 3.*	60–90 min; rest is homework	APPLY LEARNING CONSOLIDATE UNDERSTANDING
7-5	Practice Consistent Scoring + Strategies for Teaching Criteria to Students	Three in one—practice scoring; practice Six-Trait Writing criteria; consider strategies for teaching criteria to students. *Cross-reference to Chapter 7: General Principles 2, 3, and 4.*	30-60 min	CONSOLIDATE UNDERSTANDING
7-6	But, It *Has* to Match the State Assessment!— Case Discussion	Things go awry when trying to teach to the state problem solving standards by modeling the state assessment. *Cross-reference to Chapter 7: General Principles 3 and 4.*	15–30 min	CONSOLIDATE UNDERSTANDING

*Recommended

Roadmap (*Continued*)

Activity	Title	Activity Description	Time	Icons
7-7	Unit-Building Activity, Assignment 5—Performance Assessment	Continued work on your own unit, developing high-quality performance assessments. *Cross-reference to Chapter 7:* General Principles 2 and 3.	30–45 min; rest is homework	APPLY LEARNING
7-8	Pick One from Textbook Figure 7.7	Student involvement. *Cross-reference to Chapter 7:* General Principle 4.	10–20 min; rest is homework	APPLY LEARNING

*Recommended

Activity 7-1   Achievement Targets for Performance Assessment

Recommended

Goals/Rationale

Skills and products are the most obvious targets of interest for performance assessment. But, this is an excellent time to reinforce the potential of using selected response and essays to assess some of the knowledge and reasoning prerequisites of skillful performance. Also, performance assessment doesn't have to be complex and time consuming. For example, although reading fluency is a complex skill on the part of students, it is relatively easy to assess—students read and clock their words per minute. This activity reinforces the notion that not all performance assessments have to be complex and time consuming.

> **Cross-Reference to *Student-Involved Classroom Assessment*, 3d ed.**
>
> General Principle 1: Which learning targets are best assessed with performance assessment.
>
> **Additional Materials Needed**
>
> TEXTBOOK: Table 7.2, "Performance Assessment of Achievement Targets."
>
> **Time Required**
>
> 15–30 minutes.

What to Do

1.   (5–10 minutes) Look at textbook Table 7.2, "Performance Assessment of Achievement Targets." Think about or discuss these questions:

   a. Is it clear why each item is on the list?

   b. What questions do you have about targets best assessed with performance assessment?

2.   (10-20 minutes) Expand Table 7.2 for your content area. Think about or discuss these questions:

   a. What are other topics in your area(s) of expertise that require performance assessment? Why? Do your colleagues agree? Why or why not?

   b. Which of these targets is *most* worth the time and energy to develop and use a performance assessment? If you focus your performance assessment attention on these high-priority targets, what methods will you use to assess the rest?

   c. Which of these targets are simple enough that developing a performance assessment is easy? Therefore, is considering alternatives necessary or desirable?

   d. What are the knowledge/understanding and reasoning prerequisites required to perform skillfully on at least one of your high-priority targets? How will you assess these prerequisites?

Activity 7-2   A Term Paper Assignment—Case Discussion

Optional

Goals/Rationale

This activity is good for activating prior knowledge about performance assessment by raising issues near and dear to teachers' hearts— workload, student motivation, and quality.

> **Cross-Reference to *Student-Involved Classroom Assessment*, 3d ed.**
>
> General Principles 1 and 4: Targets best assessed with performance assessment and involving students.
>
> **Additional Materials Needed**
> None.
>
> **Time Required**
> 15–20 minutes.

What to Do

1. (5–10 minutes) Individually read the worksheet, "A Term Paper Assignment." Think about these questions:

    a. This teacher apparently found the best way he could to deal with the immense numbers of papers he had to read. Was he wrong, given his realities?

    b. If you were a student who worked this hard to receive this feedback, how would you react?

2. (10 minutes) Think about or discuss these questions:

    a. Specifically, what went wrong here?

    b. Which problems could have been avoided? How?

A Term Paper Assignment—Case

The assignment was very clear: Read four novels by the same author and write a comparative term paper arising from that experience. Develop a guiding thesis and use insights derived from your reading to defend your thesis. The experienced high school English teacher had been covering American literature for decades and had been assigning term papers in this way for his entire career. It had always worked well.

One high school student, an avid reader, had no trouble finding a socially conscious author and searching out and reading four compelling novels about the justices and injustices of our culture. The author was a woman and her stories focused on the female experience in United States history—the roles, challenges, and triumphs of women. However, next came the challenge for our young scholar. She had no confidence as a writer, even though adults in her family had told her that they saw evidence in her work that she could be a talented young writer.

The assignment contained no information about the attributes of a good term paper. "Just apply the lessons you learned from other teachers," said her teacher. "This is a term paper like all the others." The problem, however, was that our young writer had received almost no prior instruction in how to organize, let alone compose, such a piece. Nevertheless, she picked a prominent character from each novel and structured her paper around a comparative analysis of these women. She established the standards of comparison up front and examined key similarities and differences between and among them. To conclude, she used her comparison to speculate about the character and experience of the woman who had created these characters.

She had to turn the draft in by a specified date or have her grade for the project reduced. She met the deadline, delivered the draft to her teacher, and learned that she wouldn't get it back—after all, how could one teacher review 180 drafts! (A valid point, especially when there would be another 180 final versions to read and evaluate later.) But her teacher assured the class that as the final deadline approached, they would thank him for requiring the preliminary version.

Over the next two weeks, our student worked to polish her paper. She revised and edited slightly—reading paragraphs to her parents and worrying that it just wasn't good enough. Finally the due date arrived and our young author turned her paper over to her teacher.

Two weeks later the paper was returned. On the cover, the teacher had written two things: "B+" (certainly a very good grade by most standards, especially for a first big paper) and a single comment: "You used the word 'she' entirely too many times in this paper." There was no other feedback.

Upon returning home, our student showed the paper to her parents. They asked what she herself thought of her efforts. She dropped the paper in the wastebasket, wondered aloud what her teacher really thought of her work, said she needn't have wasted so much time worrying or working, and left the room. For her, this product-based performance assessment was a frustrating and unfulfilling experience.

Activity 7-3   Help Your Students Understand Performance Criteria

Optional

Goals/Rationale

This is a great activity to begin the study of performance criteria, whether learners are adults or children. To get the idea of the important components of performance criteria, it's useful to relate the ideas to a familiar topic, in this case, criteria for a pizza. But, any familiar topic will do—restaurants, new cars, movies, and so on.

> **Cross-Reference to *Student-Involved Classroom Assessment*, 3d ed.**
>
> General Principles 1 and 4: Targets best assessed with performance assessment and involving students.
>
> **Additional Materials Needed**
> None.
>
> **Time Required**
> 25–30 minutes; rest is homework.

What to Do

Part A: Preparation/Do with Colleagues

1. (5 minutes) Look at the worksheet, "First Draft Pizza Rubric," created by a group of kindergartners.

2. (10–15 minutes) Think about or discuss the following questions:

    a. What evidence is in the rubric that students understand the concept of levels of quality?

    b. What questions would you ask to help students distinguish between absolute *essentials* of a pizza and personal preferences?

    c. To engage your students in a similar rubric-building activity, what food, familiar item, or process would be appropriate in your setting? (The key here is to use something that students have experienced and know well so that all can contribute their ideas to the mix.)

    d. How might you build on this activity to take students into an academic target? What might be a good starting target for your students?

3. (10 minutes) Finish building a rubric that you all agree represents the essential criteria for a pizza with supporting details that make each criterion come to life.

Part B: Try with Students

Engage your students in building a rubric using the answers to items 2c and 2d, above.

First Draft Pizza Rubric[1]

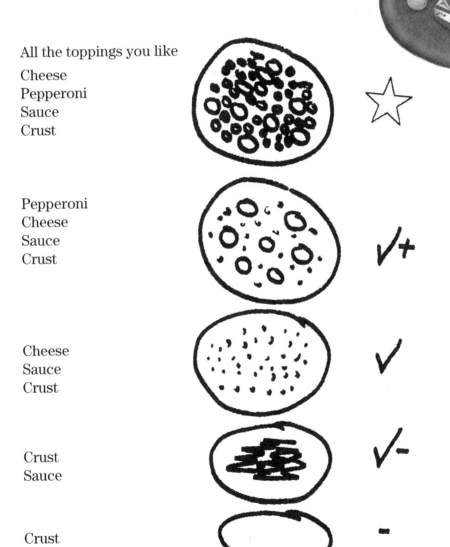

All the toppings you like

Cheese
Pepperoni
Sauce
Crust

Pepperoni
Cheese
Sauce
Crust

Cheese
Sauce
Crust

Crust
Sauce

Crust

[1]From Pauline Jacroux, Grade 1, Aikahi Elementary School, Kailua, Hawaii, March 2000.
Used with permission.

Activity 7-4   Sort Student Work

Recommended

Goals/Rationale

Activity 7-3, "Help Your Students Understand Performance Criteria," was merely a warmup for the main event—actually developing performance criteria for use in the classroom. Here, the process is modeled using the student work on the worksheet, "Third-Grade Mathematics Problem to Solve." The goal in this activity is to develop criteria for open-ended mathematics problems. However, the process is the same for any complex student outcome and models the "discovery" and "consolidation" steps in textbook Table 7.3, "Steps in Devising Performance Criteria."

Although overtly about developing criteria, this activity also helps develop clear targets—participants practice defining the essential ingredients of learning and to identify work that exemplifies different levels of skill on the target being assessed, in this case math problem-solving. Teachers nearly unanimously agree that sorting student work to develop criteria is extremely helpful in refining instruction.

Cross-Reference to *Student-Involved Classroom Assessment*, 3d ed.

General Principles 2 and 3: Developing high-quality performance assessments.

Additional Materials Needed

WORKBOOK: Appendix B, Figure B.3, "Everett's School District Problem Solving Rubric"; Appendix A, "Seven Strategies for Using Criteria as a Teaching Tool." TEXTBOOK: Figure 10.11, "Central Kitsap School District's Student-Friendly Mathematics Problem Solving Criteria"; Table 7.3, "Steps in Devising Performance Criteria."

Time Required

60–90 minutes; rest is homework.

What to Do

Part A: Preparation/Do with Colleagues

1.   (5-10 minutes) Solve the problem on the worksheet, "Third-Grade Mathematics Problem to Solve." If you are working with others, compare your solution strategies. Think about or discuss:

   a.   Are some solution strategies "better" (more sophisticated or elegant) than others? Will this matter when developing characteristics of quality student problem solving, or will any sound solution strategy be equally good?

b.   What does "clearly explain your answer" mean? Did you clearly explain your answer? Will clear explanation of the answer count? How much?

2.   (30-50 minutes) Sort the work.

a.   Sort the student work on the worksheet into three piles based on its quality and write down your reasons for placement. Why do you think some work is better than others? Be as specific as possible—What are you saying to yourself as you place a piece of work into one stack or another? What would you say to or ask students as you return their work? The goal here is not necessarily to get every piece of work into the correct stack. The goal is to come up with a good list of reasons for why you sorted each answer as you did.

Notes: (a) You can sort the work physically by cutting the samples apart or conceptually by noting next to each in which pile you would place it. (b) If you would like additional samples with which to work, you can ask students in your classes to solve the problem and use their responses. (c) Remember, you're sorting the work to develop criteria for quality which then can be used to assess other math problem solving. It's a bootstrap operation: use student work to draft criteria; use the criteria to direct future work; use future work to refine the criteria.

b.   Do you have general statements in your list, such as "logical," "communicates well," or "understood the problem"? If you used these statements with students, would they understand what you meant? Would they know what they did right or what to do differently next time? How might you dig beneath these general terms to get to indicators that describe what, specifically, in the work you saw that indicated that it was "logical" or not? Was it "the student picked out the correct information," "the student went from beginning to end without any missteps," "the student used the most sophisticated process possible," or what? Specifically, what did the student *do* that gave you the cue as to what pile to put the paper in?

Because the criteria are supposed to increase student understanding of the features of quality, we need to be clear on the indicators in the work that cue our judgments of quality. Challenging oneself to continually describe the indicators in the student work make you judge it, for example, "logical" also promotes deeper understanding of and consensus on what we mean by those terms.

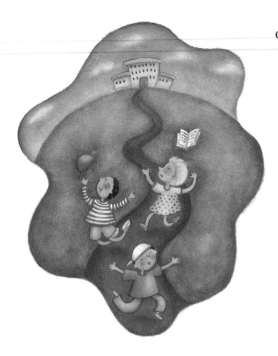

c. So far the sorting has been "holistic"[1]—you have a list of comments for high, medium, and low performance; any single paper gets only one score. Did you find that some work was strong in some ways and weak in others—for example, communication was good, but the logic was weak?

Many teachers feel that it would be very useful to be able to profile student strengths and weaknesses rather than provide one overall holistic judgment of quality. Such profiling can be facilitated by grouping comments that are similar into "traits" or "dimensions" of a successful performance. Traits that are common for mathematics are communication in mathematics, problem solving, understanding the problem, and correct computation. Do your comments group into these categories? Grouping features into important dimensions or traits of performance results in "analytical trait" performance criteria rather than "holistic" criteria. When might you want to use "holistic" scoring and when might you want to use "analytical trait" scoring?[1]

d. Compare your work to the math rubric developed by Everett School District (*Workbook* Appendix B, Sample #2, "Mathematics Problem Solving," Figure B.3) or that developed by Central Kitsap School District (textbook, Figure 10.11, p. 317).

Might you be able to use one of these rubrics instead of having to begin from scratch as we did above?

In our experience, educators usually don't have to start from scratch when developing rubrics. There are decent existing rubrics for many complex skills—writing, working in a group, oral presentation, thinking skills, etc. However, it is also our experience that merely selecting a rubric from those already in existence doesn't have the same power as first engaging in a certain amount of sorting/description and then looking for rubrics that best match one's own work. Only through sorting do educators understand that criteria *are our own*. Only through sorting do we engage in the conversations necessary to come to agreement on *what will count*.

---

[1]You might want to use holistic scoring when the skill or product to be assessed is simple and really only has a single important dimension or when the goal of the assessment is to get a "quick and dirty" overall estimate of level. You would probably want to use analytical trait scoring when the skill or product is complex and has several important dimensions; when students are going to use the rubric and it is important to break down the complex skill or product so that they can see the essential components; and when you're going to use the rubric for instructional decision making.

e. If you sorted other samples of math problem solving would you come up with the same descriptors of quality? In other words, could you use the same criteria across all math problems? Would this generality be useful? To you? To your students?

3. (20–30 minutes) *Optional.* Think about or discuss the following:

a. Did you come up with very negative words and phrases that describe the work in the weakest pile? If you used these reasons with students, what might be their reaction? How could you modify these statements to be, instead of negative descriptions of what a student can't do, merely descriptive of a lower level along a developmental continuum of ability to solve problems?

b. Would sorting these math problems be a useful activity to do with students? Why or why not?

c. The assessment team at Northwest Regional Educational Laboratory has devised seven strategies for teaching performance criteria (specifically the Six-Trait Model rubrics in writing) to students. We have recast these strategies to apply to any criteria (Appendix A, "Seven Strategies for Using Criteria as a Teaching Tool"). Discuss questions you might have about these strategies. Which of these strategies are students using when they sort work to develop performance criteria?[2]

d. How might you use the same process to develop criteria for other complex performances such as writing, reading comprehension, reading fluency, oral presentations, science process skills, and critical thinking?

e. Try the "definition" step in textbook Table 7.3; define each trait. Then mark the statements on your brainstormed list of attributes that describe each trait in your "low," "middle," and "high" piles. For example, if your first trait is "problem solving," mark the statements that are indicators of problem-solving quality. Do the same thing with each of your other traits. Viola—a rubric!

f. How much did and should you count following instructions? For example, if you are assessing persuasive writing and the student writes a narrative piece, should the student receive a lower score? When should following instructions be factored into the score and when should it not?

[2]Strategies 1 and 2.

Part B: Try with Students

1. Try the sorting activity with students. When they have finished sorting, ask them if they want to see what teachers look for. Ask them to compare their lists to the list you generated.

2. Think about the following questions:

    a. Could students sort the work successfully? If not, why not? What else would have to happen first?

    b. Did students come up with the same list of features of quality as you did? Any insights from this?

    c. Was this engaging for students? Why or why not?

Third-Grade Mathematics Problem to Solve

A teacher brought 12 apples and 15 bananas as a snack for the 20 students in his third-grade classroom. One helper passed out the apples to the 20 students, while another helper passed out the bananas. Every student got at least one of the fruits. If all the apples and bananas were given out, how many students got more than one fruit? Show all your work and clearly explain your answer.

Student response 1:

I use my fingres and + 12 + 3 = 15. So the anser is 3 because there is 3 more bananans than appls.

Student response 2:

Well, 7 children got seconds. The first time around only 12 kids got apples and 15 kids got bananas. Out of 15, 7 of them got seconds. Well, I drew 20 heads then I drew 12 apples then I did the same thing to the bananas. Then I drew a dot for the apples and a J like thing for the bananas and that's how I got my answer.

Student response 3:

There was a class activity. 20 children attended. I added 12 apples and 15 bananas. The answer was 30. Now I subtract 20 from 30. The answer was 10. 10 people were given more than one fruit.

$$\begin{array}{r} 12 \\ +15 \\ \hline 30 \end{array} \qquad \begin{array}{r} 30 \\ -20 \\ \hline 10 \end{array}$$

Student response 4:

7 kids would get two because you have 20 children so you first start with 15 bananas and add 12 to it so 15 + 12 = 27. You take the 7 away and 7 kids would get two.

Student response 5:

7. Becase

$$\begin{array}{r} 12 \\ +15 \\ \hline 27 \end{array}$$

Student response 6:

Well, you add 20, 12, 15, together. ten I found iton the cowky later. The anser wus 8 ech.

Student response 7:

Eight students can! Because if you subtit twenty-twelve you et eight.

$$\begin{array}{r} 2\,0 \\ -12 \\ \hline 8 \end{array}$$

Activity 7-5

Practice Consistent Scoring + Strategies for Teaching Criteria to Students

Optional

Goals/Rationale

This activity is three in one—a chance to practice consistent scoring as outlined in textbook Figure 7.5, a chance to practice the Six-Trait Writing rubric (textbook Figure 7.3), and a chance to consider various strategies for teaching criteria to students. The latter is a great example of student involvement.

> **Cross-Reference to *Student-Involved Classroom Assessment*, 3d ed.**
>
> General Principles 2 and 3: Developing high-quality performance assessments.
>
> **Additional Materials Needed**
>
> WORKBOOK: Appendix A, "Seven Strategies for Using Criteria as a Teaching Tool." TEXTBOOK: Figure 7.3, "Analytical Writing Assessment Rating Scales," Figure 7.5, "Steps in Training Raters of Student Performance."
>
> **Time Required**
>
> 30-60 minutes.

What to Do

1. (15–30 minutes) Use the steps outlined in textbook Figure 7.5, "Steps in Training Raters of Student Performance," to practice scoring the student writing in the worksheet, "Writing Samples," with the Six-Trait Writing rubric from textbook Figure 7.3.

2. (5–10 minutes) Discuss the following questions:

    a. Is this useful to do with colleagues? Why or why not?

    b. Would this be useful to do with students? Why or why not?

3. (5–10 minutes) As described in Activity 7-4, "Sort Student Work," the assessment team at Northwest Regional Educational Laboratory has devised seven strategies for teaching performance criteria (specifically the Six-Trait Model rubrics in writing) to students. We have reworded these strategies to apply to any criteria (see Appendix A, "Seven Strategies for

Using Criteria as a Teaching Tool"). If you did not do so in Activity 7-4, think about or discuss questions you might have about these strategies.

4.   (5–10 minutes) Which of these strategies did you practice when you scored student writing in this activity?[1]

Writing Samples

Writing Sample 1

If I could change one thing it would be . . .

If I could change one thing it would be. To let kids have their own credit cards, when they were at least eleven or twelve. They could have Jobs to. The kids could take care of the parents when they went on vacations. You could be almost any thing, even if you were a Football player you could still get payed. You could even be lawer.

You could probably be a doctor. You could have your own house if you wanted. But you could only work on weekends. Or on summer vacations. But you would still hav be to get finished with school.

Writing Sample 2

Nuclear weapons and Testing will Plunge Us Into a Global Fallout[2]

We now have a new member of the nuclear club, India. This should come as no surprise.

In 1995 India was denied the right to test nuclear weapons, and enter the nuclear race. Today, three years later, India has started to test anyway, which seems to me to be much more frightening.

If India has the technology, why need to prove it to the western world? They are basically telling the western countries that third-world countries are now capable of testing and building weapons of mass destruction. This seems to me to look like an unnecessary flex of political muscle and strikes me as a very dangerous and childish act.

Where will it end? Other political unstable countries will follow India's example, and soon every middle-eastern country will be building and testing nuclear weapons.

If we do not stop India and similar countries, it may be too late, and we will all suffer the consequences. We have seen the horror of this weapon in the past; now we are seeing it again. The only answer is the abolition of all our weapons of mass destruction.

What is the point of possessing these weapons? In my opinion a world where everyone has weapons of mass destruction will not survive for long.

---

[1]Hint: Look at strategies 1 and 2.
[2]From *The Ontario Curriculum—Exemplars, Grades 1–8, Writing*, Ottawa, ON: Ministry of Education and Training, 1999.

Writing Sample 3

If there was someone I knew who I would want to feel differently about a situation, I would give them advice to persuade them not to. My advice would be to stay from it, say no to the persons, ask questions about it, and ask it's peers if it is right.

My first piece of advice, "stay away from it", could consist of drugs, a dangerous stunt, or an abandoned place. Either way the stakes are high and it can cripple. It doesn't cut it with me if I tell my friend it is a mistake and they defend it by saying "everyone else is doing it," and I say, "you're not everyone else." My first piece of advice is very important because it can hurt the person and the people around them.

Saying no is my second piece of advice. It is important because those two words could get a person out of a lot of trouble. Such as drugs, sex, being picked up in a car by a stranger, or getting out of a crime such as shoplifting, or stealing a car, or also breaking and entering. It is all right to say no because you aren't wimping out on something, you are saving yourself from getting into something bad.

Writing Sample 4

Saving our earth and oceans is very important to our future, and a better earth. Polluting our oceans and lakes is abusing Gods creations. When you litter in our oceans and lakes you kill many innocent plants and animals, some in which are useful.

If you were a fish in the ocean helpless and harmlessly swimming around not hurting anyone. And suddenly you swim to a part where there is garbage, and harmful gasses every where. You would end up breathing in the harmful gasses, or possible eating a piece of food that would poison you. The harmful gasses would get into your lungs and destroy them. And the food would pison you so bad you would die. This happens to many animals and plants every day, each time you litter in oceans and lakes. So please don't litter and save millions of living plants and animals. Because every piece of garbage you through away in oceans, streams or lakes, is like throughing away one plant or animals life. They don't bother you so don't bother them.

Writing Sample 5

Are you fourteen and looking for an after-school job? If so, you probably know that you can't get one. Sure, you can get a permit when you're fourteen, but what good is that if you can't get a job until you're sixteen. Permit and job ages are conflicting and its proposed itself as a problem to most fourteen year olds. Something needs to be changed.

Laws today put too many restrictions on fourteen year old employees. The laws state that a fourteen or fifteen year old can only work a couple of hours a day. That is, if you can find a job. These unfair laws also limit the jobs theses young adults can do.

Also, if you are lucky enough to find a job, the salaries are very low. When paychecks are passed out its hardly worth the time and effort you've put into it. Of course these is always the paper route, berry fields, or babysitting. However, if you look at it, these jobs are harder work than most other jobs and they pay a lot less.

I also believe that if the government was to give fourteen year olds more jobs, it would keep lots of them off the streets after school and on weekends. Which, in turn, would quite possible lower the drug use and crime rate in most cities. Changing the law would allow more kids to go to college. with a job they could save for college and not leave it to parents or have to wait and try to pay their way through. Not to mention there would be more taxes coming out of more paychecks, which would mean better communities.

However, I can see the government and business owners point of views. There would be a great fear of young workers not being able to hold a job or a fear of them quiting frequently. Of course there are going to be few, but I think for the most part fourteen and fifteen year old adolescence would be eagerly inclined to do a good job.

The working laws need some serious help. They need to be changed. They need to give fourteen and fifteen year olds the option to be employed on a regular work schedule with regular wages. I feel we are not only willing but competent enough, by far, to perform most of the work tasks of everyday jobs. Something, somewhere, somehow needs to be changed.

Writing Sample 6—Green Is Good

Vegetarians. Aren't they those health-food-nut, skinny-as-a-rail joggers we all see so much of? No. Vegetarians are just everyday people like you and me, especially me. I have been a vegetarian for almost three months now and I still can't find a reason to go back to eating meat.

Why do people eat these innocent animals if they know the harm that it's doing to their bodies? Studies show that vegetarians have a lower risk of heart disease, diabetes, and some forms of cancer. Besides that, red meat will clog up your kidneys.

I really don't understand hunters. How can they see anything as precious as a deer, then shoot it, cook it, and eat it? Just hours before it was grazing in the grass, pondering the finer aspects of life and now there it is laying helplessly on your plate.

Deciding to become a vegetarian took me weeks of in-depth research. I had to keep my protein level up somehow. After reading that most of our forests were being cleared away for cattle grazing, I finally made my decision. So eat the greener way and avoid all those guilty feelings.

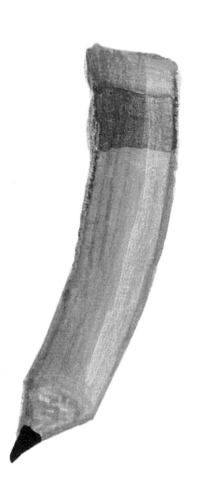

Activity 7-6

But, It *Has* to Match the State Assessment!—Case Discussion

Optional

Goals/Rationale

This case involves a well-intentioned attempt to teach to the state and mathematics problem-solving standards by modeling the state assessment and involving students in assessment. But, things went awry. This activity gives you practice in solving a classroom dilemma that really happened.

> **Cross-Reference to *Student-Involved Classroom Assessment*, 3d ed.**
>
> General Principles 3 and 4: Avoiding potential sources of bias and distortion in performance assessment and involving students.
>
> **Additional Materials Needed**
> None.
>
> **Time Required**
> 15–30 minutes.

What to Do

1. (5–10 minutes). Read the worksheet, "But, It *Has* to Match the State Assessment!," and think about the following questions:

   a. Will the problem given to the students to solve elicit problem solving? Why or why not?

   b. Do the criteria capture the characteristics of quality mathematics problem solving? Why or why not?

   c. Will this procedure assist students to learn to be better problem solvers or just be better at taking the state test? Why or why not?

   d. Is this a good example of student involvement to increase motivation and achievement? Why or why not?

   e. Do these teachers adequately understand mathematics problem-solving? Have they adequately incorporated it into assessment and instruction? Do they understand characteristics of quality assessment? Why or why not?

2. (5–10 minutes) If in a group, discuss the questions in item 1.

3. (5–10 minutes) What should these teachers do differently to involve students in a meaningful activity that matches the intent of the state math problem-solving content standards?

But, It *Has* to Match the State Assessment!— Case

Situation:

Students in ABC state did well on the recall and knowledge portions of the state mathematics assessment, but poorly on the problem-solving portions. A group of third-grade teachers at one school attempted to:

- Teach to the state mathematics problem-solving standards

- Model the state assessment so that students would be prepared

- Involve students in assessment by helping them understand the criteria for quality

Here's what they did:

1. They gave students problems to solve at least once a week. These were printed on a sheet of paper that reproduced the state criteria for scoring mathematics problems:

    - The student restates the problem.

    - The student describes how he will solve the problem.

    - The student then solves the problem.

    - The student includes a relevant drawing.

2. The teacher (or a student) reminded the students of this process by modeling it in front of the class.

3. The students were then given a new problem and were asked to complete their responses and give the paper to an aide. The aide checked for all four parts (and the right answer). If the students had all four parts and the right answer, the aide wrote "4" on the work and put it on the teacher's desk. If the students did not have all four parts and/or did not have the correct answer, the aide pointed out what was missing and gave the work back to the student to correct.

Things to Consider:

1. All of the problems were along the following lines: "Dennis Gonzales played in nine baseball games and hit a total of 36 home runs. What was the average number of home runs hit by Mr. Gonzales each game?"

2. The students seemed to blindly follow the four steps. There was no discussion of why (or whether) this illustrated good problem solving by either teachers or students.

Activity 7-7

Unit-Building Activity, Assignment 5— Performance Assessment

Optional

Goals/Rationale

This is the fifth in a series of direct applications to day-to-day life in the classroom. This unit-building activity centers around the role of performance assessment in the unit you are assembling.

> **Cross-Reference to *Student-Involved Classroom Assessment*, 3d ed.**
>
> General Principles 2 and 3: Developing high-quality performance assessments.
>
> **Additional Materials Needed**
>
> TEXTBOOK: Figure 7.2, "Performance Assessment Design Framework"; Table 7.3, "Steps in Devising Performance Criteria." OTHER: Your draft unit plan.
>
> **Time Required**
>
> 30–45 minutes; rest is homework.

What to Do

Part A: Preparation/Do with Colleagues

(30–45 minutes) Revisit your unit and zero in on targets you've identified for which performance assessment is the best match. Select one target that requires the creation of a product, and another that requires a performance. Write performance tasks and criteria using procedures described in textbook Chapter 7 and summarized in Figure 7.2 and Table 7.3. If working in a group, help each other with this development.

Part B: Try with Students

1. Try your draft task(s) with students. (Make sure students know that you will use the results to help refine the assessment, not to grade them!).

2. Score responses using your draft scoring guide. Revise your criteria/scoring guide and performance task(s) as needed. Use the following questions to guide your revisions:

    a. *Tasks*. Is there a pattern of errors in responses that could indicate misunderstanding of the task? (Did you get work back that's very different from what you expected?) Does the work provide information about student performance in relation to the selected target; is it aligned with the target?

b.   *Criteria.* Are there essentials missing from the performance criteria? (Or, might the details not really paint a clear picture of the desired quality?) Do the levels work? Do you see significant differences in the responses of English-language learning (ELL) students?

Pick One from Textbook Figure 7.7

Activity 7-8

Optional

Goals/Rationale

Performance assessment provides a great opportunity to involve students in assessment. Textbook Figure 7.7 provides many ideas. This activity encourages you to expand the list of possible ways to involve students and try one or more of them in your classroom.

> **Cross-Reference to *Student-Involved Classroom Assessment*, 3d ed.**
>
> General Principle 4: Involving students in assessment.
>
> **Additional Materials Needed**
>
> WORKBOOK: Appendix A, "Seven Strategies for Using Criteria as a Tool for Instruction." TEXTBOOK: Figure 7.7, "Ideas for Student-Involved Assessment."
>
> **Time Required**
>
> 10–20 minutes; rest is homework.

What to Do

Part A: Preparation/Do with Colleagues

1.   (5–10 minutes) Look at textbook Figure 7.7, which lists ways to involve students in performance assessment. Compare this list to "Seven Strategies for Using Criteria as a Tool for Instruction" in *Workbook* Appendix A. Match each item in Figure 7.7 to the seven strategies. In other words, what strategy does each item in Figure 7.7 represent?

2.   (5–10 minutes) Where are the holes in Figure 7.7? In other words, which strategies are not represented there? How might you amend the figure to fill the holes?

Part B: Try with Students

Pick one or more activities from your expanded Figure 7.7 to try with students.

Notes:

Personal Communication: Immediate Information About Achievement

Big Ideas in This Chapter

This chapter answers the following guiding question:

How can I best use my interaction with my students during instruction to provide information about their achievement?

The **General Principles** addressed in this chapter are as follows:

1. Personal communication-based assessments align well with knowledge, understanding and reasoning targets.

2. This kind of assessment can take a variety of forms, including instructional questions and answers, class discussions, conferences and interviews, oral exams, conversations with others about students, and student journals.

3. Using personal communication in conjunction with other methods can deepen understanding of student learning.

4. As with the other methods, this one can fall prey to avoidable sources of bias that can distort results if we are not careful.

5.   By involving our students in assessments that rely on personal communication, we can set them up for energetic and successful learning.

Anyone who has taught or studied the classroom assessment process knows that teachers gather a great deal of information about their students' achievement through everyday communication. But, personal communication assessment is subject to the same rules of evidence as all other methods. Assessments must arise from a clear target, serve a clear purpose, be capable of accurately reflecting the target in question, sample performance adequately, and control for all relevant sources of bias and distortion that can lead to incorrect conclusions. This chapter is intended to help teachers understand and adhere to these standards of quality.

Links to Previous Chapters

This is the fourth chapter on the four specific assessment methods first introduced in textbook Chapter 4. This chapter covers the "personal communication" column of textbook Figure 4.2, "A Plan for Matching Assessment Methods With Achievement Targets," more fully by:

- Expanding on the notion of student involvement. Specifically, how does one involve students in personal communication assessment?

- Going deeper into target-method match for personal communication.

- Delving into a topic only briefly mentioned in Chapter 4— sampling and potential sources of bias and distortion when using personal communication to assess students.

Portfolio Reminder

Once again, we remind you that it is important to keep potential portfolio material handy. See previous chapters for suggestions.

Roadmap

Activity	Title	Activity Description	Time	Icons
8-1	*What Types of Personal Communication Assessment Have You Experienced? + Potential Sources of Bias/Distortion	Personal experiences leading to consideration of target-method match, sources of bias/distortion, and student involvement. *Cross-reference to Chapter 8:* General Principles 1, 2 and 4.	10-20 min; rest is homework	APPLY LEARNING CONSOLIDATE UNDERSTANDING
8-2	Practice Asking Different Kinds of Questions	Practice asking questions that serve various learning functions. *Cross-reference to Chapter 8:* General Principles 2, 4, and 5.	15 min; rest is homework	APPLY LEARNING CONSOLIDATE UNDERSTANDING
8-3	Scored Discussion	Involving students in assessment of classroom discussions. *Cross-reference to Chapter 8:* General Principles 2 and 5.	20–30 min; rest is homework	APPLY LEARNING CONSOLIDATE UNDERSTANDING
8-4	Journal Icons	Using assessment to deepen thinking using journals. *Cross-reference to Chapter 8:* General Principles 2 and 5.	30–45 min; rest is homework	APPLY LEARNING CONSOLIDATE UNDERSTANDING
8-5	Unit-Building Activity, Assignment 6—Personal Communication	Continued work on your own unit, developing high-quality performance assessments. *Cross-reference to Chapter 8:* General Principles 1, 2 and 4.	30–45 min; rest is homework	APPLY LEARNING

*Recommended

Activity 8-1

What Types of Personal Communication Assessment Have You Experienced? + Potential Sources of Bias/Distortion

Recommended

Goals/Rationale

Two primary topics in textbook Chapter 8 are the types of formats for personal communication and the role of subjectivity in personal communication assessments. This activity draws on personal experience to explore the range of options for personal communication and some things that can go wrong.

> **Cross-Reference to *Student-Involved Classroom Assessment*, 3d ed.**
>
> General Principles 1, 2, and 4: Aligning targets with personal communication assessment and avoiding sources of bias/distortion.
>
> **Additional Materials Needed**
>
> None.
>
> **Time Required**
>
> 10-20 minutes; rest is homework.

What to Do

Part A: Preparation/Do with Colleagues

1. (5–10 minutes) Think about the following questions:

    a. Which of the forms of personal communication have you used in your classroom—question and answer, group discussion, conferences/interviews, journals and learning logs and/or oral examinations?

    b. For which learning targets did you use these formats?

    c. What have you found successful or positive? Why? What were your keys to success? How do your keys to success relate to those in the chapter?

    d. What problems or negative experiences have you had with these formats? Why? Was there anything in this chapter that might help you address the problem?

2. (5–10 minutes) If working in a group, discuss your responses.

Part B: Try with Students

Choose a form of personal communication assessment you haven't yet tried in your classroom. Enlist the aid of a colleague who has already used it successfully. Try this assessment form with students. Be prepared to discuss your experience.

Practice Asking Different Kinds of Questions

Activity 8-2

Optional

Goals/Rationale

This activity provides practice with one of the five types of personal communication discussed in the chapter—question and answer.

> **Cross-Reference to *Student-Involved Classroom Assessment*, 3d ed.**
>
> General Principles 2, 4, and 5: Sources of bias/distortion, student involvement.
>
> **Additional Materials Needed**
>
> TEXTBOOK: Table 8.2, "Questioning Techniques That Draw Students into Learning."
>
> **Time Required**
>
> 15 minutes; rest is homework.

What to Do

Part A: Try with Colleagues

1. (15 minutes) Review the classification scheme for questions presented in Table 8.2, "Questioning Techniques That Draw Students into Learning." Each person should prepare several questions of various types. Group members should ask each other these questions to make sure they function as intended.

2. *Optional.* Videotape or watch each other during instruction and classify the questions asked. Did you emphasize any type over others? What else did you discover?

3. *Optional.* If you intend to do Part B, below, rewrite textbook Table 8.2 using student-friendly language, as needed.

Part B: Try with Students

1. Post on the wall the student-friendly version of Table 8.2 types. Teach students the classification scheme in Table 8.2— types of questions and why teachers ask different kinds of questions. Demonstrate different kinds of questions.

2. Ask students to practice asking each other questions of various types.

3. Ask students to listen to the questions you ask during instruction and give you feedback on types and what, if anything, was left out.

4. Be ready to describe your experience with your colleagues.

Activity 8-3

Scored Discussion

Optional

Goals/Rationale

This activity provides practice with one of the five types of personal communication discussed in textbook Chapter 8—group discussion. Specifically, the activity calls for involving students in assessing discussions. The goals are for students to understand the nature of quality discussion and identify it in actual practice when it occurs. The activity also provides practice in matching assessment methods to targets— personal communication overlaps with performance assessment when it comes to oral performances such as group discussions, listening, and oral presentations.

> **Cross-Reference to *Student-Involved Classroom Assessment*, 3d ed.**
>
> General Principles 2 and 5: Forms of personal communication assessment, student involvement.
>
> **Additional Materials Needed**
>
> WORKBOOK: Appendix A, "Seven Strategies for Using Criteria as a Teaching Tool." OTHER: Video of students participating in a group discussion (optional). (You'll need to find or make your own tape.)
>
> **Time Required**
>
> 20–30 minutes; rest is homework.

What to Do

Part A: Preparation/Do with Colleagues

1. (5–10 minutes) Think about or discuss issues surrounding target-method match. Specifically, sometimes folks are confused by the relationship between personal communication and performance assessment. Actually there is an overlap here—see the Venn diagram following Part B. Think about or discuss the extent to which this Venn diagram corresponds with your understanding of the relationship between personal communication and performance assessment.

2. (15–20 minutes) Review the procedures for Part B. Review and/or discuss any questions or issues you might have. Revise the worksheet, "Rubric: Student-Friendly Guide to Group Discussions," as needed.

Part B: Try with Students

1. Begin with a brainstorm—What does it look like when people are working well together in a group discussion? What would the people be doing? What would they *not* be doing?

2. *Optional.* Show the video of students working in a group. See if there is anything else the students would like to add to the list begun in item 1 above.

3. Ask students, "Do you want to see what teachers look for?" Ask them to compare the brainstormed list to the worksheet, "Rubric: Student-Friendly Guide to Group Discussions." Where do their lists and the rubric overlap? Where were the mismatches? How might they reconcile mismatches? (Note: the rubric covers both interaction skills and understanding of content/reasoning.)

4. Ask students to "score" their own group discussions or others on video, using the rubric.

5. Have students give advice to specific individuals on the video on how to make their group discussion performance better.

6. Have students draw a picture that captures the essence of group discussion skills.

7. Have a "So What?" discussion to promote student metacognition:

    a. Ask students why they think you wanted them to do this activity. (What do they think you wanted them to learn?)

    b. Ask them how the information might be used in the future.

Part C: Reflect on the Activity

Think about the following questions:

1. Could students score the discussions successfully? If not, why not? What else would have to happen first?

2. Did students generate the same list of features of quality as you did? Can you draw any insights from this?

3. Was this engaging for students? Why or why not?

4. Which of the "Seven Strategies for Using Criteria as a Teaching Tool" (*Workbook* Appendix A) was/were used in this activity?[1]

5. Would this rubric help you help students attain state standards? Which ones? Would using the rubric help students achieve important learning targets?

6. What would you need to do before using this rubric to assess student competence in group discussion in order to avoid potential sources of bias and distortion?

Personal Communication   **Performance Assessment**

Targets Assessed:
Knowledge
Understanding
Reasoning

PC Formats to Assess These Targets:
Q&A
Class Discussion
Interview/Conferences
Student Journals
Oral Examinations

The overlap is skills that require personal communication to assess:
Group Skills
Oral Presentations
Listening
Group Discussion
Foreign Language

Targets Assessed:
Products
Skills

---

[1]Strategies 1, 2, 3, 4, and 6.

Rubric: Student-Friendly Guide to Group Discussions

Trait 1: My Understanding of the Topic

I Do This Well—I completely understand the information we're discussing.

- I understand what everyone else is talking about.

- I understand the meaning of the "technical" words being used.

- I know exactly which pieces of information I need to make a point.

- I can give good examples of what I mean.

- I can give evidence to support what I say.

I'm On My Way—I think I understand most of the information we're discussing.

- I understand some of the ideas, but not all of them.

- I understand many of the "technical" words, but not all of them.

- I can sometimes give examples of what I mean.

- I picked out some of the important information, but I might have missed some.

I'm Just Starting—I'm not sure I understand the information we're discussing.

- I'm not sure I understand what everyone else is talking about.

- I don't understand many of the "technical" words being used.

- I'm unsure which examples or information to use to make a point.

- I'm not sure that the information I use is correct.

Trait 2: My Understanding of What Group Work Is About

I Do This Well—I understand the reasons for working in a group and how to get group work done.

- I try to make sure I understand the reasons for the group work—what the group is supposed to accomplish.

- I help make sure that the discussion stays on the topic.

- I understand various ways to get group work done efficiently. For example, I know when it is useful to summarize the discussion, when the group needs additional information or help, when the group needs a leader, when the group needs to make sure all ideas are expressed, and when ideas need to be clearer.

- I know just what information is needed to contribute to the discussion.

- I know when the job of the group is done.

- I try to help make sure the group gets its work done.

- I know when it's useful to work in a group and when it is not.

I'm On My Way—I'm learning the reasons for working in a group and how to get group work done.

- I sometimes understand the goals of group work and sometimes I don't.

- I participate in the group when asked to by others, but I usually don't participate without being asked.

I'm Just Starting—I'm not sure I understand the reasons for working in a group, nor how to get group work done.

- I don't think I understand why we sometimes work in groups. I don't understand what working in a group is supposed to accomplish.

- I don't understand how to get group work done in an efficient manner.

- I usually don't follow what is going on.

- I get distracted and don't pay attention.

- I let others take responsibility for making sure the work gets done.

Trait 3: How I Interact with Others

I Do This Well—I know just how to get along with others when working in a group.

- I listen to what others have to say. I don't interrupt.

- When I disagree with someone, I know how to do it so that I don't hurt anyone's feelings.

- I make sure that everyone who wants to has a chance to talk.

- I'm polite.

I'm On My Way —I sometimes get along well with others when working in a group.

- I generally listen to others, but sometimes I get distracted.

- I sometimes interrupt.

- I try not to hurt others' feelings, but I think I sometimes do anyway.

- I understand how to be polite, but sometimes I'm not.

I'm Just Starting—I'm not sure how to get along with others in a group.

- I think I hurt people's feelings when I disagree with them, but I'm not sure.

- I try to do all the talking.

- I try to never do any talking.

- I don't listen to what others have to say.

- I don't understand what to do to be polite to others.

- I don't understand why everyone needs a chance to talk.

- I didn't realize there are things you can do to get along better in a group.

Trait 4: The Language I Use During the Discussion

I Do This Well—I know just how to say things so that others will understand.

- I say things in a way that others in the group will understand.

- I don't use more words than I need to. I know just how much to say to be clear.

- I try to use words that others will understand. I know when I need to use different words in order to be clear.

I'm On My Way —I sometimes say things in ways that others understand.

- I think I sometimes use more words than needed to make a point.

- I think I sometimes use words that others don't understand.

I'm Just Starting—I'm unsure if I say things in ways that others will understand.

- I try to use big words to impress others.

- I'm not sure how to say things in ways others will understand.

- I didn't realize that I need to pay attention to how I say things.

Activity 8-4   Journal Icons

Optional

Goals/Rationale

This activity provides practice with journals and logs—the fifth kind of personal communication discussed in Chapter 8. This example was adapted from the work of an eighth-grade teacher, Janice Evans Knight,[1] who was trying to get her students to think more deeply in their journal entries. She said: "Most students' initial efforts at writing journal entries were lengthy, literal accounts about what was read. These boring responses displaying a lack of critical thinking filled page after page in their journals. It seemed that demonstration lessons on how to [think more deeply] were needed." So, she taught students how to use a system for coding their journal entries for the types of thinking displayed. She taught the codes one at a time, using teacher modeling and having students practice writing about what was read showing a specific type of thinking. She saw a dramatic increase in the depth of thinking displayed in journal entries. "By coding the students' responses, not only does the teacher have a record of the type of thinking that went into their creation, so do the students. They can readily self-evaluate and work independently towards improving their responses. The students are also more motivated to include different kinds of thinking in their entries." This activity is modeled after Knight's.

(*Note:* This activity will only work in classrooms where teachers and students are already using reading logs.)

> **Cross-Reference to *Student-Involved Classroom Assessment*, 3d ed.**
>
> General Principles 2 and 5: Forms of assessment, student involvement.
>
> **Additional Materials Needed**
>
> WORKBOOK: Appendix A, "Seven Strategies for Using Criteria as a Teaching Tool."
>
> **Time Required**
>
> 30–45 minutes; rest is homework.

What to Do

Part A: Preparation/Do with Colleagues

1. (10-20 minutes) If you yourself are keeping a learning log, use the icons on the next page to classify the types of entries you have made.

---

[1] Janice Evans Knight, Coding journal entries, *Journal of Reading*, *34* (1), 1990: 42–47.

2. (15–20 minutes) Review the procedures for Part B. Think about or discuss any questions or issues you might have. Revise the icon list or descriptors as needed.

3. (5 minutes) Look at the "Seven Strategies for Using Criteria as a Teaching Tool" in *Workbook* Appendix A. Identify which strategies are being used in this example.[2]

Part B: Try with Students

1. Prepare a bulletin board displaying the journal icons.

2. Find examples from journal entries that are examples of the type of thinking being taught.

3. Prepare a mini-lesson that teaches students one of the cues. Plan how you'll introduce the usefulness of icons to students, how you'll model the kind of thinking you want students to practice, how you'll use the sample journal entries to allow students to practice recognizing the type of thinking being done, and how you'll ask students to generate their own journal entries that illustrate the desired thinking.

4. Perhaps add a "So What?" discussion. Ask students to explain why you wanted them to learn this. How will it help them?

5. Try out the lesson(s) and be ready to report on what happened.

R	**Recall**—Facts, plot design, sequence, details, summary. Tell the sequence of events in *The Ransom of Red Chief*.	✳	**Analysis**—Ingredients, component parts, internal functioning. How did the author create a mood of happiness?
↻	**Synthesis**—Pool or integrate information to reach a new insight. What do you conclude from the two authors' visions of leadership?	▢	**Classify**—Organize into categories. What types of stories did we read this year?
◉	**Compare**—Comparison, similarity. How are the main characters in X and Y alike?	◉	**Contrast**—Contrast, difference, distinction, discrimination, differentiation. How are the styles of A and B different?
Ex→💡	**Idea to Example**—Analogy, categorization, deduction, prediction, consequence. In our list of stories, find some examples of friendship.	💡→Ex	**Example to Idea**—Induction, conclusion, generalization, finding essence, hypothesis. What is the main theme of this story?
⚖	**Evaluation**—Value, judgment, rating. Was Ahab right to chase the whale? Why or why not? Did you like the plot? Why or why not?		

Activity 8-5

Unit-Building Activity, Assignment 6— Personal Communication

Optional

Goals/Rationale

This is the sixth in a series of direct applications to day-to-day life in the classroom. This unit-building activity centers around the role of personal communication assessment in the unit you are assembling.

> **Cross-Reference to *Student-Involved Classroom Assessment*, 3d ed.**
>
> General Principles 1, 2, and 4: Target-method match, forms of personal communication assessment, sources of bias/distortion in personal communication assessment.
>
> **Additional Materials Needed**
> Your unit plan.
>
> **Time Required**
> 30–45 minutes; rest is homework.

What to Do

Part A: Preparation/Prework

Zero in on targets in your unit for which personal communication is the best match or which may benefit from adding a personal communication component.

Part B: Preparation/Do with Colleagues

(30–45 minutes) Draft the personal communication assessment—tasks and criteria—making sure you check for quality using each of the five standards of quality. Build on ideas in textbook Chapter 8. If you are working in a group, consider assisting each other.

Part C: Try with Students

Try your draft with students and score their responses. Use the results to refine and improve the assessment. Use the following questions to guide your revisions:

1. *Tasks*. Are your questions and procedures clear? Did you find yourself rephrasing an original question to help students understand what you were asking? Do the results of your assessment provide useful information about the target—are the tasks aligned with the target?

2. *Criteria.* Are you sure that your scores are accurate? How well does your score sheet work? Are there too many things you tried to document? Did English-language learning (ELL) student performance reflect their real achievement level?

3. *Student Involvement.* How might you involve your students?

Notes:

End Part II

Activities

Roadmap

Activity	Title	Activity Description	Time	Icons
PII-1	Analyze Sample Assessments for Sampling and Bias/Distortion	Identify bias and distortion in real classroom assessments. *Cross-reference to textbook:* Uses learning from Chapters 5–8.	30–60 min	CONSOLIDATE UNDERSTANDING
PII-2	*Show What You Know	Explain and articulate what you have learned about classroom assessment. *Cross-reference to textbook:* Uses learning from Chapters 5–8.	Homework	SELF-REFLECT
PII-3	*Portfolio Building	Add material to your growth portfolio. *Cross-reference to textbook:* Uses learning from Chapters 5–8.	Homework	SELF-REFLECT
PII-4	Unit Building Activity, Assignment 7: Sampling and Bias/Distortion	Adjust your plan using your current understanding of quality classroom assessment, especially sampling and bias/distortion. *Cross-reference to textbook:* Uses learning from Chapters 5–8.	Homework	APPLY LEARNING

*Recommended

Links to Previous and Subsequent Chapters

Now you've got all the basics (see *Workbook* Figure Part II-1, "Five Standards of Quality Assessment"). Textbook Chapters 1–4 provided an overview of quality and student involvement, but they mostly covered clear and appropriate learning targets (Standard 1), clear and appropriate users and uses (Standard 2), and matching assessment methods to targets and users/uses (Standard 3). Textbook Chapters 5–8 went through each of the assessment methods in detail, including sampling (Standard 4), potential sources of bias and distortion (Standard 5), and student involvement (Standard 2). Communication will be addressed in later chapters and clear and appropriate learning targets will be revisited in later chapters as well. *Workbook* Figure Part II-2 summarizes the various sources of bias and distortion covered in textbook Chapters 5–8.

Portfolio Building

The activities in this section are intended to consolidate understanding of all the material in Part II of Rick's book. This is your chance to reflect on what you've learned so far and convert this self-reflection and assessment into portfolio entries.

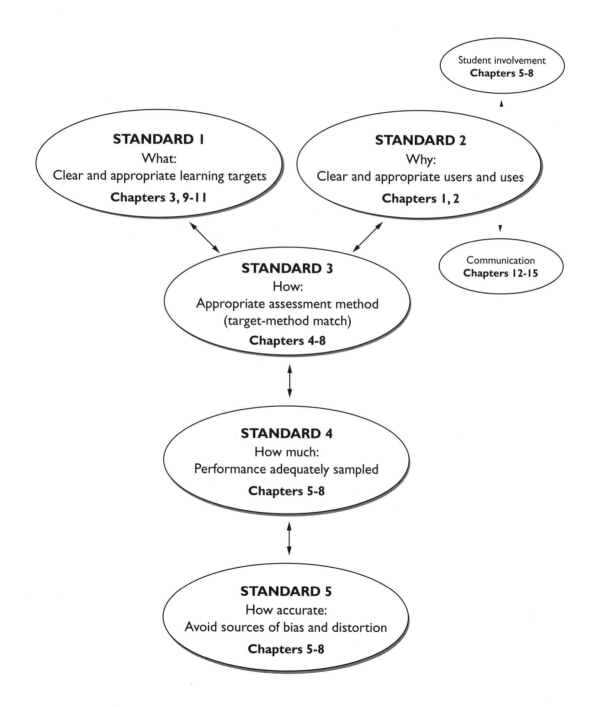

Figure Part II-1
Five Standards of Quality Assessment

Examples of Common Barriers to Assessing Accurately

1. Barriers common to all methods

   A. Potential barriers to accurate assessment that can occur within the student:
      - Language barriers
      - Emotional upset
      - Poor health
      - Physical disability
      - Peer pressure to mislead assessor
      - Lack of motivation at time of assessment
      - Lack of testwiseness (understanding how to take tests)
      - Lack of personal confidence leading to evaluation anxiety

   B. Possible barriers to accurate assessment that can occur within the assessment context:
      - Noise distractions
      - Poor lighting
      - Discomfort
      - Lack of rapport with assessor
      - Cultural insensitivity in assessor or assessment
      - Lack of proper equipment

   C. Examples of barriers to accurate assessment that arise from the assessment itself (regardless of method):
      - Directions lacking or vague
      - Poorly worded questions
      - Poor reproduction of test questions

2. Barriers to accurate assessment unique to each format

   A. Possible barriers to accurate assessment with multiple-choice tests:
      - Lack of student skills necessary to read the questions
      - More than one correct response
      - Incorrect scoring key
      - Incorrect bubbling on answer sheet
      - Clues to the answer in the item or in other items

   B. Potential barriers to accurate assessment with essay assessments:
      - Lack of student skills necessary to read the questions
      - Lack of student skills necessary to write responses
      - No scoring criteria
      - Inappropriate scoring criteria
      - Evaluator untrained in applying scoring criteria
      - Biased scoring due to stereotyping of respondent
      - Insufficient time or patience to read and score carefully
      - Students don't know the criteria by which they'll be judged

Figure Part II-2

Examples of Common Barriers to Assessing Accurately

C. Potential barriers to accurate assessment with performance assessment:

- Lack of student skills necessary to read the questions
- No scoring criteria
- Inappropriate scoring criteria
- Evaluator untrained in applying scoring criteria
- Bias due to stereotypic thinking
- Insufficient time or patience to observe and score carefully
- Student doesn't feel safe
- Unfocused or unclear tasks
- Tasks that don't elicit the correct performance
- Biased tasks
- Students don't know the criteria by which they'll be judged

D. Possible barriers to accurate assessment when using personal communication:

- Sampling enough performance
- Inaccurate record keeping
- Lack of rapport with respondent

E. Potential barriers to accurate assessment with portfolios:

- Group work that looks like individual work
- Work that belongs to someone else
- Unclear why entries were chosen
- Too much; can't wade through it all; not summarized or organized well
- Sampling "best" or "typical" performance—which is it?
- No scoring criteria
- Inappropriate scoring criteria
- Evaluator untrained in applying scoring criteria
- Bias due to stereotypic thinking
- Insufficient time or patience to observe and score carefully

Figure Part II-2

Continued

Activity PII-1   Analyze Sample Assessments for Sampling and Bias/Distortion

Optional

Goals/Rationale

This activity gives you practice in identifying bias and distortion in real classroom assessments, and then thinking about the implications for your own practice.

> **Cross-Reference to *Student-Involved Classroom Assessment*, 3d ed.**
>
> Chapters 5–8.
>
> **Additional Materials Needed**
>
> WORKBOOK: Appendix B, sample rubrics and assessments; Figure Part II-2, "Examples of Common Barriers to Assessing Accurately." TEXTBOOK: Figure 7.4, "Practical Considerations in Performance Assessment Sampling."
>
> **Time Required**
>
> 40–60 minutes.

What to Do

1. (10 minutes) Look at the rubrics in *Workbook* Appendix B, "Standard 4—How Much: Sampling," and "Standard 5—How Accurate: Sources of Bias/Distortion." Do the rubrics cover those things that truly describe sound sampling and elimination of bias and distortion? Would you add anything?

2. (10 minutes) Look at "Assessment Sample 1: Reading Rate" in Appendix B. Has the author gathered enough samples of performance to make a stable estimate of student reading rate?[1] Are there potential sources of bias and distortion?[2] Using the rubrics, plus *Workbook* Figure Part II-2, and textbook Figure 7.4, "score" the assessment for the traits of "sampling" and "bias/distortion."

3. (10–30 minutes) Analyze the other assessments in Appendix B for sampling and bias/distortion. (Writeups of each assessment are also included in Appendix B, but don't peek ahead.)

---

[1]Answer—Not really. The author only gathers a single sample a few times a year.

[2]Answer—We do have a few questions: How did the author determine the proper reading level of the books used? Did the author pick the times of day when students can do their best? Are students at ease?

4. (10 minutes) Think about or discuss the following:

    a. In what percentage of assessments you've seen or used are issues of sampling and bias/distortion explicitly addressed?

    b. Does every assessment have to address issues of sampling and bias/distortion or does there just need to be a general pattern of such attention over time?

    c. What are the implications for the assessments you use in your own classroom? What are you thinking about doing differently?

Show What You Know

Activity PII-2

Recommended

SELF-REFLECT

Goals/Rationale

Periodically we encourage you to reflect on your increasing confidence and competence as a classroom assessor. One self-reflection technique is to ask you to "show what you know"—explain and articulate what you are learning and how it connects to other things in your lives. Activity PII-2 proposes several ideas for doing this that might appeal to different learning styles. Any of the ideas can be considered prime potential portfolio material.

Cross-Reference to *Student-Involved Classroom Assessment*, 3d ed.

Chapters 5–8.

Additional Materials Needed

WORKBOOK: Appendix A, "Sample Working Folder/ Portfolio Cover Sheet"; rubrics in Appendix B; Figure Part II-2, "Examples of Common Barriers to Assessing Accurately."

Time Required

Open, it's homework.

What to Do

Items 1 and 2 are recommended. The rest are optional. *Be sure to include a cover sheet* (such as that in Appendix A, "Sample Working Folder/Portfolio Cover Sheet") *with each portfolio entry.*

1. *Recommended.* Make a list of assessments that do and don't meet standards of quality as outlined in Chapters 5–8 and shown in *Workbook* Figure Part II-2, "Examples of Common Barriers to Assessing Accurately." Briefly describe your rationale for including each on the list.

2. *Recommended.* Write a letter to a colleague, student, parent, or instructor that explains one student-involvement strategy you have tried with your class. Give an account of what you and your students did, what worked well, whether you would use it again, and what you would do differently.

3. *Optional.* Construct a concept map that shows your current understanding of how the following topics link:

▲ Selected Response	▲ Essay	Assessment Methods
▲ Performance Assessment	Products	Fill in the Blank
▲ Constructed Response	Dispositions	True/False
Reasoning	Learning Targets	▲ Personal Communication
Skills	Matching	Knowledge/Understanding
▲ Sampling	Unclear Tasks	▲ Potential Sources of Bias & Distortion
Quality Assessment	Unclear Criteria	Problems w/Test Administration

4. *Optional.* Draw pictures or make posters of your current understanding of the items above marked with a ▲.

5. *Optional.* Write a letter to a colleague, student, parent, or instructor that explains (a) the steps in developing an assessment of high quality and why following these steps is essential, or (b) how to involve students in various types of assessments and why such involvement is essential.

6. *Optional.* Outline the major learnings in Part II of *Student-Involved Classroom Assessment*, 3d ed. Include a statement of which of these might need to be considered in future assessment planning for your building or district. Include a list of questions that you might need to ask before you can determine future assessment planning in your district or building. Consider the barriers you might face in pursuing the areas that need improvement.

7. *Optional.* Prepare a half-day workshop agenda for others that teaches them how to develop high quality assessments and how to involve students. Be sure to include all four kinds of assessment: selected response, essay, performance assessment, and personal communication.

Portfolio Building

Activity PII-3

Recommended

Goals/Rationale

Here's where you make your next set of choices for your growth portfolio. Remember, your goal is to reflect on and self-assess your growth on the following targets:

- Standard 1—Clear and appropriate learning targets
- Standard 2a—Clear and appropriate users and uses
- Standard 2b—Sound communication about assessment
- Standard 2c—Student involvement in assessment
- Standard 3—Choosing the most appropriate assessment method
- Standard 4—Sampling
- Standard 5—Eliminating sources of bias and distortion

Cross-Reference to *Student-Involved Classroom Assessment*, 3d ed.

Chapters 5–8.

Additional Materials Needed

WORKBOOK: Figure Part II-2, "Examples of Common Barriers to Assessing Accurately"; Appendix C, "Self-Assessment Developmental Levels"; Appendix B, "Classroom Assessment Quality Rubrics"; Appendix A, "Sample Working Folder/Portfolio Cover Sheet," "Classroom Assessment Confidence Questionnaire," and "Assessment Principles." TEXTBOOK: Figure 7.4, "Practical Considerations in Performance Assessment Sampling."

Time Required

Open, it's homework.

What to Do:

Items 1 through 4 are recommended. The rest are optional. *Be sure to include a cover sheet* (such as that in *Workbook* Appendix A, "Sample Working Folder/Portfolio Cover Sheet") *with each portfolio entry.*

1. *Recommended.* Take another look at the previous assessments in your portfolio. Amend and date your commentary on their quality. Use *Workbook* Appendix B, textbook Figure 7.4, and *Workbook* Figure Part II-2 to help direct your commentary. Do you notice any difference in content and depth between your original and amended commentaries?

2. *Recommended.* Select a new assessment (test, quiz, essay test, or performance assessment) that you have recently used or taken. *If you are a current teacher, it must be one that you administered, scored, and recorded for use within the context of your teaching.* Using the rubrics in *Workbook* Appendix B, reflect on the quality of this assessment and write a brief analysis. What are its strengths? What things might you improve?

   Write a brief comparison of the quality of the assessments you have evaluated so far. Is the quality improving over time? How do you know?

3. *Recommended.* Retake the "Classroom Assessment Confidence Questionnaire" in *Workbook* Appendix A. How is your confidence changing over time?

4. *Recommended.* Analyze the content of your portfolio for sampling and potential sources of bias and distortion. Would a reader of your portfolio get an accurate view of your growing confidence and competence in classroom assessment? Would a reader get an accurate picture of (a) your knowledge of quality and ability to apply this knowledge in developing and selecting assessments for use, (b) your knowledge of student involvement and applying that knowledge in the classroom? As you analyze your own portfolio, consider the following:

   - *Sampling.* Do you have an adequate sample of assessment methods and users/uses to accurately show the breadth and depth of your learning? If so, why? If not, what else might you add?

   - *Bias and Distortion.* Have you avoided other pitfalls that would result in an inaccurate picture of your knowledge and growth? Would your entries convince a reader that the information, products, and displays in your portfolio accurately represent your learning? Explain. Consult *Workbook* Figure Part II-2 for potential sources of bias and distortion in portfolios. What might you do to avoid or correct these?

5. *Optional.* Self-assess using the "Self-Assessment Developmental Levels" in Appendix C. There is a developmental level continuum for each of the five standards of quality assessment. Especially attend to the developmental level continuums for sampling and bias/distortion.

6. *Optional.* Review previous portfolio entries and note your progress in confidence and competence. Answer the following questions:

   a. How has your thinking about assessment changed over time?

   b. What are you doing differently in the classroom as the result of what you've learned so far?

   c. What is the impact on students? On colleagues? What evidence do you have for this impact?

   d. What questions from before can you now answer? What new questions do you have?

7. *Optional.* Consider again the "Assessment Principles" in *Workbook* Appendix A. Now, which principles affirm your own beliefs? Why? Are there any with which you disagree either in part or in whole? Why? What concerns might you have about any of them?

8. *Optional.* What else in your working folder or learning log might you put in your portfolio to demonstrate increasing competence and confidence in your knowledge, reasoning, skills, and products associated with sound classroom assessment?

Activity PII-4   Unit-Building Activity, Assignment 7— Sampling and Bias/Distortion

Optional

Goals/Rationale

This is the seventh in a series of direct applications to day-to-day life in the classroom. This unit-building activity centers on adjusting your plan using your current understanding of classroom assessment in general and specific information on sampling and bias/distortion. In Part II, we've asked you to design, try out and refine assessments using each of the methods: selected response, essay, performance assessment, and personal communication. It's time to look across the unit with an equity lens to spot potential problems embedded in draft assessments that will limit students' ability to produce accurate information about their learning.

> **Cross-Reference to *Student-Involved Classroom Assessment*, 3d ed.**
> Chapters 5–8.
>
> **Additional Materials Needed**
> WORKBOOK: Figure Part II-2, "Examples of Common Barriers to Assessing Accurately." OTHER: Your draft unit plan.
>
> **Time Required**
> Open, it's homework.

What to Do

1. Use *Workbook* Figure Part II-2 to refine your draft assessments. Attend especially to equity issues.

    a. Are you presenting ideas, terms, or settings that are outside the experience of some of your students?

    b. Check the balance of assessment methods in your unit. Do you offer a balanced variety of ways for students to demonstrate their learning?

    c. How clear are the assessment criteria? Are you sure *all* students understand what's expected?

2. Review your unit calendar.

    a. Has each target or key element of a large target been addressed in your unit? (Will there be evidence about the targets you've selected?)

b. Which of your targets are relatively simple? These can be reasonably covered with a small assessment sampling. Which of your targets are broad and complex? Do the assessments that you've planned provide sufficient sampling of these targets? (Generally, the broader and more complex the target, the more assessment exercises are needed to make solid judgments about target achievement.)

Notes:

PART III

Classroom Applications

Assessing Reasoning Proficiency

Big Ideas in This Chapter

This chapter answers the following guiding question:

How can I help my students become confident, competent masters of their own reasoning and problem-solving proficiencies?

The **General Principles** addressed in this chapter are as follows:

1. Real-life problems are solved using certain consistent patterns of reasoning. This chapter defines and illustrates these patterns.

2. The heart of academic competence includes the ability to use knowledge and understanding to figure things out in the same patterned ways required to solve real-life problems.

3. Our classroom assessment challenges, then, are to understand those predictable patterns of reasoning, assess them accurately, and share the patterns and assessment responsibilities with our students. We want to make sure our learning targets are crystal clear and that we assess them well with student involvement.

This chapter begins our examination of classroom assessment applications from the perspective of translating achievement targets into various assessment methods. Chapter 9 can assist teachers in helping students develop one of the most critical academic capabilities: the ability to reason productively, a foundation for all other competencies. Students may be in some difficulty if their teachers possess no vision of sound reasoning to share. This chapter encourages you to develop such a vision.

Links to Previous Chapters

Chapter 9 defines and expands on the reasoning terms and concepts used in textbook Chapters 5 and 6 when developing test specifications, and Activities 8-3, "Scored Discussion" and 8-4, "Journal Icons," assessing different reasoning patterns using rubrics.

This chapter also explores the material from textbook Chapters 5–8 from a 90-degree shift in perspective. While Chapters 5–8 explored the columns in textbook Figure 4.2, "Aligning Achievement Targets and Assessment Methods," this chapter begins the exploration of the rows.

Links to Subsequent Chapters

This is the first of three chapters to explore, in depth, how to assess specific learning targets. Chapter 9 addresses reasoning, while Chapter 10 looks at skills and products, and Chapter 11 delves into dispositions.

Portfolio Reminder

Once again, we remind you that it is important to keep potential portfolio material handy. See previous chapters for suggestions.

Roadmap

Activity	Title	Activity Description	Time	Icons
9-1	*Compare The Textbook's Classification Scheme to Those You Use Now	What definitions of reasoning patterns will you use? *Cross-reference to Chapter 9:* General Principles 1 and 3.	20–30 min	CONSOLIDATE UNDERSTANDING
9-2	*Real-World Examples	Internalize the patterns of reasoning in the chapter by finding real-world examples. *Cross-reference to Chapter 9:* General Principles 1, 2, and 3.	40-60 min	CONSOLIDATE UNDERSTANDING
9-3	*Key Words	Generate key words that trigger different reasoning patterns and convert the list into questions you could ask students. *Cross-reference to Chapter 9:* General Principle 3.	30–45 min; rest is home-work	APPLY LEARNING CONSOLIDATE UNDERSTANDING
9-4	Convert Reasoning Patterns into Student-Friendly Language	Help students understand the reasoning targets they are to hit. *Cross-reference to Chapter 9:* General Principles 1, 2, and 3.	40–55 min; rest is home-work	APPLY LEARNING CONSOLIDATE UNDERSTANDING
9-5	*Assessing Reasoning in the Classroom*— Video Discussion	Video discussion of all the topics covered in Chapter 9. *Cross-reference to Chapter 9:* General Principles 1, 2, and 3.	60–120 min	CONSOLIDATE UNDERSTANDING
9-6	Unit-Building Activity, Assignment 8—Assessing Reasoning	Continued work on your own unit, developing high-quality assessments for reasoning. *Cross-reference to Chapter 9:* General Principles 1, 2, and 3.	15 min; rest is home-work	APPLY LEARNING

*Recommended

Activity 9-1

Compare the Textbook's Classification Scheme to Those You Use Now

Recommended

Goals/Rationale

A key part of Chapter 9 is the discussion of the many interrelated parts of the reasoning process. Your challenges with respect to reasoning are to: (1) develop a conceptual scheme of reasoning that you are willing to master so completely it becomes second nature to you; (2) translate this scheme into real-world examples easily and comfortably, and (3) bring it to life for your students.

Rick attempts to take his own advice by describing six patterns of reasoning he has become comfortable with, has mastered, can translate into real-world examples, and can bring to life for his students—you! If this is a comprehensive scheme you can master and use well—great! If you already have another comprehensive scheme you have mastered and can use well—great! The goal is not necessarily to use Rick's scheme; the goal is to have *some* comprehensive scheme (that matches the kinds of reasoning central to the subject(s) you are teaching) that you can bring alive for your students.

This activity gives you the opportunity to compare Rick's classification scheme for reasoning to others you might already be using.

> **Cross-Reference to *Student-Involved Classroom Assessment*, 3d ed.**
> General Principles 1 and 3: Define patterns of reasoning used in everyday life.
>
> **Additional Materials Needed**
> Other classifications of reasoning skills with which you are familiar.
>
> **Time Required**
> 20–30 minutes.

What to Do

1. (10–15 minutes) Consider other reasoning/thinking skills classifications you have used. What are their component parts? How are they alike and different from Rick's? What are their relative strengths and weaknesses? How might Rick's taxonomy supplement or replace the previous schemes you've used?

2. (10–15 minutes) What patterns of reasoning have we asked you to use in this activity? (Answers are in the footnote, but don't peek.[1])

---

[1] Analyze reasoning classification schemes, compare schemes, evaluate the strengths and weaknesses of each scheme, synthesize schemes.

Real-World Examples

Recommended

Activity 9-2

Goals/Rationale

This activity helps you to internalize the reasoning patterns discussed in the chapter by finding examples of reasoning in action.

Cross-Reference to *Student-Involved Classroom Assessment*, 3d ed.

General Principles 1, 2, and 3: Define patterns of reasoning, assess them accurately, and share them with students.

Additional Materials Needed

None.

Time Required

40–60 minutes.

What to Do

1. (10–15 minutes) What reasoning patterns are required in situations (a) and (b) below? Write down your analysis.

    a. Look at Part B of Activity 8-3, "Scored Discussion." What patterns of reasoning are students using in steps 1 through 5? (Don't peek, one set of possible answers is in the footnote.[1])

    b. What patterns of reasoning are required when preparing for an oral presentation?

2. (10–15 minutes) Think of three of your own real-world examples. Describe the patterns of reasoning at work in each example. Write down your conclusions.

3. (15–20 minutes) If you are working in a group, share your analyses with others. Anonymously circulate each person's analyses. Be "critical friends"—revise and expand your lists of patterns in each example based on the suggestions of your peers.

4. (5–10 minutes) What patterns of reasoning did you use while working on this activity? (Don't peek, one set of possible answers is in the footnote.[2])

---

[1]Steps 1 and 2—analysis; step 3—comparison, synthesis; step 4—evaluation; step 5—analysis, synthesis, inference.
[2]Analyzing samples for important component parts; comparing these component parts to the types of reasoning patterns in the chapter; classifying component parts into types of reasoning patterns.

Activity 9-3   Key Words

Recommended

Goals/Rationale

You can use a variety of methods to assess the quality of student reasoning. This activity asks you to generate words that trigger different thinking patterns, which you can then use in questions for students.

> **Cross-Reference to *Student-Involved Classroom Assessment*, 3d ed.**
>
> General Principle 3: Translating reasoning patterns into assessments.
>
> **Additional Materials Needed**
>
> TEXTBOOK: Figure 8.2, "Questioning Techniques That Draw Students into Learning," Figure 9.10, "Sample Selected Response Exercises That Require Reasoning," and Figure 9.11, "Triggers for Test Questions."
>
> **Time Required**
>
> 30–45 minutes; rest is homework.

What to Do

Part A: Preparation/Do with Colleagues

1. (10–15 minutes) What words trigger different thinking patterns? For example, to trigger evaluative thinking, you could ask students to "judge," "rate," or "evaluate." Generate as long a list as possible of such "key words" that tap or trigger different kinds of reasoning. You can use textbook Figure 8.2, Figure 9.10 or Figure 9.11, or other lists of words with which you are familiar. Combine your list with those of your colleagues.

2. (15-20 minutes) Convert your list into examples of questions that you could use to tap different patterns of reasoning in a current unit you are teaching (inservice) or material you are learning (preservice). Try to generate selected response, essay, and personal communication questions.

3. (5–10 minutes) What patterns of reasoning did we ask you to use with this activity?[1]

Part B: Try with Students

Try your questions with students. Be ready to discuss what happened, insights you obtained, what worked well, what you would want to modify, and so on.

---

[1] Analysis of various words that could be used; classification of words into patterns of reasoning tapped; deduction-generating questions that elicit different patterns of reasoning.

Convert Reasoning Patterns into Student-Friendly Language

Activity 9-4

Optional

Goals/Rationale

Reasoning is an important learning target for students. Students need to understand the targets they are to hit. This activity gives you the opportunity to translate the patterns of reasoning in Chapter 9 into student-friendly language and then see what students have to say about them.

> **Cross-Reference to *Student-Involved Classroom Assessment*, 3d ed.**
>
> General Principles 2 and 3: Understand patterns of reasoning and share them with students.
>
> **Additional Materials Needed**
> None.
>
> **Time Required**
> 40–55 minutes; rest is homework.

What to Do

Part A: Preparation/Do with Colleagues

1. (20-25 minutes) Convert the definition and examples of reasoning from Chapter 9 into language and examples that students are likely to understand. You can use pictures and/or words. Posters that represent the important elements of a pattern of reasoning with 2-3 bullets and a picture are also a good way to go. If you want, divide the patterns of reasoning up with your colleagues if you are working in a group. You can also work on student-friendly versions for different grade ranges. (One idea: Look at the icons used in Activity 8-5, "Journal Icons.")

2. (10–15 minutes) If you are working in a group, review and revise each other's student-friendly version(s).

3. (10–15 minutes) Think about or discuss how you will introduce students to the reasoning patterns and words associated with them. Will you start with a single pattern or several? How will you build on previous experiences? (For example, you might already have done Activity 8-5 with your students.) What examples of reasoning might you use? How might you model different patterns? How might students help in defining these patterns of reasoning?

Part B: Try with Students

Try out your plan with students. Be ready to discuss with your colleagues what happened.

Activity 9-5

Assessing Reasoning in the Classroom—Video Discussion

Optional

Goals/Rationale

The video, *Assessing Reasoning in the Classroom*, takes you step by step through the ideas presented in textbook Chapter 9. The video comes complete with a facilitator's guide that helps you work through key ideas.

> **Cross-Reference to *Student-Involved Classroom Assessment*, 3d ed.**
>
> General Principles 1, 2, and 3: Defining patterns of reasoning, translating them into sound assessments, and involving students.
>
> **Additional Materials Needed**
>
> VIDEO: *Assessing Reasoning in the Classroom*, available from the Assessment Training Institute, 800-480-3060.
>
> **Time Required**
>
> 60 minutes to view the video without doing the embedded activities. At least two hours if all the activities in the video are completed.

What to Do

Acquire the video and follow the steps clearly laid out in the facilitator's guide.

Unit-Building Activity, Assignment 8— Assessing Reasoning

Activity 9-6

Optional

Goals/Rationale

This is the eighth in a series of direct applications to day-to-day life in the classroom. This unit-building activity centers around assessments that focus on student reasoning. Application of learning from Chapter 9 will enable you to clarify your unit's reasoning targets and strengthen their assessment. Then from this clear vision of reasoning required for your assessments, you will review and refine the assessment of reasoning in the midst of learning—helping students develop and refine their understanding of reasoning patterns with feedback.

> **Cross-Reference to *Student-Involved Classroom Assessment*, 3d ed.**
>
> General Principles 1, 2, and 3: Defining patterns of reasoning, translating them into sound assessments, and involving students.
>
> **Additional Materials Needed**
>
> Your draft unit plan.
>
> **Time Required**
>
> 15 minutes; rest is homework.

What to Do

Part A: Do with Colleagues

(15 minutes) Review and discuss the following steps as needed.

Part B: Homework

1. What patterns of reasoning are called for by your unit targets? What prerequisite reasoning skills are called for by your skill and product targets? What patterns of reasoning have you used in your previous tables of specifications? Can you clarify any of these using the information in Chapter 9?

2. Using the ideas in Chapter 9, refine assessments of reasoning for your end-of-unit assessment and assessments to be embedded during instruction. Did you use a variety of assessment methods? Why did you choose each method? Will your unit's embedded assessments provide you information about reasoning targets and enable students to know which reasoning targets need more attention as they progress through the unit?

Notes:

Performance Assessment of Skills and Products

Big Ideas in This Chapter

This chapter answers the following guiding question:

How can I devise assessments that help my students become confident, competent masters of the performance skills and product development capabilities that I expect of them?

The **General Principles** in this chapter are as follows:

1. Performance assessment scoring criteria must be sharply focused on the right achievement targets, including all of the active ingredients needed for success.

2. Performance tasks must engage students in interesting tasks that afford them the opportunity to accurately demonstrate mastery of all key elements of skill and product achievement.

3. The heart of academic competence resides in students' ability to use their own knowledge and understanding to continuously improve their performance until they succeed. Therefore, there is a direct link between performance criteria and student involvement.

Performance assessment provides the classic example of student involvement—students themselves learning the criteria for quality work in order to self-assess and track their own progress over time. Since this benefit of performance assessment comes from the performance criteria rather than the performance task, many of the activities in Chapter 10 focus on criteria.

Links to Previous Chapters

Chapter 10 returns to the consideration of those forms of achievement that require assessment based on observation and judgment. Chapter 7 provided the design frameworks needed to understand performance assessment, exercises on developing criteria and tasks, and exercises using criteria with students. Chapter 10 gets into variations on the theme of performance assessment by presenting many examples. The chapter also illustrates its own principles by providing standards (in the form of a checklist) for performance assessment quality and samples of performance tasks and criteria that illustrate these standards.

Chapter 10 is the second of three chapters that focus on how to assess specific types of targets. The first was Chapter 9, which looked at reasoning skills. Chapter 11 covers dispositional targets.

Links to Subsequent Chapters

Clear criteria for judging the quality of products and performances is essential for good communication, dealt with in Part IV of the textbook.

Portfolio Reminder

Once again, we remind you that it is important to keep potential portfolio material handy. See previous chapters for suggestions.

Roadmap

Activity	Title	Activity Description	Time	Icons
10-1	Building on Student Strengths	Practice writing assessment tasks that address the same targets and honor diversity. *Cross-reference to Chapter 10: General Principle 2.*	25–35 min	CONSOLIDATE UNDERSTANDING
10-2	Types of Rubrics and When to Use Them	The title says it all. *Cross-reference to Chapter 10: General Principle 1.*	30–50 min	CONSOLIDATE UNDERSTANDING
10-3	Expanding a Checklist into a Rubric	One method to generate rubrics. *Cross-reference to Chapter 10: General Principles 1 and 3.*	60-80 min for each checklist	CONSOLIDATE UNDERSTANDING
10-4	*Analyze Sample Performance Criteria for Quality	Use the checklist in the chapter to analyze the strengths and weaknesses of real rubrics. *Cross-reference to Chapter 10: General Principle 1.*	45–90 min	CONSOLIDATE UNDERSTANDING
10-5	*Analyze Sample Performance Tasks for Quality	Use the checklist in the chapter to analyze the strengths and weaknesses of real performance tasks. *Cross-reference to Chapter 10: General Principle 2.*	50–90 min	CONSOLIDATE UNDERSTANDING
10-6	Unit-Building Activity, Assignment 9—Skills and Products	Continued work on your own unit, developing high-quality assessments of products and performances. *Cross-reference to Chapter 10: General Principles 1, 2, and 3.*	15–20 min; rest is homework	APPLY LEARNING

*Recommended

Activity 10-1   Building on Student Strengths

Optional

Goals/Rationale

Performance assessment gives us opportunities to get vivid pictures of student achievement on learning targets that is simply not possible with other methods. Our students walk in the classroom door with diverse experiences, strengths, patterns of language and communication, and cultural, ethnic, and geographic contexts, as well as their own unique learning styles and intelligences. To accurately assess their achievement of important targets, it's important to see and use the power of performance assessment to avoid inadvertent biases that mask actual student learning. This activity focuses on applying what we know about the variety of ways that students learn (their strengths) to create good assessments.

Cross-Reference to *Student-Involved Classroom Assessment*, 3d ed.

General Principle 1: Developing performance assessments that accurately portray student achievement.

Additional Materials Needed

None.

Time Required

25–35 minutes.

What to Do

1. (5 minutes) Read the worksheet, "An Example of Using Student Strengths." Read all parts—"The Digestive System," "Your Challenge" and the table.

2. (10–15 minutes) Individually or in small groups of 2 or 3, adapt the performance assessment task in the example so that it aims for the same target but enables students to use intelligences different from those in the example. (If you prefer, revise a performance task you have already used in your classroom.)

3. (5 minutes) If you are working in a group, do a quick sharing of your task with another group to check that the adapted tasks, while permitting students to exercise different strengths, will still provide clear and accurate information about the desired learning target.

4. (5–10 minutes) What might you do differently in your classroom based on this activity?

An Example of Using Student Strengths

The Digestive System

In a middle school Life Science laboratory program, students take a selected response test to demonstrate their knowledge of key vocabulary and concepts. The school includes students who are English-language learners from a number of different cultures. In the past, results for these students have been mostly dismal. Knowing that multiple-choice formats are a barrier to some students' accurately displaying what they have learned, Ms. Joseph, the sheltered English teacher, designed performance tasks that assess the same targets (knowledge of vocabulary and basic understanding) as the multiple-choice tests.

For example, in her class unit on the digestive system, students act out the movement of food through the digestive system. One group acts out the parts of the system itself, physically positioning themselves around the room, each with a small card that lists the name of their part of the system on one side and its function in digestion on the other. Another group of students acts out the "food," moving through the system and being processed on the journey. One by one, the "food" moves through the system, successfully navigating the digestive tract while calling out the name of each part of the system as they pass by. Students then switch roles.

Your Challenge

Identify the intelligences that students have used while acting out the digestive system. Adapt Ms. Joseph's task (or create another) that draws on one or more *other* potential strengths/intelligences of her students. The following table presents some possibilities.

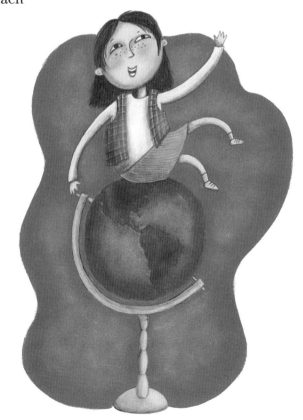

Intelligence	Ways Students Can Respond
Visual-Spatial: Thinking in pictures; seeing and showing ideas with shapes, colors, size; learning by seeing	Posters, drawings, murals, maps...
Verbal-Linguistic: Thinking in words and using language to express ideas	Reports, essays, journals, oral presentations, storytelling...
Mathematical-Logical: Using logic and reasoning to learn and problem solve; making sense of thing by calculating, measuring, analyzing	Charts, logs, tables, diagrams, mind maps, webs...
Musical-Rhythmic: Using hearing, tone, rhythm, and patterns to learn	Songs, chants, using musical instruments, patterned sounds...
Bodily-Kinesthetic: Using body and hands to learn and show learning	Demonstrations, role plays, puppet shows, physical demonstrations, hands on displays, dances...
Interpersonal: Understanding and learning best through interaction with others; and through group activity and chances to work with a partner	Group presentations, choral readings, joint projects...
Intrapersonal: Learning through reflection; thinking about what you've done; your work and what can make it better; knowing your feelings: metacognition (able to think about your own thinking)	Journal writings, one-on-one interviews, conferences, writings, self assessment, reflection logs...
Naturalistic: Awareness of nature; learning from observation; being attuned with surroundings and the environment	Demonstrations with materials from the environment (guiding others around an area and pointing out natural phenomena)...

Activity 10-2   Types of Rubrics and When to Use Them

Optional

Goals/Rationale

There are different types of rubrics; the trick is to know which type to use when. This activity begins by defining types of rubrics and asking you to find examples in the textbook and this *Workbook*. Then, we discuss when to use the various types.

> **Cross-Reference to *Student-Involved Classroom Assessment*, 3d ed.**
>
> General Principle 1: Performance criteria need to have the right content.
>
> **Additional Materials Needed**
>
> TEXTBOOK: Figure 10.12, "Going to School," Figure 10.4, "ACTFL Foreign Language Proficiency Guidelines for Speaking," Figure 10.5, "Oral Presentation Performance Criteria," Figure 10.3, "Writing Assessment Criteria," Figure 10.11, "Central Kitsap Problem Solving Criteria."
>
> **Time Required**
>
> 30–50 minutes.

What to Do

1. (15–30 minutes) Consider the definitions for different kinds of rubrics—holistic, analytical trait, task specific, general—in the worksheet, "Rubrics Square." In each shaded cell are examples of these rubric types from the textbook and this *Workbook*. Make sure you understand the definitions and can find other examples in the textbook, *Workbook*, or other sources. Add the examples you find into the cells of the worksheet. Please note that <u>all</u> rubrics are either holistic or analytical trait <u>and</u> either task-specific or general, so you will <u>always</u> have to make two choices. Also note that you can have task-specific, holistic <u>or</u> analytical trait rubrics. You can also have general holistic or analytical trait rubrics.

2. (10–15 minutes) Now that you've had the opportunity to solidify your understanding of different types of rubrics, the next step is to think about when you'd want to use each type. Think about or discuss the following questions:

   a. What do you think the developers of textbook Figure 10.12, "Going to School," were trying to assess? Can you tell for sure by looking at the task or the task-specific rubric?[1] Can you tell what is being assessed by the general rubrics in textbook Figure 10.4, "ACTFL Foreign Language Proficiency Guidelines for Speaking," or Figure 10.5, "Oral Presentation Performance Criteria?"[2] What implications does this have for your use of task-specific or general rubrics?

[1]This is one of the shortcomings of task-specific rubrics—you can't necessarily tell from the task nor the rubric what is being assessed. The developers of "Going to School" were attempting to assess problem solving and communication in mathematics. Did you guess right?

[2]This is one of the strengths of general rubrics—to be general, they have to define the skills being assessed in terms that can be applied across the board. That's why such rubrics are so good to use with students; they help students generalize from one task to the next.

b. Complete the problem in the worksheet, "Combine Two Triangles." Score your response using the included task-specific rubric. Look at the sample student responses. How would they have to be scored using the rubric? Are they correct responses nevertheless?[3] What implications does this have for your use of task-specific or general rubrics?

c. Considering (2a) and (2b) above, when would you want to use task-specific and general rubrics? The worksheet, "Task-Specific or General?" (p. 227) summarizes some points, but be sure to list your own uses first.

d. When would you want to use holistic or analytical trait rubrics? The worksheet, "Holistic or Analytical Trait?" (p. 228) summarizes some uses, but be sure to list your own first.

3. (5 minutes) What patterns of reasoning (see Chapter 9) did you use in this activity?

[3]This is a another weakness of task-specific scoring—it is frequently difficult to list all the possible correct answers because it's hard to think of them all. In fact, that's a reason one test publisher told us they were moving away from task-specific scoring. Raters go on automatic pilot and don't notice when student answers are correct yet not listed on the official list of correct answers.

Rubrics Square*

	CHOICE 2	
	Holistic Rubric: One score is given to an entire product or performance that summarizes one's judgment of its overall quality.	**Analytical Trait Rubric:** A score is given to each of several important dimensions of a product or performance. Each score summarizes one's judgment of that dimension apart from the others.
Task Specific Rubric: a rubric that can only be used with a single exercise, product, or task.	**Textbook Figure 10.12, "Going to School"**—You can only use this rubric to score the "Going to School" problem. The whole solution gets a single score that summarizes your judgment of overall quality. Therefore "Going to School" is task-specific.	**Textbook Figure 10.12, "Going to School 2"**—You can only use this rubric to score the "Going to School" problem. You give the performance a separate score for (a) the graph, (b) Graham and Paul, and (c) the Rationale. Therefore, "Going to School" is task-specific analytical trait.
General: a rubric that can be used across all similar tasks, exercises, and products.	**Textbook Figure 10.4, "ACTFL Foreign Language Proficiency Guidelines for Speaking"**—You can use this rubric for any language in any communication setting. A person's ability to speak a foreign language is summarized into a single level. Therefore, the ACTFL rubric is general holistic.	**Textbook Figure 10.5, "Oral Presentation Performance Criteria"**—You can use this rubric for any oral presentation. Each oral presentation gets three scores (language, delivery, and organization). Therefore, the Oral Presentation rubric is general analytical trait.

(Row label at left: CHOICE 1)

*Title thanks to Dr. Joe Hansen, Silverton School District, Oregon.

Combine Two Triangles*

Problem

Put together two triangles that have the same size and shape to create a new shape. In the space below, draw your new shape.

How many sides does your new shape have? _____

How many corners does your new shape have? _____

Scoring Guide

2 = Student creates shape using two triangles (same size and shape) showing two sides and/or two points touching and answers both questions correctly based on that shape.

1 = Student creates shape using two triangles (same size and shape) showing two sides and/or two points touching and answers one question correctly based on that shape.

0 = Other

Sample Correct Responses

Actual Student Answers

*From Gail Lynn Goldberg, Maryland State Department of Education, paper American Educational Research Association Annual Meeting, 1996.

Task-Specific or General?

Here's some advice:

GENERAL	TASK SPECIFIC
Definition: Similar performance tasks use the same rubric.	**Definition:** Each performance task has its own rubric. The rubric for one task can't be used for another.
Examples: Textbook Figure 10.3, "Writing Assessment Criteria," Figure 10.4, "ACTFL Foreign Language Proficiency Guidelines for Speaking," and Figure 10.5, "Oral Presentation Performance Criteria."	**Examples:** Textbook Figure 10.12, "Going to School," variations 1 and 2.

GENERAL

When to Use:
- When the rubric is being used instructionally to help students understand the nature of quality and generalize from one task to the next
- When students will not all be doing exactly the same task; when students can choose the evidence to show competence on a particular skill or product
- When teachers are trying to be consistent in judging different work in different classes or grades where the tasks are all different

Disadvantages:
- Takes longer to learn; but therein is also the strength—learning the rubric is also learning the skill
- Takes longer to score.

TASK SPECIFIC

When to Use:
- When speed of getting a score is more important than thinking through what is being scored
- When you want to know if students know particular facts, equations, methods, or procedures
- When consistency of scoring is of utmost importance

Disadvantages:
- Can't give to students ahead of time because it "gives away" the answer
- Must develop a new rubric for each task; this takes time and sometimes isn't possible, e.g., with portfolios when students select different work samples
- Does not make the rater think— scoring is on automatic pilot
- Correct answers not in the scoring guide are sometimes missed
- Does not help define the nature of quality in general; only states what quality looks like for a particular task

Holistic or Analytical Trait?

For any given product or performance, the second rubric choice is:

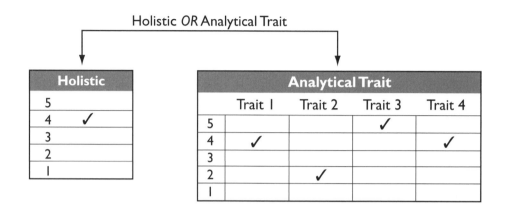

Holistic OR Analytical Trait

Holistic	
5	
4	✓
3	
2	
1	

Analytical Trait			
Trait 1	Trait 2	Trait 3	Trait 4
5			✓	
4	✓			
3				
2		✓		
1				

HOLISTIC

Definition: One score or rating for the entire product or performance.

Examples: Textbook Figure 10.4, "Foreign Language Proficiency Guidelines," Figure 10.12, "Going to School," variation 1.

When to Use:
- For a quick snapshot of overall status or achievement

- When speed of scoring is more important than having a profile of strengths and weaknesses

- When the skill or product to be assessed is simple; when it has only a single dimension

Disadvantages:
- Two students can get the same score for vastly different reasons

- Not as good for identifying strengths and weaknesses and planning instruction

- Not as useful for students to use

ANALYTICAL TRAIT

Definition: Several scores or ratings for a product or performance. Each score represents an important dimension or trait of the performance or product.

Examples: Textbook Figure 10.5, "Oral Presentation Criteria"; and Figure 10.11, "Central Kitsap Problem-Solving Criteria."

When to Use:
- Planning instruction—shows relative strengths and weaknesses

- Teaching students the nature of a quality product or performance—they need the details

- Detailed feedback to students or parents

- When knowing how to precisely describe quality is more important than speed

- For complicated skills, products, or performances for which several dimensions need to be clear

Disadvantages:
- Scoring is slower

- Takes longer to learn

Expanding a Checklist into a Rubric

Activity 10-3

Optional

Goals/Rationale

Have you ever had a checklist or rubric that you wished was a little clearer? This activity provides a strategy for "filling out" a checklist or rubric to add the clarity needed for both teachers and students to understand the nature of quality. In this activity we will "fill out" textbook Figure 10.2, "A Quality Control Checklist for Performance Criteria," and Figure 10.13," A Quality Control Checklist for Performance Tasks." We're going to use the sample performance criteria and tasks in Chapter 10 to help us "fill them out."

In other words, the portrait we paint of quality performance criteria and tasks using the checklists is only a beginning—they only describe what strong performance criteria and tasks look like. They don't help us with understanding what "middle quality" or "weak" performance criteria and tasks look like. We're going to practice one strategy for sharpening this portrait—using actual samples of performance criteria and tasks to help us describe other levels of quality besides "strong".

This is a strategy that you can also use in your classroom to sharpen up unclear criteria or convert checklists into rubrics. For example, in one state with which we were working, teachers were given the state rubrics for reading, math and writing plus scored samples of student work with explanations for those scores. The rubrics themselves, however were sketchy in terms of the detail that would help teachers and students understand the targets being assessed on the state assessment. Teachers "filled out" the state rubrics using the scored samples of student work. This made the criteria much clearer for teachers and students.

Cross-Reference to *Student-Involved Classroom Assessment*, 3d ed.

General Principles 1 and 3: Defining quality performance criteria, student involvement.

Additional Materials Needed

TEXTBOOK: Figure 10.2, "A Quality Control Checklist for Performance Criteria," Figure 10.13, "A Quality Control Checklist for Performance Tasks," Figure 10.5, "Oral Presentation Performance Criteria"; textbook pages 301–332, on criteria and tasks.

Time Required

60-80 minutes for each checklist.

What to Do

1. (10 minutes) Look at the worksheet, "Rubric for Performance Criteria." We have begun to fill in the descriptors for the "strong" rating using terms from the checklist—Figure 10.2, "A Quality Control Checklist for Performance Criteria." For example, Figure 10.2 includes the following descriptors for a strong "on target" rubric: *each element to be scored is vividly and understandably described; the scoring guide is well organized both within and across rating scales; examples illustrate each level of quality; the criteria center on what experts in the field would consider the most important or telling,* and so on. Finish writing in the descriptors for "strong" using the words in Figure 10.2. Note that the checklist (Figure 10.2) *only* describes what strong performance criteria look like.

   Most checklists only describe one level of quality—strong. A feature is either there or it is not. Checklists seldom describe "medium" or "weak" performance.

2. (10–20 minutes) So, what do medium and weak performance criteria look like? Textbook pages 301-322, on criteria, contain examples of "medium" and "weak" rubrics, and we describe exactly what makes each so. For example, the "oral presentation" criteria in the textbook Figure 10.5 are "medium" on the trait of being "On Target." The reasons cited in the textbook (p. 310) are, "contains much that is relevant, but leaves out an entire trait that is essential—content." "Why are '4' and '3' grouped together?" These statements can be used to "fill out" the descriptors for "medium"—see how we've done that in the worksheet, "Rubric for Performance Criteria."

   Look through the descriptions for the other "medium" and "weak" performance criteria in Chapter 10 and see if you can add descriptors to the "medium" and "weak" categories of the worksheet, "Rubric for Performance Criteria."

3. (5 minutes) Discuss or think about the following questions:

   a. Would this be a useful activity to do with colleagues? Why?

   b. Would this be a useful activity to with students? Why?

   c. How would you apply this method to other performance criteria that are a little unclear?[1]

4. (5 minutes) What reasoning skills did we ask you to use in this activity? (Refer to Chapter 9.)[2]

[1]Hint: Gather samples of student work; find several strong, medium, and weak performances; describe why they are strong, medium, and weak; use your descriptions to "fill out" your rubric.

[2]One set of possibilities: analysis (analyzing samples of work); inferences (inductive reasoning—inferring general characteristics from specific examples; evaluation (evaluating the quality of rubrics).

5. (30-40 minutes) *Optional.* Repeat this exercise (as desired) with textbook Figure 10.13, "A Quality Control Checklist for Performance Tasks." You'll need to make a new rubric template worksheet. Merely change the title of "Rubric for Performance Criteria" to "Rubric for Performance Tasks." The rest of the new worksheet will be the same. As before, use the descriptors in Figure 10.13 to fill out the "strong" rating levels. Then use the "medium" and "weak" examples of performance tasks in Chapter 10 (p. 322-332) to add descriptors to the "medium" and "weak" levels of the worksheet, "Rubric for Performance Tasks."

Rubric for Performance Criteria

Trait 1: On-Target	Descriptors
Strong	Each element to be scored is vividly and understandably described. All language is specific and accurate. The guide is well organized both within and across rating scales. The criteria center on what experts in the field would consider the most important aspects of quality.
Medium	Contains much that is relevant, but leaves out a major component of quality. Levels are grouped in a way that doesn't make sense.
Weak	

Trait 2: Practical	Descriptors
Strong	The level of detail and precision in ratings fit the use. Teachers feel the time required to learn to use the rubrics is worth it. The criteria have been translated into language that students can understand. The criteria lead to fair evaluations for all students.
Medium	
Weak	

Activity 10-4 Analyze Sample Performance Criteria for Quality

Recommended

Goals/Rationale

In some assessments the author is very aware of quality issues surrounding performance criteria. But in many other assessments, rubrics have weaknesses in content, clarity, and user friendliness. This activity gives you practice in identifying weaknesses in real rubrics and then fixing them.

Cross-Reference to *Student-Involved Classroom Assessment*, 3d ed.

General Principles 1 and 3: Defining quality rubrics, student involvement.

Additional Materials Needed

WORKBOOK: Appendix A, "Seven Strategies for Using Criteria as a Teaching Tool"; Appendix B—sample assessments. TEXTBOOK: Figure 10.2, "A Quality Control Checklist for Performance Criteria."

Time Required

45–90 minutes.

What to Do

1. (10–15 minutes) Use textbook Figure 10.2, "A Quality Control Checklist for Performance Criteria," (or your filled-out rubric from Activity 10-3) to analyze the "Rubric for Application Letter" in "Assessment Sample 6: Interview" in *Workbook* Appendix B. What are its strengths? Weaknesses? What score (strong, medium, or weak) would you give it on the traits of "On Target" and "Practical?" Why?[1]

2. (10–30 minutes) Look at the other performance assessments in Appendix B. What do you notice about them with respect to the quality of the performance criteria included? (Writeups of each assessment are also included in Appendix B, but don't peek ahead.)

3. (5-10 minutes) What is the quality of other rubrics you've seen or used? Gather samples and critique them with colleagues.

4. (10–20 minutes) Look at one of the rubrics that you judge to be weak. What advice would you give the authors on how to make it stronger? Revise the rubric using your own advice.

[1]Our analysis of this rubric is included in the "Analysis of Assessment Sample 6: Interview," under Standard 5, (*Workbook* Appendix B). How does your analysis compare to ours?

5. (10–15 minutes) *Optional.* Think about or discuss the following questions:

    a. Does every performance assessment have to include high quality performance criteria or does there just need to be a general pattern of high-quality rubrics over time?

    b. Which of the "Seven Strategies for Using Criteria as a Teaching Tool" (*Workbook* Appendix A) did we use in this activity?[2] (We're trying to use the same strategies to teach you, our learners, the characteristics of sound performance criteria.)

    c. What are the implications for the assessments you use in your own classroom? What are you thinking about doing differently?

    d. What patterns of reasoning (see textbook Chapter 9) did you use in this activity?

Analyze Sample Performance Tasks for Quality

Activity 10-5

Recommended

Goals/Rationale

In some assessments the author is very aware of quality issues surrounding performance tasks. But in many other assessments, tasks have weaknesses in content, clarity, and feasibility. This activity gives you practice in identifying weaknesses in real performance tasks and fixing them.

> **Cross-Reference to *Student-Involved Classroom Assessment*, 3d ed.**
>
> General Principle 2: Defining quality performance tasks, student involvement.
>
> **Additional Materials Needed**
>
> WORKBOOK: Appendix A, "Seven Strategies for Using Criteria as a Teaching Tool"; Appendix B, sample assessments. TEXTBOOK: Figure 10.12, "Going to School," Figure 10.13, "A Quality Control Checklist for Performance Tasks."
>
> **Time Required**
>
> 50–90 minutes.

[2] Strategies 2 and 3.

What to Do

1. (10–15 minutes) Use textbook Figure 10.13, "A Quality Control Checklist for Performance Tasks" (or your filled-out rubric from Activity 10-3, "Rubric for Performance Tasks") to analyze the performance task in textbook Figure 10.12, "Going to School." What are its strengths? Weaknesses? What score (strong, medium, or weak) would you give it on the traits of "On Target" and "Practical?" Why?

2. (10–30 minutes) Look at the other performance assessments in Appendix B. What are the quality of their performance tasks? (Writeups of each assessment are in Appendix B, but don't peek ahead.)

3. (10 minutes) Think about other assessments you've seen or used. What are the tasks like? What is their quality? Gather samples and critique them with colleagues.

4. (10–20 minutes) Look at one of the tasks that you judged to be weak. What advice would you give the authors to make the task stronger? Revise the task using your own advice.

5. (10–15 minutes) *Optional.* Think about or discuss these questions:

    a. Does every performance assessment have to include high quality performance tasks or does there just need to be a general pattern of high-quality tasks over time?

    b. Which of the "Seven Strategies for Using Criteria as a Teaching Tool," (*Workbook* Appendix A), did we use in this activity?[1] (We're trying to use the same strategies to teach you, our learners, the characteristics of sound performance assessment.)

    c. What are the implications for the assessments you use in your own classroom?

    d. What patterns of reasoning (see textbook Chapter 9) did you use in this activity?[2]

---

[1]Strategies 2 and 3
[2]Analysis, comparison, evaluation

Unit-Building Activity, Assignment 9— Skills and Products

Activity 10-6

Optional

Goals/Rationale

This is the ninth in a series of direct applications to day-to-day life in the classroom. This unit-building activity centers on the quality of unit assessments designed to tap product and performance skill targets. Applying ideas and information from Chapter 10, you will examine and refine performance assessments as appropriate throughout the unit.

> **Cross-Reference to *Student-Involved Classroom Assessment*, 3d ed.**
>
> General Principles 1, 2, and 3: Defining quality criteria and quality tasks, student involvement.
>
> **Additional Materials Needed**
>
> Your draft unit plan.
>
> **Time Required**
>
> 15–20 minutes; rest is homework.

What to Do

Part A: Preparation/Prework

Revisit the work that you've drafted thus far to identify product and performance assessments in need of further refinement based on the information in Chapter 10. Consider both end-of-unit assessments and assessments embedded throughout instruction. Are the tasks clear, appropriate for your students, and practical? Are the criteria comprehensive, clear, relevant, and practical for students and others to use? Will the current product and performance assessments provide accurate evidence of unit target achievement? Are there any potential biases or components of the tasks and criteria that may mask the learning of some students? Do the embedded assessments set students up for success on the final unit assessment?

Part B: Do with Colleagues

(15–20 minutes) Pair up with a partner. Take a stroll around the room or (if weather permits) outside for a coaching "walk-talk" exchange. Each partner identifies a product or performance assessment that *isn't quite there yet*. While you walk and talk, gather ideas for refinement.

Part C: Homework

Refine your performance assessments as needed.

Notes:

Assessing Dispositions

Big Ideas in This Chapter

This chapter answers the following guiding question:

Why, when, and how should I assess the emotions and dispositions of my students?

The **General Principles** in this chapter are as follows:

1. Student dispositions are inevitably connected to their academic achievement and so can help us maximize their success if we consider them carefully.

2. As with achievement, we must carefully define affective student characteristics to assess them accurately. When assessing affect, we need to pay attention to all possible sources of bias and distortion, including clear understanding of cultural differences in the expression of affect.

3. The heart of academic competence resides in students' ability to use their own knowledge and understanding to continuously improve their performance until they succeed. Therefore, there is a direct link between performance criteria and student involvement.

Student dispositions toward learning are inexorably tied to achievement. If we expect high achievement, we must promote positive attitudes about it, and we must motivate students to try to achieve. From time to time we need to check how we're doing in this regard. To consider assessment in the classroom without attending to student attitudes, interests, motivation, and academic self-concept would be akin to trying to understand the workplace and make it productive without regard to workers' attitudes and motivations.

However, it is also true that dispositions are very personal, so we must limit our attention to those matters over which teachers and schools have responsibility, such as academic self-concept and motivation to learn.

Finally, "attitudes toward knowledge and learning are part of one's cultural heritage. They are shaped by the same influences that form all values, attitudes, and skills; family, friends, community, religion, life experiences, and education are some of these."[1] Because of this, assuming that attitudes and other forms of dispositions are commonly shared across groups is an invitation to bias and distortion. Accurate assessment of dispositional targets takes great care.

Links to Previous Chapters

Chapter 11 echoes themes first introduced in Chapter 1—the relationship between student motivation and school success. Chapter 11 adds specific detail on how to define relevant affective characteristics of students and how to assess these characteristics.

This is the final chapter of three that focuses on how to assess specific types of targets.

Portfolio Reminder

Once again, we remind you that it is important to keep potential portfolio material handy. See previous chapters for suggestions.

---

[1]From *Pacific Standards for Excellence in Teaching, Assessments, and Professional Development*, Pacific Resources for Education and Learning, Honolulu, HI, 1996.

Roadmap

Activity	Title	Activity Description	Time	Icons
11-1	*What's Appropriate?	What affective targets are appropriate in your context? *Cross-reference to Chapter 11: General Principle 1.*	20–40 min	
11-2	*Types of Dispositions	How does Rick's scheme compare to others with which you are familiar? *Cross-reference to Chapter 11: General Principle 2.*	20–40 min	
11-3	*Analyze Sample Surveys for Quality	Critique the "Classroom Assessment Confidence Questionnaire." *Cross-reference to Chapter 11: General Principle 2.*	20-30 min	
11-4	Evaluate, Then Try, the "Critical Spirit Checklist"	Analyze the quality of the "Critical Spirit Checklist" and try it out with your colleagues or students. *Cross-reference to Chapter 11: General Principles 1, 2, and 3.*	30–60 min; rest is homework	
11-5	Unit-Building Activity, Assignment 10—Building A Measure of Affect and Assessing Affect	Step-by-step practice and/or work on your unit. *Cross-reference to Chapter 11: General Principles 1, 2, and 3.*	10-15 min; rest is homework	

*Recommended

Activity 11-1   What's Appropriate?

Recommended

Goals/Rationale

We all have questions in our minds regarding the appropriateness of assessing student dispositions (affect). Some may consider it personally and professionally risky. For this reason, it's a good idea to begin with a frank discussion of some of these concerns. This activity provides an opportunity to think through the types of dispositional targets that would be useful and appropriate to assess in one's local context. Typically, this discussion leads to an exploration of the relationship between positive affect and positive achievement, to a discussion of all the influences of student dispositions that extend beyond the control of teachers, and ends up in a discussion of how affect is manifested differently in different cultures.

> **Cross-Reference to *Student-Involved Classroom Assessment*, 3d ed.**
>
> General Principle 1: Dispositions are connected to student achievement.
>
> **Additional Materials Needed**
>
> TEXTBOOK: Table 11.1, "The Range of Dispositions."
>
> **Time Required**
>
> 20–40 minutes.

What to Do

1. (5–10 minutes) Think about or discuss the advantages and disadvantages of assessing dispositions.

2. (5–10 minutes) Choose three categories of dispositions (center column) in Table 11.1, "The Range of Dispositions." For each category, decide on two appropriate (school-related) topics that would be useful to know about students to plan instruction, and two inappropriate (nonschool-related) topics that should *not* be asked of students. For example, for anxiety, two appropriate things might be anxiety about test taking and speaking in front of a group. Two inappropriate things might be anxiety about home life and sexuality. If you are working in a group, compile a complete list with colleagues. What is in-bounds in your setting?

3. (5–10 minutes) Read the worksheet, "Cultural Considerations About Assessing Dispositional Targets." What implications might this information have for assessing dispositions accurately and using them to plan instruction?

4. (5–10 minutes) If you and your colleagues choose to assess some aspects of dispositions, how would you explain to a parent what you are doing and why? How would you explain it to students?

Cultural Considerations About Assessing Dispositional Targets

Public expressions of affect	In some cultures, public expression of private thoughts, attitudes and concerns is extremely difficult and may be viewed as inappropriate. *Consider providing students with other—more private and culturally compatible—ways of expressing positive and negative responses to what they are learning and their reactions to it. One option is to use learning log prompts or dialog journals.*
Interpreting nonverbal communication	When we assess dispositions through nonverbal behaviors that occur naturally in the classroom (i.e., assuming that student eye contact with the teacher equals interest in the content of the lesson), cultural differences can interfere with the accuracy of our judgments. In some cultures a raised eyebrow signifies agreement and interest. In others, silence is the appropriate response to a statement you agree with. In short, *don't rely on nonverbal indicators to assess dispositions.*
Authority, status, and accurate assessment	Young people in a number of cultures are expected to express only positive responses to those in authority—in the classroom, in the home and in the community. Inviting such students to fill out a scaled attitude survey is likely to result in only high-end scoring—it is disrespectful of the knowledge and position of the authority figure to provide negative feedback. *One possibility is to remove the personal aspect of the survey by providing fictional scenarios that ask students to make choices for the characters.*
Focus on work and learning	Assessment of dispositions needs to be carefully limited to those dispositions and habits of mind that clearly affect the quality of student work and ongoing learning.

Activity 11-2 Types of Dispositions

Recommended

Goals/Rationale

In textbook Chapter 11, Rick presents eight types of school-related dispositions that might usefully and appropriately be assessed in the classroom. As with other topics, Rick chose these because they seem to cover what's important, and they have been clearly defined in the research literature. The eight types of dispositions are a way to give us a vocabulary to discuss complex ideas.

You don't necessarily need to use Rick's set of eight dispositions, but you *do* need to use *some* comprehensive set. This activity is designed to

both deepen understanding of the eight dispositional characteristics described in Chapter 11 and compare them to other classification schemes with which you may be familiar. The goal is not to quibble over definitions, but to think through a scheme that covers the bases and provides a framework you and your colleagues can use successfully. This activity also points out cultural differences that might interfere with your ability to draw sound conclusions about student affect.

Cross-Reference to *Student-Involved Classroom Assessment*, 3d ed.

General Principle 2: Types of school-related dispositions.

Additional Materials Needed

TEXTBOOK: Table 11.1, "The Range of Dispositions."

Time Required

20–40 minutes.

What to Do

1. (10–20 minutes) To deepen your understanding of the eight dispositions in Chapter 11, complete the worksheet, "Dispositions—How Can We Tell?" If you're working in a group, you could divide up the list. (Note: You could also do this with students. What would you need to do first for this activity to be useful?)

2. (10–20 minutes) Think about or discuss the following questions:

    a. How does Rick's list of eight dispositions in textbook Table 11.1, "The Range of Dispositions," compare to others you've seen, learned, or are using? (For example, "Habits of Mind"—such as persistence, curiosity, and open mindedness?) How might you combine Rick's list of eight dispositions with others you are comfortable with to come up with a comprehensive whole?

    b. What patterns of reasoning (see Chapter 9) did you use in this activity?[1]

---

[1]At least: comparative thinking (how does one list compare to another?); synthesis (how can lists be combined to form a comprehensive whole?)

Dispositions—How Can We Tell?

Unfavorable. A student whose attitude toward science is unfavorable would be likely to say _____ . Would this be true of students from all cultures?	ATTITUDES	Favorable. A student whose attitude toward science is favorable would be likely to say _____ . Would this be true of students from all cultures?
How might a student whose culture favors individual achievement above group accomplishment act when taking a test?	VALUES[2]	How might a student whose culture favors group collaboration above individual accomplishment act when taking a test?
Negative. How might a student with a negative view of herself as a learner act when faced with learning challenging content?	ACADEMIC SELF-CONCEPT	Positive. How might a student with a positive view of herself as a learner act when faced with learning challenging content?
External. What might a student say who attributes academic success to luck or forces outside his control?	LOCUS OF CONTROL	Internal. What might a student say who attributes academic success to his own effort?
Can't do. What actions or words would indicate that a student believes she is unlikely to succeed? Might telling words or actions be different in a culture where humility is valued?	SELF-EFFICACY	Can do. What actions or words would indicate that a student believes she is likely to succeed? Might these words or actions be misleading in a culture which requires public expressions of confidence and discourages public admission of uncertainty?
Disinterested. In what ways does a student indicate disinterest? What nonverbal cues do you look for? Is our mental set of "interest" cues influenced by our cultural expectations? How?	INTERESTS	Interested. How might a teacher interpret a child's interest in reading if, when asked (for example, "Darren, would you like to read the next paragraph?"), the child will not read aloud? How would this interpretation change if the teacher knew that the child is from a culture where a question such as the teacher asked is viewed as an invitation, not a request, and that it is okay to decline invitations?
No more. When asked about their future academic goals, what are likely responses from students whose aspirations for themselves are low?	ASPIRATIONS	More. What are some of the things that students with high academic aspirations are likely to say and do?
Threatened. How might a student act who is anxious about speaking in front of a group?	ANXIETY	Safe. How might a student act who is not anxious about speaking in front of a group?

[2]Please note that while all other categories have "negative" on the left and "positive" on the right, this category, values, has value-neutral situations described on both the left and right.

Analyze Sample Surveys for Quality

Activity 11-3

Recommended

Goals/Rationale

We've encouraged you, the user of this *Workbook*, to self-assess your own dispositions using the "Classroom Assessment Confidence Questionnaire" in *Workbook* Appendix A. When learning about assessing dispositions, it is useful to critique existing examples. Using the quality criteria for assessments (Five Standards of Assessment Quality), this activity asks you to analyze the strengths and weaknesses of the "Confidence Questionnaire." You also have the opportunity to analyze other sample surveys and questionnaires.

> **Cross-Reference to *Student-Involved Classroom Assessment*, 3d ed.**
>
> General Principle 2: Types of school-related dispositions.
>
> **Additional Materials Needed**
>
> WORKBOOK: Appendix A, "Classroom Assessment Confidence Questionnaire"; Introduction Figure 2, "Five Standards of Quality Assessment."
>
> **Time Required**
>
> 30 minutes for each survey.

Part A: Analyze the "Confidence Questionnaire"

1. (10-15 minutes) Analyze the "Classroom Assessment Confidence Questionnaire" in *Workbook* Appendix A. Think about the following:

    a. What type(s) of format(s) is/are used?

    b. What type(s) of disposition(s) is/are being assessed?

    c. What is the quality of the survey? Consider: is the target defined well, is the use clear, is the target matched well to the format, do the questions cover the ground, and what are the potential sources of bias and distortion? (These match the "Standards for Quality Assessment" in *Workbook* Introduction Figure 2.)

2. (10–15 minutes) Complete the questionnaire again. Do the results really represent your current level of confidence? Has your confidence changed since the beginning of study? Are these results useful?

Part B: Analyze Other Surveys and Questionnaires

(20-30 minutes per survey) Find examples of surveys and questionnaires designed to assess various types of dispositions—political surveys, product surveys, student academic self-concepts, and so on. Critique them for quality—clear target, clear purpose, target-method match, sampling, and bias/distortion.

Activity 11-4

Evaluate, Then Try, the "Critical Spirit Checklist"

Optional

Goals/Rationale

Activity 11-3, "Analyze Sample Surveys for Quality," focused on surveys and questionnaires to assess dispositions. This activity looks at checklists and rubrics. You begin by analyzing textbook Figure 11.3, "Checklist for Evaluating Critical Spirit," for quality. Then, you self-assess your own critical spirit. Finally, you try out the checklist with students. (Note: by "critical spirit" we mean "critical thinking," "evaluative thinking," or "evaluative spirit"—how disposed a person is to objectively evaluate evidence before drawing a conclusion.)

> **Cross-Reference to *Student-Involved Classroom Assessment*, 3d ed.**
>
> General Principles 1, 2, and 3: The connection between student dispositions and student achievement, types of school-related dispositions, possible sources of bias/distortion, student involvement.
>
> **Additional Materials Needed**
>
> WORKBOOK: Appendix A, "Seven Strategies for Using Criteria as a Teaching Tool." TEXTBOOK: Figure 10.2, "A Quality Control Checklist for Performance Criteria," Figure 11.3, "Checklist for Evaluating Critical Spirit."
>
> **Time Required**
>
> 30–60 minutes; rest is homework.

What to Do

Part A: Preparation/Do with Colleagues

1. (10–15 minutes) Evaluate textbook Figure 11.3, "Checklist for Evaluating Critical Spirit," in terms of the criteria for good rubrics in Chapter 10 (Figure 10.2, "A Quality Control Checklist for Performance Criteria"):

   a. Does this Figure 11.3 capture the essence of "critical spirit?" Does the content represent current best thinking about critical spirit?

   b. Is it clear what the items on the checklist in Figure 11.3 mean?

   c. Is it practical for teachers and students? If not, what would you need to do to make it usable?

2. (5–10 minutes) Self-evaluate using Figure 11.3, "Checklist for Evaluating Critical Spirit." Do the results really represent your current level of critical spirit? What might be possible sources of bias and distortion that result in an inaccurate picture of your critical spirit?

3. (10–20 minutes) *Optional*. Plan how you might collect information on the critical spirit of your students.

   a. Be clear on purpose—will you do this just to try out a dispositional rubric, will you use the information for a decision, or will you use the rubric to involve students?

   b. How/where will you observe students? What will they be doing? How many students will you observe at a time? How will you ensure that you've sampled student behavior adequately?

   c. Try out your plan and be ready to discuss what happened.

4. (5–15 minutes) *Optional*. Even if you are not planning to do Part B of this activity, look at it and think about the following questions:

   a. How does the procedure illustrate the "Seven Strategies for Using Performance Criteria as a Teaching Tool" (*Workbook* Appendix A)?[1]

   b. What patterns of reasoning (Chapter 9) are used in each step?

[1]The procedure involves strategies 1, 2, 4, 5, 6, and 7.

Part B: Try with Students

Do this part of the activity only if (a) students have had prior practice using performance criteria; (b) you've taught lessons on critical thinking skills or used criteria for critical thinking (for example, Activity 8-4, "Journal Icons"); (c) students already have been used to thinking about the affective component of learning; (d) this is an affective area you plan to stress throughout the school year; and (e) this is an affective area that is appropriate to address in your local context.

1.   Develop a student-friendly version of textbook Figure 11.3, "Checklist for Evaluating Critical Spirit."

2.   Show students examples (models) what it looks like when one is and is not exhibiting a "critical spirit." Discuss the differences. Begin a list.

3.   Discuss the importance of critical spirit. Why is this disposition important for success in Western culture?

4.   Have students bring in examples of critical spirit.

5.   Add to the list of features.

6.   Show students your student-friendly version of the "Checklist for Evaluating Critical Spirit." Ask students to compare it to their list of features.

7.   Ask students to outline the circumstances under which a critical spirit is important to use.

8.   Critique anonymous examples of critical spirit.

9.   Have students privately self-assess their own critical spirit.

Activity 11-5

Unit-Building Activity, Assignment 10— Building A Measure of Affect and Assessing Affect

Optional

Goals/Rationale

This is the tenth in a series of direct applications to day-to-day life in the classroom. This unit-building activity centers on the role of assessing affect in the unit you are assembling. **You can also do this activity even if you are not doing the whole unit-building sequence.**

The process of developing, administering and interpreting the results of a measure of dispositions can be a very instructive enterprise for those just learning about this domain. This activity outlines such a process.

Cross-Reference to *Student-Involved Classroom Assessment*, 3d ed.

General Principles 1, 2, and 3: The connection between student dispositions and student achievement, types of school-related dispositions, possible sources of bias/distortion, student involvement.

Additional Materials Needed

Your draft unit plan.

Time Required

10-15 minutes; rest is homework.

What to Do:

Part A: Preparation/Prework

If you are working on your unit plan, you may already have done some of the following steps. Review all the steps anyway, just to see if you have missed anything.

1.   *Identify a context* within which the assessment of dispositions would be relevant. If you are teaching, make it your classroom. If you are a student yourself, you might conduct an assessment of the dispositions of your classmates. If you are working on your unit, this would be a good context.

2.   Within that context, *identify a purpose* for conducting such an assessment. If this is just a practice exercise for you, try to think through why a teacher in this context might seek out information about student affect; try to make the practice as real-world as possible. Be sure to keep the ground rules for assessment dispositions in mind—when is assessing dispositions appropriate?

   If you are working on your unit, what is the role of assessing dispositions in your unit? Are you clear on the purpose for such assessment—is it one of the important unit outcomes, or are you assessing affect to better adjust instruction during the unit, or is your purpose to involve students?

3.   Referring to the textbook or to the targets identified in your unit, *identify which kind of disposition* you wish to assess.

4.   Now *devise your assessment* instrument or process. Your objective is to tap the direction and intensity of respondent feelings about the object(s) you have selected. Again, consult the text for your format options.

Part B: Do with Colleagues

(10–15 minutes) When you have drafted your instrument or process for gathering information, have one potential respondent (one of your students or a classmate) *review your assessment* for you. That is, have that person read each question or item aloud, tell you what they think it means, and then respond. This will tell you whether they are interpreting the question as you had intended, so you can adjust as needed before you administer it.

Homework

1. After making any needed adjustments for clarity, *administer your questionnaire or interview* to enough respondents to give you some data to summarize. Again, remember that this is a practice activity. So be reasonable in gathering responses.

2. *Summarize your results.* If you relied on selected response, tally the number of respondents who selected each response option for each item. If you opted for open-response questions (via questionnaire or interview) or performance observations, translate each response into its essential information about the direction and intensity of feelings communicated. If you have any uncertainty about the direction and intensity of feelings conveyed by any particular response, *have another qualified person* (colleague, professor, classmate) *review your interpretation*. Given the results of this second interpretation, what conclusions would you draw regarding the interrater reliability of your assessment?

3. When you have completed your summary, *share your results* with the respondents to see what conclusions they draw regarding the overall direction and intensity of feelings.

4. *Reflect on the entire process* to identify lessons learned and keys to your successful assessment of dispositions in the future. If you are working on your unit, will your dispositional assessments embedded during instruction lead to student success? Will the current assessments provide accurate evidence of dispositions; are there any unconscious biases that might provide inaccurate information for some students?

End Part III

Activities

Roadmap

Activity	Title	Activity Description	Time	Icons
PIII-1	*Show What You Know	The title says it all. *Cross-reference to textbook:* Uses information in Chapters 9-11.	Homework	
PIII-2	*Portfolio Building	The title says it all. *Cross-reference to textbook:* Uses information in Chapters 9-11.	Homework	

*Recommended

Portfolio Building

The activities in this section are intended to consolidate understanding of the material in Part III of Rick's book. This is your chance to reflect on what you've learned so far and convert this self-reflection and assessment into portfolio entries.

Activity PIII-1   Show What You Know

Recommended

Goals/Rationale

Periodically we encourage you to reflect on your increasing confidence and competence as a classroom assessor. One self-reflection technique is to "show what you know"—explain and articulate what you are learning and how it connects to other things in your lives. Activity PIII-1 proposes several ideas for doing this—ideas that might appeal to different learning styles. Any of the "show what you know" activities can be considered prime potential portfolio material.

> **Cross-Reference to *Student-Involved Classroom Assessment*, 3d ed.**
>
> Chapters 9–11.
>
> **Additional Materials Needed**
>
> WORKBOOK: Appendix A, "Sample Working Folder/Portfolio Entry Cover Sheet," "Seven Strategies for Using Performance Criteria as a Teaching Tool."
>
> **Time Required**
>
> Open, it's homework.

What to Do

Item 1 is recommended. The rest are optional. *Be sure to include a cover sheet* (such as that in *Workbook* Appendix A) *with each portfolio entry.*

1. *Recommended.* List and explain the three key points you want to remember from Part III.

2. *Optional.* Based on your learning from Chapters 9–11, add to or revise any of your previous concept maps.

3. *Optional.* Based on your learning from Chapters 9–11, add to or revise any of your previous pictures or posters.

4. *Optional.* Write a letter to a colleague, student, parent, or instructor that explains the following:

    a. Various types of learning targets, why each is important, and how they interrelate.

    b. The use of rubrics with students—why you might want to teach students to use rubrics, when you might want to, and how you might do it. Include both academic and affective targets. Use the vocabulary associated with (a) quality rubrics, and (b) strategies for using criteria as tools for learning (see "Seven Strategies" in *Workbook* Appendix A).

5. *Optional.* Outline the major learnings in Part III. Include a statement of which of these might need to be considered for future assessment planning in your building or district. Include a list of questions that you might need to ask before you can determine future assessment planning in your district or building. Consider the barriers you might face in pursuing these areas that need improvement.

6. *Optional.* Prepare a half-day workshop agenda for others that helps them define each target type, and learn how to choose the most appropriate assessment method(s) for each target type.

Activity PIII-2   Portfolio Building

Recommended

Goals/Rationale

Here's where you make your next set of choices for your growth portfolio. Remember, the goal is to reflect on and self-assess your growth on mastering or understanding the following targets:

- Standard 1—Clear and appropriate learning targets
- Standard 2a—Clear and appropriate users and uses
- Standard 2b—Sound communication about assessment
- Standard 2c—Student involvement in assessment
- Standard 3—Choosing the most appropriate assessment method
- Standard 4—Sampling
- Standard 5—Eliminating sources of bias and distortion

Cross-Reference to *Student-Involved Classroom Assessment*, 3d ed.

Chapters 9–11.

Additional Materials Needed

WORKBOOK: Appendix A, "Classroom Assessment Confidence Questionnaire," "Assessment Principles," "Sample Working Folder/Portfolio Cover Sheet"; Appendix B, "Classroom Assessment Quality Rubrics"; Appendix C, "Self Assessment Developmental Levels."

Time Required

Open, it's homework.

What to Do

Items 1 through 4 are recommended. The rest are optional. *Be sure to include a portfolio entry cover sheet* (such as that in Appendix A, "Sample Working Folder/Portfolio Cover Sheet") *with each portfolio entry.*

1. *Recommended.* Take another look at the previous assessments in your portfolio. Amend (and date) your commentary on their quality. Use the rubrics for evaluating the quality of assessments in Appendix B to help direct your comments. (Do not remove your previous samples or commentaries.) What differences do you notice in content and depth between your original commentary and your amended commentaries?

2. *Recommended.* Select a new assessment (test, quiz, essay test, or performance assessment) that you have recently used or taken. *If you are a current teacher, it must be one that*

you administered, scored, and recorded for use within the context of your teaching. Using the assessment quality rubrics provided in *Workbook* Appendix B, reflect on the quality of this assessment and write a brief analysis. Is this a sound assessment, in your opinion? Is it unsound? Does it meet your standards of quality?

Write a brief comparison of the quality of all the assessments in your portfolio. Is the quality improving over time? How do you know?

3. *Recommended.* If you didn't take the "Classroom Assessment Confidence Questionnaire" in *Workbook* Appendix A as part of Activity 11-3, "Analyze Sample Surveys for Quality," take it now. How is your classroom assessment confidence changing over time?

4. *Recommended.* Go back through your portfolio and identify the patterns of reasoning (textbook Chapter 9) you used to produce at least two of the entries. What is your confidence level in defining and assessing reasoning in the classroom?

5. *Optional.* Self-assess using the "Self Assessment Developmental Levels" in *Workbook* Appendix C. There is a developmental level continuum for each of the five standards of quality assessment.

6. *Optional.* Review previous portfolio entries and note your progress in confidence and competence:

   a. What are you thinking about assessment now that is different from before?

   b. What are you doing differently in the classroom as the result of what you've learned so far?

   c. What is the impact on students? On colleagues? What evidence do you have for this impact?

   d. What questions from before can you now answer? What new questions do you have?

7. *Optional.* Consider again the "Assessment Principles" in *Workbook* Appendix A. Now, which principles affirm your own beliefs? Why? Are there any with which you disagree either in part or in whole? Why? What concerns might you have about any of them?

8. *Optional.* What else in your working folder or learning log might you put in your portfolio to demonstrate increasing competence and confidence in your knowledge, reasoning, skills, and products associated with sound classroom assessment?

Notes:

PART IV

Effective Communication About Student Achievement

Introduction to Part IV: Effective Communication About Student Achievement

Big Ideas in the Introduction to Part IV

The **General Principles** addressed in this chapter are as follows:

1. Accurate information derived from quality classroom assessments is an essential prerequisite of effective communication.

2. Involving students in communicating about their own achievement provides a powerful boost to their motivation and achievement.

3. To be effective, communication about student achievement must adhere to several important conditions.

Links to Previous Chapters

First, Part IV presents the final aspect of the student-involvement picture—communication (the other two aspects have been student-involved assessment and student-involved record keeping). Second, Part IV reinforces the need for sound assessment: communication about achievement is only as good as the assessments on which it is based. Third, the conditions for effective communication link directly to the five standards for quality assessment discussed throughout the textbook (see Figure Intro IV-1, "Conditions for Effective Communication" for this connection).

Links to Subsequent Chapters

This section presents general principles for sound communication that will be applied throughout Chapters 12–15. These principles are summarized in Figure Intro IV-1, "Conditions for Effective Communication."

Portfolio Reminder

Once again, we remind you that it is important to keep potential portfolio material handy. See previous chapters for suggestions.

Roadmap

Activity	Title	Activity Description	Time	Icons
Intro IV-1	*What Is My Current Practice?	The title says it all. *Cross-reference to Part IV Introduction:* General Principles 1, 2, and 3.	20 min	QUICK CHECK
Intro IV-2	4, 3, 2, 1, X— Case Discussion	Use principles of sound communication to give advice on this case. *Cross-reference to Part IV Introduction:* General Principles 1, 2, and 3.	20-30 min	CONSOLIDATE UNDERSTANDING
Intro IV-3		Use principles of sound communication to give advice on this case. *Cross-reference to Part IV Introduction:* General Principles 1, 2, and 3.	20-30 min	CONSOLIDATE UNDERSTANDING

*Recommended

Conditions for Effective Communication

1. Everyone agrees what is to be communicated about
    (**Standard 1**—clear and appropriate learning targets):

    a. The targets to be discussed

    b. Definitions of those targets

2. Assessments underpinning the communication are accurate:

    a. Rely on a proper method
        (**Standard 3**—target-method match)

    b. Sample performance appropriately
        (**Standard 4**—sampling)

    c. Control for potential sources of bias and distortion
        (**Standard 5**—bias and distortion)

    d. Based on good record keeping

    e. Information is summarized properly

3. There is an interpersonal environment conducive to good
    communication:

    a. Clear and agreed on reasons for sharing information
        (**Standard 2**—clear and appropriate users and uses)

    b. A shared language—everyone understands what the
        symbols mean

    c. A focused opportunity to share

    d. The message senders and receivers have checked for
        understanding of the message

Figure Intro IV-1[1]
Conditions for Effective Communication

---

[1]Summarized from the textbook introduction to Part IV.

Activity Intro IV-1   What Is My Current Practice?

Recommended

Goals/Rationale

This activity prepares you to study sound communication about student achievement by considering your current practice.

> **Cross-Reference to *Student-Involved Classroom Assessment*, 3d ed.**
>
> General Principles 1, 2, and 3: Effective communication requires accurate assessments, student involvement boosts achievement, effective communication must adhere to several important conditions.
>
> **Additional Materials Needed**
>
> WORKBOOK: Figure Intro IV-1, "Conditions for Effective Communication."
>
> **Time Required**
>
> 20 minutes.

What to Do

(20 minutes) Think about or discuss the following questions:

1. How do I currently document student assessment information?

2. Why do I document my student information in this way?

3. Am I currently documenting what I really value and expect in student learning?

4. How do I currently communicate to my students and parents what students have learned?

5. How do my current communication practices match up to the "Conditions for Effective Communication" in Figure Intro IV-1?

6. What are local barriers to more effective communication?

4, 3, 2, 1, X—Case Discussion

Activity Intro IV-2

Optional

Goals/Rationale

This activity requires you to use conditions for sound communication to analyze what went wrong in the case study and decide how to fix it.

> **Cross-Reference to *Student-Involved Classroom Assessment*, 3d ed.**
>
> General Principles 1, 2, and 3: Effective communication requires accurate assessments, student involvement boosts achievement, effective communication must adhere to several important conditions.
>
> **Additional Materials Needed**
>
> WORKBOOK: Figure Intro IV-1, "Conditions for Effective Communication."
>
> **Time Required**
>
> 20-30 minutes.

What to Do

1. (5–10 minutes) Read the case, "4, 3, 2, 1, X"—A letter written to the Assessment Training Institute by a parent describing a situation in her child's classroom.

2. (15-20 minutes) Think about or discuss the following questions:

   a. Using Figure Intro IV-1, "Conditions for Effective Communication," what might be contributing to the situation depicted in the case? Were the targets clear? Was the communication based on sound assessment information? Did everyone agree on what to communicate about? Was there a clear reason for sharing information? Did everyone understand the message?

   b. What are some solutions?

4, 3, 2, 1, X—Case

Natalya's fourth-grade teacher, Mary, is a wonderful, loving person with a lot of creativity. Natalya loves her. But many of us parents are about to go crazy from not being able to tell what's going on in class. Homework is so erratic that one week Natalya is spending three to five hours a night and the next she's barely got anything. Due dates get changed without anyone telling the parents. We haven't gotten a single assignment returned so far this year to gauge how our kids are doing.

We've been working closely with Mary and have a good relationship—so far. I'm worried about hurting her feelings or having her feel threatened by us (or other parents), but I'm not sure what to do next.

First of all, our school district changed its elementary report card this year. On the positive side, it is more closely aligned to the district curricular frameworks, and, ultimately, to the state's essential academic learning requirements. The district gave us a support document that outlines some of the expectations from the curricular frameworks, and even though the document is not perfect (it's probably confusing to most parents), it's much better than anything we've ever had in the past. For example, it delineates various levels of reading and mathematics achievement and approximately where students should be at various grade levels in school (for example, at Reading Level F by third to fifth grades).

This is a step in the right direction, but we were offered no examples of what work looks like at those various levels, so it's still way too abstract. I'm not sure that the teachers themselves were even trained with any concrete examples, so it appears they are still going on "intuition" more than anything else.

I don't know how our school district chose the rating scales they used (although I hear from a friend that it's also used in another district), but it's bound to lead to confusion. The scale goes "4, 3, 2, 1, X." Well, of course, that looks a lot like the 4.0 grade scale used by high schools and colleges. It's a stretch for parents to NOT associate 4 with A, 3 with B, 2 with C, etc. I don't know if the intent was to loosely map the grades that way.

Here is the key to markings:

> 4—Exceeds standards for this grade
>
> 3—Meets standards for this grade—proficient
>
> 2—Does not meet standards but making progress
>
> 1—Does not meet standards/not progressing
>
> X—Not covered this reporting period

A marking of 3 or 4 indicates that this student is meeting standards and on schedule to exit. (You've probably heard that our district has instituted "Exit Standards" for grades 3, 5, 8, and 11+.)

Now here's the rub. The only assessment that our teacher could show us was an initial assessment she did with Natalya on reading and mathematics. The reading assessment showed that Natalya was 6.5 grade equivalent overall (8.5 in comprehension), but her marks on the report card were all 3 for reading. What on earth does that mean? When my husband tried to ask the teacher gently what it would be like for someone to get a 4, she really couldn't say. The teaching intern offered that it might be a student who had picked multiple books off the Newberry reading list, made regular trips to the library (which Natalya does), and so on.

In any case, Natalya ended up with all 3s on her report card. Yet, not three weeks ago we had received a letter from the Highly Capable Program director saying that Natalya had been recommended by her teacher for the program, which requires students to be operating at about two years ahead of grade level. What gives?

I did talk with the parent of a friend of Natalya's who had always been a good student like Natalya. She's in the other fourth grade class this year. Her mother was surprised about the new report card. She was mostly surprised because in past years Ai-Li had always gotten all 1s (Excellent) and maybe a few 2s (Good) on the previous reporting scale. This time she got a number of 3s in addition to 4s (but at least she got some 4s. . .). It certainly appears that these two teachers—who teach next door to each other and collaborate on many things and teach in what is considered one of the "model" alternative programs in the city—had very different understandings of how to use the new reporting system.

The Challenge of Dealing with the Media—Case Discussion

Activity Intro IV-3

Optional

Goals/Rationale

This activity requires you to use conditions for sound communication to analyze what went wrong and decide how to fix it.

> **Cross-Reference to *Student-Involved Classroom Assessment*, 3d ed.**
>
> General Principles 1, 2, and 3: Effective communication requires accurate assessments, student involvement boosts achievement, effective communication must adhere to several important conditions.
>
> **Additional Materials Needed**
>
> WORKBOOK: Figure Intro IV-1, "Conditions for Effective Communication." TEXTBOOK: Chapter 1, p. 7-10.
>
> **Time Required**
>
> 20-30 minutes.

What to Do

1. (5–10 minutes) Read the case, "The Challenge of Dealing with the Media."

2. (15-20 minutes) Think about or discuss the following questions:

a. Using Figure Intro IV-1, "Conditions for Effective Communication," what went wrong with the communication about achievement between Emily and the reporter in Rick's opening vignette (textbook p. 7-10) and the rest of the story in the attached case, "The Challenge of Working with the Media"? Was the communication based on sound assessment information? Did the school and the reporter agree on what to communicate about? Was there a clear reason for sharing information? Did the reporter understand the message?

b. What are some solutions?

The Challenge of Dealing with the Media— Case

Please reread the opening scenario of Chapter 1 in the textbook (p. 7-10)—the story of Emily and the school board meeting. When you have done so, return to this case and read on.

A newspaper reporter was in attendance at the school board meeting. The next day, a story appears in the local paper under the headline, "Local Students Fail Writing Test."

At the beginning of the article, he analyzes Emily's beginning-of-year (pretest) writing sample point for point according to its flaws. Then, in an example of balanced reporting, he points out that the author of this flawed piece demonstrates better writing skills later in the year, though he presents no evidence of improved skills.

As you read on, you find out why this particular reporter selected this headline. It was not because Emily had done poorly at the board meeting, for he acknowledges that she did very well. Rather, the reporter has two separate but related reasons for highlighting student failure.

First, he wants to point out how inadequate Emily's writing instruction must have been before the tenth grade. What, he asks, had been going on in writing instruction in the elementary and middle schools to produce a writer so incapable of composing coherent text?

The reporter's second reason for complaining was more fundamental— the apparent narrowness of the new writing program at the high school. The only form of writing Emily had been taught to do well was narration—storytelling and personal point of view. What, the reporter asks, about expository writing for use in business contexts, persuasive writing, and creative or poetic writing?

The entire tone of the story is quite negative, despite the extremely positive experience everyone had at last night's board meeting. Reading it leaves many of the meeting's participants feeling frustrated.

Classroom Perspectives on Standardized Testing

Big Ideas in This Chapter

This chapter answers the following guiding question:

What role should periodic large-scale standardized tests play in communicating about student achievement?

The **General Principles** addressed in this chapter are as follows:

1. Historically, standardized tests have played a major role at several levels of the evolution of American education. This chapter reviews the history of large-scale standardized tests.

2. The scores they produce can provide valuable information to some very important decision makers, although they are of limited value day to day in the classroom. The chapter reviews the various types of scores on standardized tests and what they mean.

3. As professional educators, it is our responsibility to see that standardized tests are administered and used appropriately. The chapter covers what we need to know about them.

Although standardized tests offer little useful information for day-to-day instruction, they remain a very visible part of the current testing scene. They play a significant role in school public relations at all levels, because the public desires and expects to see high scores—for many, high scores signal that students are in good hands. Therefore, we need to understand them to use them appropriately.

Terminology Check

We've been using a lot of phrases that have "standards" in them—content standards, standards for quality assessment, standardized tests. Now's a good time to check to make sure our vocabulary is clear.

- *Large-scale, standardized test*—A test that is given the same way at roughly the same time across classrooms, such as norm-referenced tests from test publishers, state assessments, and the National Assessment of Educational Progress (NAEP). Standardized tests can come in any format—multiple choice, essay (for example, open-ended math problems), performance assessment (for example, writing), or personal communication (for example, assessing working in a group). In the case of "standardized" tests, *standard* means *uniform*.

- *Content standards*—Statements of what we want students to know and be able to do, as in, "These statements set the 'standards' for what to teach." Either standardized tests or classroom assessments can assess "content standards." *Standard* here again means *uniform*—uniform standards for content.

- *Standards* can also refer to *standards of quality assessment*—Statements of what quality looks like, as in, "This test 'sets the standard' for quality." *Standard* here means *a goal to shoot for*.

Links to Previous Chapters

Chapter 12 expands on the policy uses of assessment first mentioned in Chapter 2, and repeats the need for balance between large-scale and classroom assessment. This chapter also relates standardized tests back to principles of sound communication provided in the textbook introduction to Part IV. Finally, the chapter relates standardized tests back to principles of sound assessment (first outlined in Chapters 2–4): clear targets, clear users and uses, picking the best method, sampling, and avoiding potential sources of bias and distortion. These standards for quality assessments apply to *all* assessments, both classroom and standardized.

Relationship to Subsequent Chapters

This is the first of four chapters on communicating about student achievement. Standardized tests are one way to do this.

Portfolio Reminder

Once again, we remind you that it is important to keep potential portfolio material handy. See previous chapters for suggestions.

Roadmap

Activity	Title	Activity Description	Time	Icons
12-1	*Visualizing Invisible Targets/ Analyzing Standardized Tests	What achievement targets can standardized tests measure well? Not measure well? *Cross-reference to Chapter 12:* General Principle 3.	30–45 min	APPLY LEARNING / CONSOLIDATE UNDERSTANDING
12-2	*Interpreting Standardized Test Score Reports	Practice interpreting and using scores on standardized tests. *Cross-reference to Chapter 12:* General Principle 2.	50-90 min; rest is home-work	APPLY LEARNING / CONSOLIDATE UNDERSTANDING
12-3	Panel Hears Exam Horrors— Case Discussion	Solve another real dilemma. *Cross-reference to Chapter 12:* General Principles 2 and 3.	15–30 min	CONSOLIDATE UNDERSTANDING

*Recommended

Activity 12-1 Visualizing Invisible Targets/Analyzing Standardized Tests

Recommended

Goals/Rationale

This activity provides practice in checking actual test questions against the test developer's vision of what is to be tested, and looking for what of importance might not be covered on the test.

> **Cross-Reference to *Student-Involved Classroom Assessment*, 3d ed.**
>
> General Principle 3: It's our responsibility to see that standardized tests are administered and used appropriately.
>
> **Additional Materials Needed**
>
> OTHER: A sample published standardized test booklet, test specifications for that test which describe what targets it covers (be sure to ask for "test or item specifications"), and your local content standards.
>
> **Time Required**
>
> 30–45 minutes.

What to Do

(30–45 minutes) Place the test, test specifications, and content standards side by side.

1. Compare the test and "test specifications" to your content standards. What does the test cover that is not included in your content standards?

2. What is included in your content standards that is not on the test? If there are holes, what are they and what is the role of classroom assessment in filling these gaps? If classroom assessment has a role to play in generating information for large-scale uses, what needs to be true of classroom assessments in order to make results reliable and valid?

3. How well do the test and the content standards match to what you teach?

4. What can you conclude about the alignment of test, content standards, and instruction?

5. What questions do you have? How will you find out the answers?

Interpreting Standardized Test Score Reports

Activity 12-2

Recommended

Goals/Rationale

Everyone needs to know how to interpret and use the scores found on standardized tests, if for no other reason than to help others avoid misinterpreting and misusing such scores. Part A covers test score meanings; Part B asks you to find information on your local test score report and discuss implications for instruction; Part C gives you a chance to practice describing test scores and results in student- and parent-friendly language.

> **Cross-Reference to *Student-Involved Classroom Assessment*, 3d ed.**
>
> General Principles 2: Types of test scores and how to interpret and use them.
>
> **Additional Materials Needed**
>
> TEXTBOOK: Figure 12.2, "The Derivation of Grade Equivalents," Figure 12.4, "Test Score Summary"; Table 12.2, "Understanding Percentile Scores," Table 12.3, "Understanding Stanines." OTHER: The score report for your local standardized test (if you have one; if not, use textbook Figure 12.3, "Sample Score Report.")
>
> **Time Required**
>
> 50-90 minutes; rest is homework.

What to Do

Part A: Understanding Standardized Test Scores

(10–20 minutes) Take the quiz on the worksheet, "Test Score Quiz." If working in a group, discuss your answers. Use textbook Table 12.2, "Understanding Percentile Scores," Table 12.3, "Understanding Stanines," Figure 12.2, "The Derivation of Grade Equivalents," and Figure 12.4, "Test Score Summary," as needed. (The correct answers appear on the worksheet, "Answers to Test Score Quiz," but don't peek.)

Part B: Find Information on Your Local Test Score Report

1. (5-10 minutes) Find each of the following on a sample standardized test score report. (If you don't have a local score report, use textbook Figure 12.3, "Sample Score Report.") Note: Not all test score reports will have each of these types of scores:

    a. Number correct

    b. Grade equivalents

    c. National stanines

    d. National percentiles

    e. Performance on individual content standards or objectives

    f. What does "——•——" under "National Percentile" mean?

2. (5–10 minutes) Think about or discuss the following: What do you understand from this report? What don't you understand? How will you find out?

3. (5-10 minutes) How big a difference between scores represents a difference you need to be concerned about? There are two parts to this. First, how much of the differences between scores might just be due to errors of measurement? Second, how big a difference is educationally and practically important?

4. (10-15 minutes) What are the possible implications for instruction of the results on this test? To answer this question, consider both the results and the specific questions used to assess each standard or objective.

    a. In what areas did students perform well? Why?

    b. In what areas did students perform less well? Why?

    c. What prerequisite skills do students need to have to be prepared for the types of questions on the test? To what extent are you integrating these into ongoing instruction?

Part C: Practice Explaining Test Scores to Students and Parents

1. (5-10 minutes) Pretend that you are explaining test scores to a parent. How would you explain the following:

    a. Raw scores, percent correct, percentiles, and grade equivalents

    b. When each score should be used

    c. The implications of test scores for instruction

2. (10–15 minutes) Plan explaining standardized test scores to students.

    a. Plan how you might explain test scores to students and how you'll check they understand.

    b. You might have older students practice explaining test scores to their parents. (What knowledge and skills would students be practicing by doing this?)

Part D: Try with Students

Try your plan with students and be ready to discuss what happened.

Test Score Quiz

From "Hill's Handy Hints," a compilation of articles by John R. Hills that appeared in *Educational Measurement: Issues and Practice*, September 1983 (Volume 2, No. 1) to Fall 1984 (Volume 3, No. 3).

Instructions. Mark *True* or *False* for each question. Explain your reasoning.

T   F   1. Tim is a sixth grader. He obtained a grade-equivalent score of 9.2 in reading. This means that Tim scored well above average sixth graders in reading.

T   F   2. Tim's grade equivalent score of 9.2 in reading means that Tim could well be put in a class of ninth graders for material in which reading skills were important.

T   F   3. Tim obtained a grade equivalent score of 7.3 in arithmetic on the same test battery from which his reading grade equivalent score was 9.2. This means that in reading Tim is nearly two years ahead of his performance in arithmetic.

T   F   4. The Jones school mean (average) grade equivalent score in reading in first grade was .6. The mean increased each year until by the sixth grade it was up to 3.2. Because the Jones students are falling farther behind the national average each year, the reading program is inadequate to meet the learning needs of the Jones school students.

T   F   5. Juanita is a sixth grader. She got a percentile score of 70 in reading on a published standardized test. This means that Juanita got 70 percent of the items correct.

T   F   6. The principal at Hartford Elementary set a goal of getting every pupil up to the 50th percentile within four years. This is a reasonable goal for most modern schools.

T   F   7. Susie, a third-grade student, scored at the 30th percentile in arithmetic at the end of the school year. Scores this low are regarded as failing, and therefore Susie should be retained for another year in arithmetic instruction so that she will not be handicapped in the future.

T   F   8. Mary is a sixth grader who received a stanine score of zero on her standardized test in math. This means that Mary's score is very low compared to other sixth graders.

T   F   9. Each stanine range contains ten percent of students.

T   F   10. Mr. Rivera noticed that most of his students received the same stanine score each year. This means that they are not making much progress in school.

T   F   11. Patricia went down from the fifth stanine last year to the fourth stanine this year. Her teacher should be concerned about this.

T   F   12. Mr. Rivera wondered about his student, Elena, whose stanine score in reading comprehension went up from the fourth stanine to the sixth stanine. That big a difference is important.

Answers to Test Score Quiz

1. *True.* A grade equivalent score is the average performance of students on the test at each of several grade levels. A sixth grader who has gotten a grade equivalent of 9.2 has performed like a ninth-grade student on the sixth-grade test. Therefore, he has performed above average for students in his grade.

2. *False.* A grade equivalent of 9.2 means that Tim does as well as ninth graders on sixth-grade work. It does not necessarily mean that he can do ninth-grade work.

3. *False.* Tim's score of 9.2 on reading and 7.3 on arithmetic could be equal scores if one used another score scale such as percentiles. The difference between the two grade equivalent scores may be due to the fact that students tend to differ less within a grade on arithmetic than on reading. In addition, grade equivalent scores above a student's grade do not necessarily mean that he or she has really mastered skills beyond his or her own grade level.

4. *False.* The range of achievement in a classroom gets larger as grade level increases. Thus, the spread of achievement in first grade might only be one-half year while in grade six it might be three or four years. A below-average class can stay at exactly the same average percentile (which means that they are maintaining their relative position over time) and still appear to be falling behind in terms of grade equivalents. Similarly, an above-average class can stay at the same percentile and still appear to be getting farther ahead in terms of grade equivalents.

5. *False.* Percentile scores indicate the relative standing in a group, not the percent of items that are correct.

6. *False.* The 50th percentile is defined as being the average score. In order to be the average, some scores must be below it and some above. It is unrealistic to try to get everyone up to the average. If everyone does improve, or if only the bottom half improves, the 50th percentile also increases. While the change in the 50th percentile will not appear on the form of the test now being used, the next time the test is normed, the 50th percentile will move up.

7. *False.* Scores at the 30th percentile are really not far below average. The 30th percentile means that the student has scored better than 30% of similar students taking the test. Usually no more than a few percent of a class are failed, say 3 or 4 percent, not anywhere near 30 percent. Besides, a nationally standardized test may not accurately sample the arithmetic skills covered in Susie's class.

8. *False.* There is no such thing as a stanine score of zero. There has been a scoring error.

9. *False.* The first and ninth stanine of each have about 4 percent of student scores; the second and eighth about 8 percent; the third and seventh about 12 percent; the fourth and sixth about 16 percent; the fifth about 20 percent. Envision a bell-shaped curve.

10. *False.* Students who receive the same stanine each year are maintaining their relative position in the group; they are learning just the amount that would be expected of someone with this standing. If, however, the stanine jumps substantially, then they are learning more than would be expected of someone with their beginning level of performance.

11. *This depends.* Sometimes the change from one stanine to another can result from getting a single extra question right or wrong. In that case there's probably nothing to be worried about! However, if the student goes from high in the range of stanine five to low in the range of stanine four, there might be something to worry about.

12. *True.* When scores differ by two stanines, we tend to think of there being a real difference, not an error of measurement. A difference that large is unlikely to be an accident so it deserves further investigation. Perhaps Elena has benefited from some effective teaching, or she may have become more motivated, or she may have found more time to read, or something in her life that was impeding her progress may have been removed.

Activity 12-3   Panel Hears Exam Horrors—Case Discussion

Optional

Goals/Rationale

"The Board of education will hold further hearings today on the high school graduation test. . . ." This is enough to strike fear into anyone's heart. This activity gives you the opportunity to analyze what went wrong in a real situation and decide what might have been done to avoid the problem.

> **Cross-Reference to *Student-Involved Classroom Assessment*, 3d ed.**
>
> General Principles 2 and 3: The meaning of test scores and how to use them well.
>
> **Additional Materials Needed**
>
> WORKBOOK: Figure Intro IV-1, "Conditions for Effective Communication." TEXTBOOK: Chapter 12.
>
> **Time Required**
>
> 15–30 minutes.

What to Do

1. (5–10 minutes) Read the case, "Panel Hears Exam Horrors."

2. (10–20 minutes) Think about or discuss the following questions:

    a. Which of the three responsibilities of educators with regard to standardized tests went wrong? (See the relevant textbook pages, 400–405.)[1]

    b. What other keys to sound assessment were violated?[2]

    c. What other conditions for sound communication were violated (Figure Intro IV-1, "Conditions for Effective Communication")?

[1]Responsibility 1—Fulfilling course requirements vs. being competent; math taken in grades 9 and 10 but not tested until grade 12; accuracy, only 4 points away; accuracy, clear targets; accuracy, what do "higher standards" mean (trickier, harder, or application of knowledge)?; student self-confidence. Responsibility 2—Were students given adequate notice?

[2]Appropriate uses; targets not clear; bias and distortion—is the test or are grades a better measure of competence?

d. What should school officials (and teachers) do to avoid such problems?[3]

Panel Hears Exam Horrors—Case

By Lisa Kim Bach (*Las Vegas Review Journal*, April 16, 1999)

With just seven weeks to go until graduation, a _____ high school senior with a 3.5 grade-point average is ready to drop out. Joan _____'s daughter can't pass the math portion of the state's High School Proficiency Examination, and she's not alone. About 14 percent of the state's high school seniors are in the same predicament.

"My daughter's crying hysterically over this and she's ready to quit," [Joan] told State Board of Education members Thursday. "She can walk down the aisle, but she'll be walking on a false basis. She's not getting a diploma. . ."

[Joan] came specifically to tell the board that her daughter fulfilled all the recommended course work at her high school. Her math courses included basic math and pre-algebra. As a freshman and sophomore, that met state requirements. Now, as a senior, [Joan]'s daughter is four points short of passing the math test. She's never had geometry, she's never had algebra, and at this point in the game, [Joan] thinks it's heartless to change the rules.

She didn't get much disagreement from the Board of Education. "I'm extremely sympathetic to what you're saying," said Bill _____, a board member and career math educator. "But the state Legislature has mandated that we put this into effect."

[Bill] and other board members believe the testing was implemented too soon. He supports higher standards, but thinks the test should have been phased in after more stringent high school requirements had a chance to kick in.

And if students think this year was rough going, [Bill] has words of warning: "Wait until next year." The state's new standards, which take effect next year, include trigonometry—that could potentially make the exam more difficult. That will be coupled with students having to earn higher scores to pass. . . ."

The set of circumstances prompted [Bill] to ask the board to consider several recommendations:

*   Allow the use of calculators on the test for special education students with individual education plans that permit them to use calculators in math classes.

---

[3]Clarify what is meant by "higher standards." Make a clearer link between classroom assessments resulting in grades and the competency test. Do they measure the same thing? How high a grade must be obtained to be reasonably sure a student will "pass" the competency test? Make sure students and parents have adequate notice. Establish a procedure to resolve discrepancies between multiple measures of the same skills and knowledge.

- Add one more test opportunity before the end of the school year for seniors who haven't passed. State law allows students five opportunities to take the test, but the fifth test this year won't be offered until June.

- Lift the cap on the number of times a student can take the test. . . .

Tom _____, state test director, briefed the board Thursday on the scores from the February round of graduation exams. Of 3,320 students tested in math, 2,366 failed. Of the 1,839 tested in reading, 1,095 failed. "The question is, is that too many kids?" [Tom] said.

Board member, Gary _____ said that while the numbers are sobering, they're also a sign to teens to take the test seriously. Before the graduation test was revised, fewer than one percent of students failed the exam. "We have students who are graduating with a higher proficiency and this is one of the costs," [Gary] said. "Maybe for the first time, students are taking this more seriously than they have in the past."

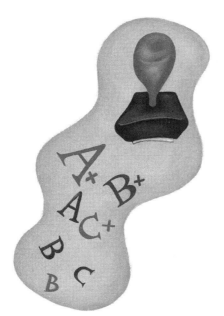

Report Cards

Big Ideas in This Chapter

This chapter answers the following guiding question:

How can I communicate about student achievement using report cards in a manner that helps my students succeed?

The **General Principles** addressed in this chapter are as follows:

1. Historically, we have assigned report card grades based both on evidence of achievement and on teacher judgment about student ability, effort, compliance, and attitude. This practice has done far more harm than good in building effective lines of communication.

2. There is a single best way to develop report card grades. In fact, in a standards-driven educational environment, there is only one acceptable way.

3. As professional educators, it is our ethical and pedagogical responsibility to understand and apply only acceptable grading practices.

4. Grades represent just one of several ways to communicate using report cards. In some situations, others work better.

An entire chapter is given to report cards and grades, not because they represent the best of our communication options, but because they have been, still are, and for the immediate future will continue to be, the most frequently used communication option. Therefore, it is in our students' best interests that we strive to communicate as effectively as we can when using report card grades.

Grading is complex, for several reasons. First, we have much to communicate. Second, we assess many things in many ways. Third, the list of valued achievement targets continues to grow and each target continues to become more complex. As these changes unfold, it becomes increasingly important that we understand how to define, assess, and communicate effectively about student achievement. If grades are to be our medium, we must master sound grading practices.

Links to Previous Chapters

Good grading depends on quality assessment as defined in Chapters 3–8. Also, grading and report cards can be evaluated using the standards for effective communication in Figure Intro IV-1, "Conditions for Effective Communication."

Links to Subsequent Chapters

This is the second of four chapters on communicating student achievement.

Portfolio Reminder

Once again, we remind you that it is important to keep potential portfolio material handy. See previous chapters for suggestions.

Roadmap

Activity	Title	Activity Description	Time	Icons
13-1	*Report Card Grading*—Video Discussion	The video parallels Chapter 13 and provides structured activities to consolidate understanding. *Cross-reference to Chapter 13:* General Principles 1, 2, 3, and 4.	60–120 min	CONSOLIDATE UNDERSTANDING
13-2	What's in a "B"?—Case Discussion	What should be included in a grade? *Cross-reference to Chapter 13:* General Principles 2 and 3.	15-25 min	CONSOLIDATE UNDERSTANDING
13-3	When Grades Don't Match the State Assessment Results—Case Discussion	What communication problems led to the case? *Cross-reference to Chapter 13:* General Principles 2 and 3.	10-20 min	CONSOLIDATE UNDERSTANDING
13-4	*Chris Brown's Science Class—Case Discussion	Look at an anonymous grade book to see if you agree with the grades the teacher gave. *Cross-reference to Chapter 13:* General Principles 2 and 3.	15-30 min	CONSOLIDATE UNDERSTANDING
13-5	Converting Rubric Scores to Grades—Case Discussion	What are the options? *Cross-reference to Chapter 13:* General Principles 2 and 3.	30–50 min	CONSOLIDATE UNDERSTANDING
13-6	Report Card Stew—Case Discussion	What are various options for report card formats and how do they satisfy standards for sound reporting? *Cross-reference to Chapter 13:* General Principle 4.	25–40 min	CONSOLIDATE UNDERSTANDING
13-7	Make Your Own Report Card Grading Plan (and/or Unit-Building Activity, Assignment 11)	Develop a grading system for your ongoing unit project, a course you are taking, or another course. *Cross-reference to Chapter 13:* General Principles 1, 2, 3, and 4.	Open, it's home-work	APPLY LEARNING

*Recommended

Activity 13-1   *Report Card Grading*—Video Discussion

Optional

Goals/Rationale

The video, *Report Card Grading: Strategies and Solutions*, takes you step by step through the ideas presented in Chapter 13. The video comes complete with a facilitator's guide that helps you work through key ideas.

> **Cross-Reference to *Student-Involved Classroom Assessment*, 3d ed.**
>
> General Principles 1, 2, 3, and 4: Developing and using report card grades appropriately; other ways to communicate about student achievement besides grades.
>
> **Additional Materials Needed**
>
> VIDEO: *Report Card Grading: Strategies and Solutions*, available from the Assessment Training Institute, 800-480-3060.
>
> **Time Required**
>
> 60 minutes to view the video without doing the embedded activities. At least two hours if all the activities in the video are completed.

What to Do

Acquire the video and follow the steps clearly laid out in the facilitator's guide.

What's in a "B"?—Case Discussion

Activity 13-2

Optional

Goals/Rationale

We have a long history in schools of reflecting a wide range of factors in report card grades—achievement, aptitude, effort, and attitudes. This activity provides an opportunity for discussion of what factors should be considered when grading.

> **Cross-Reference to *Student-Involved Classroom Assessment*, 3d ed.**
>
> General Principles 2 and 3: Developing and using report card grades appropriately.
>
> **Additional Materials Needed**
>
> WORKBOOK: Figure Intro IV-1, "Conditions for Effective Communication."
>
> **Time Required**
>
> 15–25 minutes.

What to Do

1. (5 minutes) Read the case, "What's in a 'B'?"

2. (5–10 minutes) Put yourself into the group in the case. Does the list on the left reflect what you think grades should tell us about students? Now look at the list on the right. Would the factors actually included in grades result in providing the information we need for the decisions on the left? What would need to be done differently? What factors *must* be included? What factors distort the communication? What things on either list are troubling to you? Why?

3. (5–10 minutes) Think about or discuss why the situation might be occurring—consider the extent to which conditions for sound communication (Figure Intro IV-1, "Conditions for Effective Communication") are violated. Are other standards of quality assessment being violated?

What's in a "B"?—Case

A group of teachers, other educators, and parents were attending a grading workshop at a regional conference. A parent asked if the educators in the room could tell her what's in a B and how it's different from an A or C. Participants were asked to record their answers to two questions:

1. What should a grade tell us about students?

2. What are the factors that are actually used to determine student grades in your setting?

The answers were compiled into two charts, reproduced here:

What should grades tell us about students?	What factors are actually included in grades?
• What things they know and can do • Whether they have improved during the marking period • What their strengths are and the things they need to work on • Whether they can solve real-world problems • What level their work is • Whether they are ready to move on • How they help one another • Whether they've reached a standard • How well they can apply what they know	• Attendance and lateness • Behavior/attitude • End of marking period test scores • Homework • Family status • Ability • Appearance • Personality • Teacher attitude toward the student

When Grades Don't Match the State Assessment Results—Case Discussion

Activity 13-3

Optional

Goals/Rationale

This activity asks a question about a phenomenon that is occurring with increasing frequency across the country: What happens when students consistently get high grades but fail to meet competency on a state test?

> **Cross-Reference to *Student-Involved Classroom Assessment*, 3d ed.**
>
> General Principles 2 and 3: Developing and using report card grades appropriately.
>
> **Additional Materials Needed**
>
> WORKBOOK: Figure Intro IV-1, "Conditions for Effective Communication."
>
> **Time Required**
>
> 10-20 minutes.

What to Do

(10-20 minutes) Read the case paragraph "When Grades Don't Match the State Assessment Results" and think about or discuss these questions:

1. Why might the situation be occurring—consider the extent to which conditions for sound communication (Figure Intro IV-1) are violated. Are other standards of quality assessment being violated?[1]

2. What would you do to repair this situation?[2]

---

[1] (a) The state assessment only includes achievement, while grades might include factors other than achievement. (b) Class work might not be aligned with priorities in the state assessment, so classroom assessments might measure different things than the state assessment. (c) The classroom assessments underpinning the grades aren't accurate. (d) It is unclear how the state performance standard cutoff relates to teachers' grading cutoffs.

[2] (a) Clarify state assessment and classroom learning targets. Do they match? If not, should they? Is instruction aligned? (b) Check classroom assessments for accuracy. Do they meet the five standards for quality? (c) Calibrate classroom assessments to the state assessment so that teachers and students know the level needed to perform on classroom assessments to meet state standards.

When Grades Don't Match the State Assessment Results—Case

"It seems important to let you know of a phenomenon I'm experiencing in my school as we deal with the data about students who do and do not meet standards on the state assessment and the relationship of these standards to the grades they earn. While it remains true that most of the kids who are meeting standards are those who also get As, we are discovering a significant number of students who do get As who don't meet the standards, and a similar number who get rather poor grades who do meet the standards. What should we do?"

Activity 13-4

Chris Brown's Science Class—Case Discussion

Recommended

Goals/Rationale

This activity involves looking at an anonymous gradebook to explore the complexity of assigning grades. All sorts of considerations about the vagaries of the grading process are made obvious.

> **Cross-Reference to *Student-Involved Classroom Assessment*, 3d ed.**
>
> General Principles 2 and 3: Developing and using report card grades appropriately.
>
> **Additional Materials Needed**
>
> WORKBOOK: Figure Intro IV-1, "Conditions for Effective Communication."
>
> **Time Required**
>
> 15–30 minutes.

What to Do

1. (5–10 minutes) Read the attached case, "Chris Brown's Science Class."

2. (10–20 minutes) Think about or discuss the following questions:

   a. Do the grades awarded fairly reflect the results from which they were derived? Why or why not?[1]

   b. What grading issues arise from this case study? (Consider conditions for effective communication in Figure Intro IV-1.[2] What other issues do you identify?[3])

   c. What should teachers do to avoid such problems?

Chris Brown's Science Class*—Case

This study considers the mark and grades of a teacher using a very traditional approach to grading. The marks and grades in the chart are for Chris Brown's science class in Ontario. If you are not a science teacher, put the appropriate labels for your subject in place of the lab reports, care of equipment, and so forth along the top of the table. Note carefully the information that is shown below the gradebook extract regarding the miscellaneous items, the way absence is dealt with, and the grading scale. Enter to the right of the chart the letter grade each student would get using the grading scale in use in your district/school.

Name	Lab Reports										Total Labs	Test/Exams			Total Tests	Miscellaneous*					Total Misc.	Final Total	Final Grade	
																1	2	3	4	5				
Out of	*10*	*10*	*10*	*10*	*10*	*10*	*10*	*10*	*10*	*10*	*100*	*50*	*50*	*100*	*200*	*20*	*20*	*20*	*20*	*20*	*100*	*400*	*%*	*Letter*
Robin	6	6	6	6	5	6	6	7	6	6	60	33	39	81	153	15	15	12	0	10	52	265	66	C
Kay	2	3	5	5	6	6	7	8	9	10	61	11	29	86	126	15	13	18	10	10	66	253	63	C
Marg	10	10	A	10	10	10	A	10	A	A	60	50	A	100	150	0	0	0	0	15	15	225	56	D
Jim	9	8	9	8	9	10	9	10	8	9	89	24	24	49	97	20	17	17	20	20	94	280	70	B
Peter	10	10	9	9	8	8	7	7	6	5	79	45	36	32	113	20	10	15	10	5	60	252	63	C
Lorna	10	10	10	10	10	10	10	10	10	10	100	32	29	59	120	20	20	20	20	20	100	320	80	A
John	8	8	8	7	9	9	8	9	10	8	84	32	30	57	119	20	8	7	0	5	40	243	61	C

A=Absent=0 (for Lab Reports and Tests/Exams)

*Miscellaneous: 1-Attendance; 2-Care of Equipment; 3-Attitude/Participation; 4-Notebook; 5-Reading Reports (4x5 marks)

Letter Grade Legend (in Ontario): A=80%-100%; B=70%-79%; C=60%-69%; D=50%-59%; F=0%-49%

[1]"Marg got the D, but on her achievement alone she probably earned the A. Lorna got the A, but had only a 60% average on tests and exams; is she a weak student who is compliant, or is she a very capable student who suffers from severe test anxiety? Kay and Peter both get the same grade, but Kay is getting high 80s at the end, whereas Peter is receiving failing marks; is this fair?

[2]Is it clear what achievement targets the grades are intended to represent? What is the quality of the assessments on which the entries in the gradebook are based? Were the scores combined logically to produce the final grades? What should count in the grades—achievement only or other things as well?

[3]Why did the teacher average zeros?

*From *The Mindful School: How to Grade for Learning* by Ken O'Connor. ©1999 SkyLight Training and Publishing Inc. Reprinted by permission of SkyLight Professional Development.

Activity 13-5   Converting Rubric Scores to Grades—Case Discussion

Optional

Goals/Rationale

This activity provides practice in converting ratings on rubrics to grade scales in ways that make sense.

> **Cross-Reference to *Student-Involved Classroom Assessment*, 3d ed.**
>
> General Principles 2 and 3: Developing and using report card grades appropriately.
>
> **Additional Materials Needed**
>
> TEXTBOOK: Figure 13.3, "Sample Decision Rules for Converting Rating Profiles to Grades"; Table 13.1, "Emily's Writing Assessment Record."
>
> **Time Required**
>
> 30–50 minutes.

What to Do

1. (15–30 minutes) Calculate Emily's grade using the data in textbook Table 13.1, "Emily's Writing Assessment Record," for each of the following methods.

   a. *Method 1: Overall Percentage of Points Possible.* Add up the total points Emily received from all assignments and divide it by the total points possible from all assignments. What grade would Emily get?[1]

   What if Emily failed to turn in paper 7 and got zeros for Voice and Sentence Fluency? Now what grade would Emily get?[2] Should missing one paper make this much difference?

   b. *Method 2: Average Percentages of Points Possible on Each Assignment.* Calculate the percentage of points Emily earned on each assignment. (Total earned on each assignment divided by the total possible for each assignment.) Average these percentages. What grade would Emily get?[3]

---

[1] 167/200 = 84%

[2] 157/200 = 78%

[3] 1157/13 papers = 89%

Say paper 1 got a "5" on Sentence Fluency instead of a "4". Now what grade would Emily get?[4] How can so small a change make such a big difference?

c. *Method 3: Weight Ideas and Organization Twice as Heavily as the Rest.* Divide the total number of points earned by the total number of points possible. What grade would Emily earn?[5]

d. *Method 4, Logic 1:* Use textbook Figure 13.3, "Sample Decision Rules for Converting Rating Profiles to Grades" to assign Emily a grade.

e. *Method 4, Logic 2:* Use the following rules for converting scores directly to percentages. (These conversions were based on how the wording in the rubric seemed best to describe A, B, etc.) Divide the number of points earned by the number of points possible. What grade would Emily get?[6]

5 = 100%; 4 = 90%; 3 = 80%; 2 = 70%; 1 = 60%

f. *Method 5: Later Papers Count More.* Because the goal might be to report current ability to write (not to average current ability with beginning ability), it might be logical only to count papers 9–13 in the grade. Using each of the methods above, the following percentages would result:

Method 1 = 86/105 = 82% Grade = _____

Method 2 = 437/500 = 87% Grade = _____

Method 3 = 109/135 = 81% Grade = _____

Method 4 = 21 scores given; 19 4's and 5's = 90% 4's and 5's. Grade = _____

Method 5 = 1910/2100 = 91%. Grade = _____

2. (15–20 minutes) Think about or discuss the following questions:

a. In many districts, the purpose for using the rubric scoring scheme is motivating students, providing feedback (accurate communication of achievement in relationship to standards), encouraging students to self-assess, and using assessment to improve achievement. Although the primary purpose for grading should be accurate communication of student learning, might there be hidden purposes for grading that might conflict with the instructional purposes for the rubric?

---

[4] 1177/13 papers = 91%

[5] 207/250 = 83%

[6] 3550/4000 = 89%

b. What are the advantages and disadvantages of each method for converting rubric scores to grades if the purpose for grading is to accurately report student achievement status and support the other classroom uses of the rubric?

c. The bottom line: Which method best represents Emily's current writing achievement? Why?[7]

Activity 13-6

Report Card Stew—Case Discussion

Optional

Goals/Rationale

Many educators are considering how to revise traditional report cards. In this activity, you are asked to consider how various formats satisfy conditions for sound communication about student achievement.

> **Cross-Reference to *Student-Involved Classroom Assessment*, 3d ed.**
>
> General Principle 4: Other ways to communicate about student achievement besides grades.
>
> **Additional Materials Needed**
>
> WORKBOOK: Figure Intro IV-1, "Conditions for Effective Communication." TEXTBOOK: Figure 13.4, "Reporting Specific Competencies Attained," Figure 13.5, "Juneau Primary Reading Continuum," Figure 13.6, "Sample Narrative Report," Figure 13.7, "Sample Narrative Report in the Form of a Letter to a Sixth Grader," Figure 13.8, "The Spoken Language Bands," Figure 13.9, "English Profile—Spoken Language."
>
> **Time Required**
>
> 25-40 minutes.

[7]Note: We recommend against methods 1–3, although they might seem easiest. The primary reason is that a "1" would convert to 20%. Usually an "F" is defined as 60%. If "1" is seen as "failing," averaging a 20% in with other percentages unfairly weights failing grades. It would take a lot of 4s and 5s to bring an average containing even a single "1" up to 60%. We recommend the use of one of the logic rules as the best representation of Emily's ability to write.

What to Do

1. (5–10 minutes) Read the case, "Report Card Stew." Referring to Figure Intro IV-1, "Conditions for Effective Communication," what might be going wrong with several of these report card formats? What conditions of sound communication might be being violated?[1]

2. (20–30 minutes) Analyze the report card formats presented in the textbook (Figures 13.4 to 13.9) using *Workbook* Figure Intro IV-1 and the following questions:

    a. How are the formats alike and different?

    b. What does each convey about the student's knowledge, skills, and understanding? Which help you to understand the learning targets being reported on?

    c. Who is the target audience? Would the target audience understand the message sent in each format?

    d. Which format(s) would best encourage learning, involve students, and support student success?

    e. Which format(s) would best avoid undesirable side effects?

    f. What needs to be in place to make these reporting formats work productively? Where might each of these formats run into trouble?

4. *Optional.* What patterns of reasoning did you use during the course of this activity?[2]

Report Card Stew—Case

By Linda Cagnetti (*Cincinnati Enquirer*, November 30, 1997)

If men are from Mars and women are from Venus, the men and women who create report cards must be from a more distant galaxy. As some of the report cards reviewed in our Forum section today demonstrate, schools and parents are sometimes not on the same planet at grading time.

---

[1]Message receivers are not understanding the message. Symbols don't have common meaning to message senders and receivers. Message receivers were not involved in the design of the reporting format. There was no check that the message was being received as intended.

[2]Analyzing various formats for important features. Comparing these features to conditions for sound communication. Synthesizing information from the formats with information from Figure Intro IV-1. Evaluating the strengths and weaknesses of various formats.

First of all, they're no longer called report cards; they're "progress reports." Students don't pass or fail they are now "recommended for promotion" or "assigned to the same level." Ds and Fs are replaced with "areas of concern" or "needs more time to develop." Behavior is now "social habits."

Most of these kinder-gentler report cards are computer generated, with check-marked "comments" such as "pleasure to have in class," or "uses self control." None look alike; each district and sometimes each school, designs its own.

Reactions from parents vary. Some say they're much better than the old-fashioned, too-simple ABC versions. Others find them ridiculous. Most parents are simply bewildered.

"I don't have a clue what half of this means," one parent told us. "I'm not sure how my child is doing, but, hey, they say this is progress."

Kentucky Enquirer columnist Karen Samples recently wrote about the…reformed report cards from a dozen or so districts in (local) counties, along with (national) ones. It's quite a smorgasbord. Some cards are easy to understand with both letter and number grades; others are overwhelming and mystifying.

Schools are working hard to communicate more to parents about new standards. Good idea. But more doesn't automatically translate to better. For example, the common sense alarm buzzes when you read that an elementary student is graded on 72 different skills, and the explanations are so fuzzy that a college-educated parent is befuddled.

Smoke-and-mirror report cards are another example of the gap between what education reformers believe is important and what ordinary people want. No wonder Joe and Jane public don't feel public schools belong to them anymore.

Student report cards are the most basic and precious link between schools and parents. When they're reduced to meaningless symbols and babble, educators deserve an old-fashioned, unequivocal F for failure.

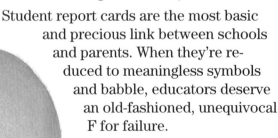

Make Your Own Report Card Grading Plan (and/or Unit-Building Activity, Assignment 11)

Activity 13-7

Optional

Goals/Rationale

This is the eleventh in a series of direct applications to day-to-day life in the classroom. This unit-building activity centers on the role of report card grading in the unit you are assembling.

This activity provides practice in developing report card grading plans. The text spells out a five-step process for developing such a plan and then illustrates it with two examples. In this activity, your task is to create your own illustration. You can create your own grading system for the unit you are developing as an ongoing *Workbook* activity, for the classroom assessment course you are taking, or for another class you are teaching or taking.

In many ways, this activity represents a summary of most of the material covered in the book up to this point. To design a sound grading procedure, you must clarify your achievement expectations, align them with proper assessment methods, build good records, summarize assessment results, and prepare to communicate about achievement.

Cross-Reference to *Student-Involved Classroom Assessment*, 3d ed.

General Principles 1, 2, 3, and 4: Developing and using report card grades appropriately; other ways to communicate about student achievement besides grades.

Additional Materials Needed

WORKBOOK: Figure Intro IV-1, "Conditions for Effective Communication."

Time Required

Open, it's homework.

What to Do

Using the outline given here and the illustrations provided in textbook Chapter 13, reason through a plan for assigning report card grades for the unit you are developing as an ongoing *Workbook* activity, for the classroom assessment course you are taking, or for another class you are teaching or taking.

1. Frame your specific achievement expectations:

    a. What knowledge should students understand? (A brief description will suffice for this practice; but in real life, the more detail you can muster, the easier it will be to implement your plan and help your students succeed.)

    b. What patterns of reasoning will be relevant for students to master during this period of instruction?

    c. Will you expect students to master any performance skills?

    d. What product development capabilities will you expect?

2. What sequence of assessments will you use to gather evidence of student success in hitting the above targets? Make a written plan that specifies what assessments will be used when—make a schedule of assessment events for knowledge, reasoning, performance skill, and/or product targets.

3. Write a brief description of each assessment. For each, specify the following:

    a. How it will sample achievement?

    b. What kinds of exercises will you use?

    c. What sources of bias do you plan to guard against and how will you do it?

    d. What specific records do you plan to maintain and how will you maintain them?

4. How will you summarize your achievement records into a composite index of student achievement at the end of the grading period? Include how you plan to deal with the following:

    a. Making sure each student's record reflects the most current information on achievement.

    b. Grading on achievement status versus improvement over time.

    c. Borderline cases.

    d. Achievement demonstrated in collaborative contexts.

5. How will you transform each student's composite achievement index into a grade for the report card?

    a. Based on fixed standards? If so, what standards?

    b. Based on the student's place in the rank order of achievement of all students?

Portfolios: Capturing the Details

Big Ideas in This Chapter

> This chapter answers the following guiding question:
>
> *How can my students and I communicate effectively about their achievement using portfolios—that is, through examining work samples and from their own self-reflections about the quality of that work?*

The **General Principles** addressed in this chapter are as follows:

1. The real power of a portfolio communication system resides in its potential for student involvement in record keeping and communication.

2. Portfolios come in many forms—all of which can serve us well if we carefully select from among the options.

3. The challenge of portfolios resides in the need to weave them into day-to-day classroom practice in practical ways. But, careful planning can remove any roadblocks.

With this chapter, we begin to make the point that grades and report cards are by no means our only communication options. In fact, we have other alternatives that sometimes can serve far more effectively than grades. One, portfolios, is a superior method whenever the information sender and receiver need to share greater detail about student achievement.

This chapter emphasizes that when using portfolios, intended use and connection to the teaching and learning process are *everything*.

Links to Previous Chapters

Portfolios must adhere to the same standards of high quality assessment as all other assessments (defined in textbook Chapters 3–8). Also, portfolios can be evaluated using the standards for effective communication in Figure Intro IV-1, "Conditions for Effective Communication."

Links to Subsequent Chapters

This is the third of four chapters in the textbook on communicating student achievement. Portfolios are used extensively in the conferences discussed in textbook Chapter 15.

Portfolio Reminder

Once again, we remind you that it is important to keep potential portfolio material handy. See previous chapters for suggestions.

Roadmap

Activity	Title	Activity Description	Time	Icons
14-1	Is This a Portfolio?	Activate prior knowledge about portfolios. *Cross-reference to Chapter 14:* General Principles 1, 2, and 3.	20–45 min	QUICK CHECK
14-2	*Job Interview Simulation	When it comes to portfolios, purpose is everything. *Cross-reference to Chapter 14:* General Principle 2.	30–45 min	CONSOLIDATE UNDERSTANDING
14-3	How Good Is My Work?—Case Discussion	A case discussion of student self-reflection. *Cross-reference to Chapter 14:* General Principle 1.	10–20 min; rest is home-work	APPLY LEARNING / CONSOLIDATE UNDERSTANDING
14-4	Analyzing Your Own Growth Portfolio (And/or Unit Building Activity, Assign-ment 12)	How well did we do designing your growth portfolio? *Cross-reference to Chapter 14:* General Principles 1, 2, and 3.	25–40 min; rest is home-work	APPLY LEARNING / CONSOLIDATE UNDERSTANDING
14-5	Dealing with Practicalities	Solutions to barriers of portfolio use. *Cross-reference to Chapter 14:* General Principle 3.	20–35 min	CONSOLIDATE UNDERSTANDING

*Recommended

Activity 14-1　Is This a Portfolio?

Optional

Goals/Rationale

This activity kicks off the study of portfolios by having you think about what you already know and looking at examples.

> **Cross-Reference to *Student-Involved Classroom Assessment*, 3d ed.**
>
> General Principles 1, 2, and 3: Student involvement, types of portfolios, classroom management of portfolios.
>
> **Additional Materials Needed**
>
> WORKBOOK: Figure Intro IV-1, "Conditions for Effective Communication." OTHER: Sample portfolios, gathered locally. (A variety is good. Choose three or four that vary on grade level, subject area, or targets covered; purpose; amount of student involvement; and nature of the evidence represented.)
>
> **Time Required**
>
> 20–45 minutes.

What to Do

1. (5 minutes) Complete the worksheet quiz, "Is This a Portfolio?"

2. (5–10 minutes) Individually list and then, if working in a group, discuss what everyone already knows about portfolios, and what questions they have.

3. (10–30 minutes) Look at samples of portfolios gathered locally and think about how well each portfolio communicates about student achievement. If the portfolio communicates well, why? If the portfolio doesn't communicate well, what could be done to improve communication? Use the following questions and Figure Intro IV-1, "Conditions for Effective Communication" to guide this thinking.

   a. What is the grade level? Subject area?

   b. Is it clear what the purpose for the portfolio is—celebration, certifying competence, documenting a project, growth, and so on? If the purpose is clear, how was it made clear? If the purpose is not clear, how might the purpose be made clear?

c. Is it clear who the portfolio is to communicate to? Will it communicate adequately to that audience? If so, why? If not, what would need to change?

d. Is it clear what learning targets are being documented by the portfolio? If the targets are clear, how were they made clear? If the targets are not clear, how might they be made clear?

e. How much were students involved in assembling the portfolio? Can you tell? What are the clues?

f. Does the portfolio provide convincing evidence of achievement? Why or why not?

Is This a Portfolio?

Instructions: Which of the following are portfolios and which are not? Why or why not?

Figure 14-1

Cartoons of kids and their stuff

Activity 14-2   Job Interview Simulation

Recommended

Goals/Rationale

When it comes to portfolios, purpose is everything. This activity makes it clear that the purpose for a portfolio determines what goes in it, who puts it there, who develops performance criteria, who judges the content, and the role of student involvement. Finally, the activity has you relate common examples of portfolio systems to the four types of portfolios outlined in the textbook.

> **Cross-Reference to *Student-Involved Classroom Assessment*, 3d ed.**
> General Principle 2: Types of portfolios.
>
> **Additional Materials Needed**
> TEXTBOOK: Pages 474-476, "Sense of Purpose."
>
> **Time Required**
> 30-45 minutes.

What to Do

1. (10 minutes) Think about or discuss the "Job Interview Discussion Question" posed following this section.

2. (5–10 minutes) Think about or discuss the following questions:

    a. Did (or would) everyone put the same things in their portfolios? Why or why not?[1]

    b. Would you have put different things in your portfolio if the purpose were different? For example, instead of applying for a job, you were documenting the favorite things you did this year (celebration portfolio), a project (project portfolio), or what you had learned about assessment last year (growth portfolio)?[2]

    c. Would you have liked someone else to have designed your job application portfolio? Why or why not? If you were developing the portfolio for a different purpose—celebration, project or growth—would you like someone else to design your portfolio for you? Why or why not?[3]

---

[1]We don't necessarily all put the same things in our portfolios because each of us is different. This is obviously also true of students.

[2]Purpose affects our choices of what to put in portfolios.

[3]Usually we want direct control over our portfolios; after all, they represent who we are. Would students feel the same?

  d. In the job interview portfolio, who develops criteria for judging quality?[4] Who judges quality? If the purpose changed—celebration, project or growth—who would develop criteria?

  e. What would you do if you asked individuals on the interview committee for criteria and they couldn't give them to you? What would you do if each member of the committee told you different criteria?

  f. What would you do if you got your interview portfolio back from the committee with a single grade on it? What would you do if you got your portfolio back with only comments on what you didn't do well? What kind of evaluation would you like? What information would be useful?

  g. What are the implications of this discussion for (1) the importance of purpose; and (2) how to design and use portfolios with students?

3. (10–15 minutes) Based on this activity, complete the worksheet, "Types of Portfolios and Implications for Decisions," that summarizes the impact of purpose on how you will design and carry out your portfolio system. (Part of the table has been completed as an example. Textbook pages 474-476 provide assistance.)

4. (5–10 minutes) There are many, many examples of portfolios out there. The worksheet, "Portfolio Matching Quiz," helps you identify the purpose for each portfolio example. This in turn will assist in designing those portfolios.

Job Interview Discussion Question

You are an educator applying for a new job (in education). Instead of a regular application form, the selection committee has asked you to submit a portfolio that illustrates who you are as an educator right now.

What would you include in the portfolio? What would tell the story of who you are as an educator? What would you submit to the committee to apply for the job?

---

[4]The interview committee—an outside agency. Sometimes this will be the same in the classroom. For some purposes, folks outside the classroom will develop criteria for quality. For other purposes, students and teachers will develop criteria.

Types of Portfolios and Implications for Decisions

Implications of Purpose for Portfolio Design				
Portfolio purpose	What story will the portfolio tell?	What kinds of evidence must it contain?	Who develops performance criteria and judges quality?	Student involvement
Celebration	What did I like best this year? What do I feel best about?	Anything the student want at anytime. Student portfolios could look very different.	The student. There might not be any outside criteria.	Students make all choices. This validates student choices as being important. Students have to think about what they value and why.
Growth	Growth on particular learning targets. Targets need to be specified.			Student-involved record keeping.
Project	How did I go about this project? What were the steps?	Items that document the project— journals, drafts, reviews by others, photos, etc.		
Status			May have criteria developed by others, for example when documenting student competence.	
Other				

Portfolio Matching Quiz

Instructions: Match each portfolio example on the right to its major purpose on the left.* Add your own examples on the right. How does this matching help you design portfolios?

Portfolio Purpose	Example
a. Celebration b. Growth c. Project d. Status	____ 1. Student-led conferences ____ 2. Certify competency for high school graduation ____ 3. Job interview ____ 4. Personal favorites ____ 5. Science fair ____ 6. Tracking student progress toward standards in mathematics ____ 7. College entry ____ 8. Help students see themselves as readers. Students choose anything in their world that documents themselves as readers ____ 9. Alternative credit ____ 10. Identify gifted students using multiple intelligences ____ 11. ____ 12. ____ 13.

*1 (b, a), 2 (a), 3 (d), 4 (a), 5 (c), 6 (b), 7 (d), 8 (a), 9 (a), 10 (d)

Activity 14-3   How Good Is My Work?—Case Discussion

Optional

Goals/Rationale

This activity helps you to structure prompting questions that provoke student self-assessment. It also has you discuss ways to involve students in portfolios as a strategy to maximize achievement, and perhaps try out some of those ideas.

> **Cross-Reference to *Student-Involved Classroom Assessment*, 3d ed.**
>
> General Principle 1: Student involvement.
>
> **Additional Materials Needed**
> None.
>
> **Time Required**
> 10–20 minutes; rest is homework.

What to Do

Part A: Do by Yourself or with Colleagues

1. (5–10 minutes) Read the worksheet, "Questions that Spark Self-Assessment." Think about or discuss the following:

    a. How would you characterize the differences between the questions in the left and right columns of the table?

    b. What insights will you take away from these contrasting examples to apply to your own portfolio reflection prompts? Why?

2. (5–10 minutes) Read the case, "The Dilemma of Student Selection and Clear Communication," in which teachers are dismayed by the shallowness of young students' portfolio selections and reflections. Think about or discuss the following questions:

    a. What do you think contributed to the weaknesses of these portfolios?

    b. What advice would you give the teachers about preparing learners for self-assessment?

Part B: Try with Students

Pick one or more self-assessment questions to try with students from the worksheet, "Questions That Spark Self-Assessment." Self-assessment is useful even if students are not assembling portfolios. Think about the following questions and be ready to report back:

1. What did students say?

2. Was the self-assessment a good use of instructional time? Why or why not?

Questions That Spark Self-Assessment

Questions That Invite Vague Answers	Questions That Invite Insights
Analysis of Skills and Processes: • Why do you like the things in your portfolio? • What's the best item in it? • What's the worst item? • Why didn't you include more writing samples? • What will you do next?	**Analysis of Skills and Processes:** • What makes this your best piece? • What makes your best piece different from your least effective piece? • What can you do in math now that you couldn't do before? • How good is your answer? What would make it better? • If you could work further on this piece, what would you do? • How does this relate to what you've learned before? • Of the work we've done recently, what do you feel most confident about? What do you still not understand?
Analysis of Processes: • Why did you do it this way? • Did you like working in a group? • What didn't work?	**Analysis of Processes:** • What steps did you go through in completing this assignment? Did this process work and lead to successful completion or were there problems? What would you change next time? • What are the ways you find working with others useful? Not useful?
How Skills and Processes Have Changed Over Time: • What's different now? • How do you feel about your work now? • What progress have you made?	**How Skills and Processes Have Changed Over Time:** • How is your work at the end of the year different from your work at the beginning? • Has the way you've planned work changed over time? If so, how? • In which area have you noticed the most improvement? How do you know?
Affective and Other Areas: • What's fun to do in school? • Do you like math? • Are you a good learner?	**Affective and Other Areas:** • Do you think you keep going on tasks differently now than in the past? If so, why? • What subject do you like the most? Why? • What type of work do you enjoy doing the most? Least? Why? • What impact has this project had on your interests, attitudes, and views of this area?

The Dilemma of Student Selection and Clear Communication—Case

It's almost time for quarterly reporting. The teachers in this elementary school have enthusiastically embraced the notion of using portfolios as part of their assessment system. They've attended a portfolio workshop, and have spent time brainstorming and agreeing on portfolio purposes (showing growth over time, involving students in self-assessment, communicating more richly about student learning with parents, and having students involved in selecting and reflecting on their work). The PTA helped buy colorful folders for storing student products, and the staff developed sets of criteria for looking at certain kinds of work (problem solving, reading, and mathematics). But now that it's time to send the portfolios home, the results of the first round of student selection seem to be revealing some serious weaknesses:

"How can I send these portfolios home?" says one teacher, face to face with what she views as disaster. "Yesterday, I asked my students to make selections from their working folders. It seemed to go okay. Then I had them write brief reflections on why each piece was chosen. When I looked them over, I was horrified. They've chosen things that I never would have. Some of the most important work we've done all quarter isn't there. Parents will get a really poor picture of what we've been doing and what their children are learning. They're going to think we're not doing our jobs. And the reflections! The reasons are so trivial. 'I like it.' 'It got the best grade.' 'The colors are my favorites.' Where are their insights? They don't know what to say. I thought this portfolio idea was going to be the answer for us. Now I'm wondering if there's any way to salvage this mess."

"My students don't know how to make good selections," says another teacher. "I'm really not sure what to do now. Their thinking is very unsophisticated. I thought I had done a good job of helping them understand what a portfolio is all about, but it's obvious they don't have the same criteria in their heads that I have in mine. I value their involvement in the process, and want them to feel ownership, but these portfolios just don't do the job."

A second grade teacher adds her thoughts: "I really did a lot to help them select portfolio pieces. I even set up some that had to be included—especially their unit books. We put together booklets that students make covers for and include the things they've done related to the unit. So everyone's portfolio includes some of the same stuff. Then they get to choose some other pieces. They're still not very good at reflection, but I'm a little bit more secure about sending things home now. Still, there are things that are really important that I don't know how to deal with, like group projects and things they construct. I'm also starting to worry about whether we're going to need a whole new building to house the portfolios at the end of the year—never mind next year!"

In frustration and with worries about changes in their own thinking about portfolios, the group asks for a chunk of time on the next faculty meeting agenda. There are questions inside of questions that need to be examined: Should we all send home portfolios? Can we individually choose not to? Since we've spent so much time on portfolios, how will we come up with other information for parents if we don't use them? Formal reporting is just around the corner and something has to be decided.

Activity 14-4

Analyzing Your Own Growth Portfolio (and/or Unit-Building Activity, Assignment 12)

Optional

Goals/Rationale

In our portfolio design for you, we have attempted to model the effective design of a portfolio system. How well did we do? In this activity, you analyze our scheme for its effectiveness and consider how you might design a portfolio system for your students.

This is the last in our series of direct applications to day-to-day life in the classroom. This unit-building activity centers on the role of portfolio assessment in the unit you are assembling.

> **Cross-Reference to *Student-Involved Classroom Assessment*, 3d ed.**
>
> General Principles 1, 2, and 3: Student involvement, types of portfolios, classroom management of portfolios.
>
> **Additional Materials Needed**
>
> WORKBOOK: Figure Intro IV-1, "Conditions for Effective Communication."
>
> **Time Required**
>
> 25–40 minutes; rest is homework.

What to Do

Part A: Do by Yourself or with Colleagues

1. (10–20 minutes) Using Figure Intro IV-1, "Conditions for Effective Communication" analyze how we, the authors of this *Workbook* set up the assessment growth portfolio we are asking you to complete. Consider the following:

   a. Were we clear on the learning targets we asked you to communicate about? (Figure Intro IV-1, items 1a–b) What are they?

   b. Were we clear on the purpose(s) for your portfolio? (Figure Intro IV-1, item 3a) What are they? Were we clear on the implications of purpose for the types of entries, when to put them in, who puts them in, whether/how to take things out, who develops criteria for quality, and who judges the quality of entries in the portfolio?

   c. How have we asked you to ensure that the entries in your portfolio accurately reflect your learning? (Figure Intro IV-1, items 2a–e)

   d. What performance criteria did we ask you to use to track your growth in learning about assessment?

   e. How have we involved you in the assembly of your own portfolio? How have we tried to check for your understanding of the process?

   f. How have we asked you to use your portfolio to communicate about your growth? (Figure Intro IV-1, items 3a–d)

2. (10–15 minutes) What would you add to our instructions for a growth portfolio in assessment literacy that would make the process clearer, more manageable, and/or more beneficial for learners?

3. (5 minutes) What impact on your motivation to learn about assessment has derived from your portfolio development?

Part B: Try with Students

1. From your experience developing your own growth portfolio, would your students benefit by doing portfolios? Why or why not? (If you are working on the unit-building sequence, consider this question in the context of your unit.) If yes, answer the following questions:

   a. For what purpose?

   b. For what learning targets?

c. What performance criteria will you use, and who will develop them?

d. What types of things should go into the portfolios? When? Who should put them in? What cover sheet will you use for entries?

e. How will you ensure adequate sampling of the learning targets the portfolio will cover? How will you avoid potential sources of bias and distortion?

f. What types of self-assessment will you ask students to do? When?

2. Be ready to report on your plans.

Activity 14-5

Dealing with Practicalities

Optional

Goals/Rationale

In the last section of textbook Chapter 14, Rick discusses practicalities of portfolio use in the classroom. Practicalities relate to time, ownership, grading, etc. This activity asks you to consider solutions to these barriers.

> **Cross-Reference to *Student-Involved Classroom Assessment*, 3d ed.**
>
> General Principle 3: Classroom management of portfolios.
>
> **Additional Materials Needed**
> TEXTBOOK: pages 483-486.
>
> **Time Required**
> 20–35 minutes.

What to Do

1. (5 minutes) In the last section of textbook Chapter 14 (p. 483-486), Ms. Weatherby and Rick discussed a few practicalities of portfolio use in the classroom. Make a worksheet that lists these practicalities, using the following column headings (1) Practicality/Barrier; (2) Issues/Solutions in the Text; and (3) Other Solutions. Down the left side, under the heading "Practicality/Barrier" list: Time, Grading, Ownership, Storage, and Other.

2. (15–30 minutes) Next to each practicality/barrier in the worksheet, note issues and the solutions in the textbook. Then brainstorm other solutions.

Notes:

Communicating with Conferences

Big Ideas in This Chapter

This chapter answers the following guiding question:

How can my students and I communicate effectively about their achievement through the use of various conference formats?

The **General Principles** addressed in this chapter are as follows:

1. As with report cards and portfolios, certain conditions must be satisfied if we are to confer effectively about student achievement.

2. We have choices—we can team students, parents and teachers in a variety of combinations to meet our communication needs. Each conference format brings with it strengths and challenges.

Chapter 15 discusses three additional information-sharing alternatives that serve best when both sender and receiver need to share detailed information about student achievement—student-teacher, teacher-parent, and student-led parent conferences. Rick considers student-led parent conferences as the most important breakthrough in communicating about student achievement of the past century. Students' partnership in this communication seems to alter their sense of accountability in significant ways. It seems to create a sense of responsibility for and a pride in accomplishment that cannot be achieved in any other way.

Grading and report cards are often seen as the end of a process, the completion of a cycle. Conferences are different. Done well, they are springboards for instructional action—using the insights gained from the conference to set goals for students, teachers, and parents.

Links to Previous Chapters

First, this is the final of four chapters on communicating about student achievement. Second, conferences must adhere to standards of high-quality assessment as defined in textbook Chapters 3–8. Third, conferences can be evaluated using the standards for effective communication in Figure Intro IV-1, "Conditions for Effective Communication."

Fourth, Chapter 15 emphasizes student involvement the heaviest of any chapter; it's the third leg in the three-part student involvement triangle—student involvement in development of assessment, tracking one's own progress, and communicating about achievement. The chapter emphasizes impact of student involvement and student motivation on achievement.

Portfolio Reminder

Once again, we remind you that it is important to keep potential portfolio material handy. See previous chapters for suggestions.

Honoring Diversity

As you well know, the interpersonal nature of conferences requires sensitivity to cultural differences:

- The language in which communication takes place
- Appropriate ways to invite family participation
- Traditional roles of parents in students' education
- Appropriate role for children when interacting with adults

How might you find out what is appropriate among the families you serve?

Roadmap

Activity	Title	Activity Description	Time	Icons
15-1	*Student-Involved Conferences—* Video Discussion	This video takes you step-by-step through conference planning. *Cross-reference to Chapter 15: General Principles 1 and 2.*	60–120 min	CONSOLIDATE UNDERSTANDING
15-2	*My Experiences with Conferences	Analyze your past experiences with conferences and fine tune them. *Cross-reference to Chapter 15: General Principles 1 and 2.*	20–40 min	APPLY LEARNING CONSOLIDATE UNDERSTANDING
15-3	What's Going Right in This Teacher-Student Conference?— Case Discussion	Analyze the dialogue in the book for adherence to principles of sound communication. *Cross-reference to Chapter 15: General Principles 1 and 2.*	15–25 min	CONSOLIDATE UNDERSTANDING
15-4	The High School Faculty Debate on Student-Led Conferences— Case Discussion	Do high school student-led conferences work? *Cross-reference to Chapter 15: General Principles 1 and 2.*	10–20 min	CONSOLIDATE UNDERSTANDING
15-5	Let the Conference Begin!— Case Discussion	Analyze the dialogue in the book for adherence to principles of sound communication. *Cross-reference to Chapter 15: General Principles 1 and 2.*	15–25 min	CONSOLIDATE UNDERSTANDING

*Recommended

Activity 15-1   *Student-Involved Conferences*—Video Discussion

Optional

Goals/Rationale

The video, *Student-Involved Conferences*, takes you step by step through the ideas presented in textbook Chapter 15. Specifically, it details alternative conference structures, shows students practicing for and conducting conferences, and illustrates typical student, teacher, and parent reactions to student involvement in this process. The video comes complete with a facilitator's guide that helps you work through key ideas.

> **Cross-Reference to *Student-Involved Classroom Assessment*, 3d ed.**
>
> General Principles 1 and 2: Ensuring communication quality, types of conferences.
>
> **Additional Materials Needed**
>
> VIDEO: *Student-Involved Conferences*, available from the Assessment Training Institute, 800-480-3060.
>
> **Time Required**
>
> 60 minutes to view the video without doing the embedded activities. At least two hours if all the activities in the video are completed.

What to Do

Acquire the video and follow the steps clearly laid out in the facilitator's guide.

My Experience with Conferences

Activity 15-2

Recommended

Goals/Rationale

Many of you have already experimented with conferences of various types—student-teacher, teacher-parent, and/or student-involved. This activity gives you the opportunity to analyze those experiences in order to fine tune them. Part of this fine tuning might involve developing a conference plan for the optional unit building activity that has run throughout the textbook and this *Workbook*.

Cross-Reference to *Student-Involved Classroom Assessment*, 3d ed.

General Principles 1 and 2: Ensuring communication quality, types of conferences.

Additional Materials Needed

WORKBOOK: Figure Intro IV-1, "Conditions for Effective Communication." TEXTBOOK: All of Chapter 15; Figure 15.3, "Student-Led Parent Conferences in a Nutshell."

Time Required

20–40 minutes.

What to Do

1. (5–10 minutes) Individually complete the first three columns in the worksheet, "My Experiences with Conferences." Use your experience either on the planning or receiving end. Be sure to include observations on what works with diverse types of students.

2. (5–10 minutes) If you are working in a group, post chart paper on the wall titled, "Keys to Success in Student-Teacher Conferences," "Keys to Success in Teacher-Parent Conferences," and "Keys to Success in Student-Led Parent Conferences." Write in suggestions based on the information in textbook Chapter 15 and on your own experiences.

3. (5–10 minutes) Based on everyone's suggestions, complete the final column in the worksheet, "My Experiences with Conferences."

4. (5–10 minutes) If you are completing the unit-building activities, decide how you might use these conference formats in your unit.

5.   If you plan to do Activities 15-3, 15-4, and/or 15-5, you might want to revisit the worksheet, "My Experiences with Conferences," after completing them.

My Experiences with Conferences

Conference type	I have tried this	How I set it up	What went well? What didn't? What diversity issues arose?	Based on information in this chapter[1], I might change...
Student-Teacher	Y N			
Parent-Teacher	Y N			
Student-Led	Y N			
Other	Y N			

[1]Refer to Figure Intro IV-1, "Conditions for Effective Communication," textbook Figure 15.3, "Student-Led Parent Conferences in a Nutshell," and other "keys to success," "anticipating the challenges," and "dealing with practicalities," in textbook Chapter 15.

What's Going Right in This Teacher-Student Conference?—Case Discussion

Activity 15-3

Optional

Goals/Rationale

The first type of conference discussed in Chapter 15 is teacher-student. This activity asks you to analyze the dialogue presented in the chapter for adherence to principles of sound communication and keys to success for teacher-student conferences.

Cross-Reference to *Student-Involved Classroom Assessment*, 3d ed.

General Principles 1 and 2; Ensuring communication quality, types of conferences.

Additional Materials Needed

WORKBOOK: Figure Intro IV-1, "Conditions for Effective Communication." TEXTBOOK: Chapter 15, teacher-student conference dialogue (p. 496-498); Chapter 15, section "Dealing with The Practicalities" (p. 504-506).

Time Required

15–25 minutes.

What to Do

1. (5–10 minutes) Reread the student-teacher conference dialogue in the textbook, pages 496-498.

    a. Which conditions for sound communication are clearly demonstrated by the dialogue and sample? What is the teacher doing well? (Refer to Figure Intro IV-1.)

    b. Which conditions for sound communication are implied by the dialogue and sample?[1] What questions would you like to ask the teacher and/or student? (Clearly relate each question to Figure Intro IV-1.)

    c. What might be improved?

2. (5–10 minutes) If working in a group, discuss your observations.

3. (5 minutes) *Optional.* What new insights might you add to the chart pages first begun in Activity 15-2, "My Experience with Conferences"?

---

[1]Figure Intro IV-1, 1a, 1b, and 3a–c. "Dealing with practicalities": thoughtful preparation, examine student work beforehand, use preestablished criteria, good listening, prepare a few thoughtful questions in advance. Common vocabulary: you can see the echo of the writing performance criteria in the dialogue.

Activity 15-4   The High School Faculty Debate on Student-Led Conferences—Case Discussion

Optional

Goals/Rationale

The third type of conference discussed in textbook Chapter 15 is student-involved parent conferences. This activity provides an opportunity to discuss the pros and cons of these conferences.

> **Cross-Reference to *Student-Involved Classroom Assessment*, 3d ed.**
>
> General Principles 1 and 2: Ensuring communication quality, types of conferences.
>
> **Additional Materials Needed**
>
> WORKBOOK: Figure Intro IV-1, "Conditions for Effective Communication."
>
> **Time Required**
>
> 10–20 minutes.

What to Do

1. (5–10 minutes) Read the case, "The High School Faculty Debate on Student-Led Conferences," and think about the following questions:

   a. Analyze each of the two teachers' experiences with student-led conferences using conditions for sound communication (Figure Intro IV-1, "Conditions for Effective Communication").

   b. What may be motivating the principal here? How good is the celebration idea from the teachers', students', and community's points of view? What would it take for the "School Success Celebration" to be successful? (Refer to Figure Intro IV-1.)

2. (5–10 minutes) Make a chart with "Students" and "Teachers" across the top and "Benefits" and "Problems" down the side. Use it to analyze pluses and minuses of the "School Success Celebration" idea from each point of view. Based on your analysis, is this a good idea? If you feel it would be beneficial, what would it take to make it happen? (Think about the conditions for sound communication presented in Figure Intro IV-1.)

3.   *Optional.* What new insights might you add to the chart pages first begun in Activity 15.2, "My Experiences with Conferences?"

The High School Faculty Debate on Student-Led Conferences—Case

A high school principal recently returned from a national conference on assessment full of excitement about an innovative new idea—student-led parent conferences—and he put the topic on the agenda for the next faculty meeting. After introducing it and discussing some of its positive aspects, the principal invited the faculty to comment.

One teacher was negative about the idea based on his experience at a previous school. There, students assembled portfolios that included all subjects and met with their parents in home room at year's end to review their achievement. Conferences were 20 minutes, so it took a long day and evening to complete them all.

For this teacher, such conferences just didn't work. First, 20 minutes was not enough to cover six different subjects. Further, students didn't know what work to place in their portfolios or how to share it, so the meetings turned out to be very brief discussions of the report card grades—completely from the student's point of view. Finally, homeroom teachers were not equipped to answer parents' questions in subjects other than their own, so parents' needs were not satisfied. All in all, it was a disaster and was abandoned after one try.

Another teacher offered a different experience. She had one student who seemed full of academic potential but didn't seem to care about school. The student's only comment was, "If my parents don't care, why should I?" When the teacher called the parents it became obvious that there had been a severe breakdown in communication in the family.

In a risky move, the teacher bet the student that her parents did care and that she could prove it. During the next grading period, the two of them assembled a growth portfolio showing the student's improvement. Further, the teacher asked her to think about how she might present herself as an improving student and to write biweekly self-reflections about the work in her portfolio. As the term ended, the teacher asked the student to invite her parents in for a special student-parent-teacher conference. The conference was a success for all.

In response to these comments, the principal made a proposal: The faculty could institute student-led conferences to bolster three initiatives already in place. First, twelfth graders are required to complete special senior projects. Second, the guidance staff has all college-bound students assemble "college admissions portfolios." Finally, students are required to complete a certain number of community service hours and assemble evidence of the productivity of their work. All three might provide an excellent basis for a school and community-wide, end-of-year acknowledgement of a productive school year.

Specifically, he proposed a three-day "School Success Celebration." Senior projects might culminate in "showcase" student-led conferences in which students presented their work for review and discussion. College admissions portfolios might be shared with parents or review boards. Community service portfolios might be presented in a group session.

The principal asked for volunteers to see if this idea was both feasible and useful.

Activity 15-5

Let the Conference Begin!—Case Discussion

Optional

Goals/Rationale

In this activity, we ask you to analyze the dialogue in the book for adherence to principles of sound communication and keys to successful conferences.

Cross-Reference to *Student-Involved Classroom Assessment*, 3d ed.

General Principles 1 and 2: Ensuring communication quality, types of conferences.

Additional Materials Needed

WORKBOOK: Figure Intro IV-1, "Conditions for Effective Communication." TEXTBOOK: Chapter 15, student-led parent conference dialogue (p. 491-494).

Time Required

15–25 minutes.

What to Do

1. (5–10 minutes) Reread the dialogue and interviews in textbook Chapter 15 (p. 491-494) that describe Terri Austin's experiences with student-led conferences. Think about the following questions:

   a. Which conditions for effective communication are clearly demonstrated by the dialogue and interview? What is the teacher doing well? (Refer to *Workbook* Figure Intro IV-1, "Conditions for Effective Communication.")

   b. Which conditions for effective communication are implied by the dialogue and sample? What questions would you like to ask the teacher and/or student? (Clearly relate each question to Figure Intro IV-1.)

   c. What might be improved?

2. (5–10 minutes) If working in a group, discuss your observations.

3. (5 minutes) *Optional.* What new insights might you add to the chart pages first begun in Activity 15-2, "My Experience with Conferences?"

Notes:

End Part IV

Activities

Roadmap

Activity	Title	Activity Description	Time	Icons
PIV-1	*Show What You Know	Two parts: Learning from Chapters 12–15 and end-of-book summary (Chapters 1-15).	Homework	
PIV-2	*Portfolio Building	Two parts: Learning from Chapters 12–15 and end-of-book summary (Chapters 1-15).	Homework	

*Recommended

Portfolio Building

Congratulations, you've finished *Student-Involved Classroom Assessment*, 3d ed.! This is a time for celebration. The activities in this section are intended to consolidate understanding of the material in Part IV of Rick's book, assist you to reflect over your entire learning experience, and celebrate your learning by sharing your portfolios and/or final units with each other.

You will design the final portfolio sharing. You can choose to have the experience be a celebration just for yourselves, or be a mock student-led conference in which each of your colleagues presents the most compelling case they can that they have become a more proficient classroom assessor as a result of participation in the learning experience. Either way will give you firsthand experience of the power and challenges of the format you choose.

Feedback to Us

Did you reach your goals? What were your challenges? What were your triumphs? What were the key elements that contributed to your success? What helped the most in this *Workbook*? What helped the least? What do you wish we had more of? What do you wish we had less of? What resources should we know about?

Help us continue to grow in our ability to help you learn about classroom assessment in a relevant and useful manner. It would be extremely helpful to us for your group to copy and complete the "Feedback to the Authors" form and mail it back. Or, just e-mail your comments to us at ati@assessmentinst.com. Thank you!

Feedback Form to the Authors

Question	RATING				
	Excellent	Good	Okay	Fair	Poor
1. How useful was the Introduction?	5	4	3	2	1
2. How useful were the activities?	5	4	3	2	1
3. How easy was it to find the activities you wanted?	5	4	3	2	1
4. How well did the formatting of the *Workbook* draw you in and make you want to use it?	5	4	3	2	1

5. Did you reach your goals? What were your challenges? What were your triumphs? What were the key elements that contributed to your success?

6. What helped the most in this *Workbook*? What helped the least? What do you wish we had more of? What do you wish we had less of? What confused you most?

7. What resources should we know about?

Thank you! Please return your responses to the Assessment Training Institute, 50 S.W. 2nd, Suite 300, Portland, OR 97204.

Activity PIV-1   Show What You Know

Recommended

Goals/Rationale

This is the final "show what you know" activity for the book. Once again, we encourage you to stop and reflect on your increasing confidence and competence as a classroom assessor. As pointed out at the beginning, the reasons for self-reflection are twofold: First, we believe that self-reflection, self-assessment, and tracking one's own progress toward expertise—in short, learner involvement in assessment—can enhance learning and motivate learners. Second, we're giving you an opportunity to try this out and see for yourself how it works, in case you want to try it with your own students. You can experience firsthand both the resistance and the benefits of doing this kind of activity.

This activity involves explaining and articulating what you are learning and how it connects to other things in your life. We propose several ideas for doing this—ideas that might appeal to different learning styles. Any of the "show what you know" activities can be considered prime potential portfolio material.

> **Cross-Reference to *Student-Involved Classroom Assessment*, 3d ed.**
>
> Chapters 1–15.
>
> **Additional Materials Needed**
>
> WORKBOOK: Figure Intro IV-1, "Conditions of Effective Communication"; Appendix A, "Sample Working Folder/Portfolio Cover Sheet."
>
> **Time Required**
>
> Open, it's homework.

What to Do

Part IV

Item 1 is recommended. The rest are optional. *Be sure to include a portfolio cover sheet* (such as that in Appendix A, "Sample Working Folder/Portfolio Cover Sheet") *with each portfolio entry.*

1. *Recommended.* At the beginning of Part IV, in Activity Intro IV-1, "What Is My Current Practice?" we asked you to answer the following questions. Answer them again based on your current understanding. How have your ideas and practices changed?

Do you have any new insights on how to overcome the barriers described in question (f)?

   a. How do I currently document student assessment information?

   b. Why am I documenting my student information in this way?

   c. Am I currently documenting what I really value and expect in student learning?

   d. How do I currently communicate to my students and parents what students have learned?

   e. How do my current communication practices match up to the "Conditions" in Figure Intro IV-1?

   f. What are local barriers to more effective communication?

2. *Optional.* Based on your learning from Chapters 12–15, draw a concept map to show your current understanding of how the following ideas link:

▲ Student Involvement	Grades
▲ Portfolios	▲ Standardized Tests
Accurate Assessments	▲ Agree on What to Communicate About
▲ Report Cards	▲ Conferences
Quality Assessment	▲ Proper Interpersonal Communication Environment

Relate these ideas to the "Five Standards for Quality Assessment," in Introduction Figure 2; link this concept map to the ones you did before. At the same time, add to or revise any of your previous concept maps based on your current understanding.

3. *Optional.* Based on your learning from Chapters 12–15, draw pictures, make posters, or create collages of the items in the table marked with a triangle.

4. *Optional.* Write a letter to a colleague, student, or parent that explains the following:

   a. Why good communication about student achievement is necessary

   b. Conditions for sound communication

   c. Communication alternatives and their strengths and weaknesses

5. *Optional.* Outline the major learnings in Part IV. Include a statement of which of these might need to be considered for future assessment planning in your building or district. Include a list of questions that you might need to ask before you can determine future assessment planning in your building or district. Consider the barriers you might face in pursuing these areas that need improvement.

6. *Optional.* Prepare a half-day workshop agenda for others that helps them understand the following:

   a. Why good communication about student achievement is necessary

   b. Conditions for sound communication

   c. Communication alternatives, their strengths and weaknesses, and keys to success

End of Book

Item 1 is recommended. The rest are optional. *Be sure to include a portfolio cover sheet (such as that in Appendix A, "Sample Working Folder/Portfolio Cover Sheet") with each portfolio entry.*

1. *Recommended.* Write an essay or a letter to a new teacher on one of the following topics:

   a. Students are key assessment users.

   b. Clear and appropriate learning targets for students are essential.

   c. High-quality assessment is a must.

   d. Sound assessments must be accompanied by good communication about student achievement.

2. *Optional.* How have your concept maps changed over time?

3. *Optional.* How might you change previous pictures or posters based on what you know now? Why?

Portfolio Building

Activity PIV-2

Recommended

Goals/Rationale

Here's where you make your final set of choices for your growth portfolio. Remember, the goal is to reflect on and self-assess your growth on the following targets:

- Standard 1—Clear and appropriate learning targets
- Standard 2a—Clear and appropriate users and uses
- Standard 2b—Sound communication about assessment
- Standard 2c—Student involvement in assessment
- Standard 3—Choosing the most appropriate assessment method
- Standard 4—Sampling
- Standard 5—Eliminating sources of bias and distortion

> **Cross-Reference to *Student-Involved Classroom Assessment*, 3d ed.**
>
> Chapters 1–15.
>
> **Additional Materials Needed**
>
> WORKBOOK: Figure Intro IV-1, "Condition for Effective Communication"; Appendix A, "Assessment Principles," "Sample Working Folder/Portfolio Cover Sheet," "Classroom Assessment Confidence Questionnaire"; Appendix B, "Quality Assessment Rubrics"; Appendix C, "Self-Assessment Developmental Levels."
>
> **Time Required**
>
> Open, it's homework.

What to Do:

Part IV

Items 1 to 3 are recommended. The rest are optional. *Be sure to include a portfolio cover sheet* (such as that in Appendix A, "Sample Working Folder/Portfolio Cover Sheet) *with each portfolio entry.*

1. *Recommended.* Reanalyze at least one of the assessments already in your portfolio. (Do not remove your previous samples or commentaries.) Add commentary about what you see now that you didn't see before. Overall, what differences do you notice in your ability and/or confidence to analyze assessments for quality?

2. *Recommended.* Choose a final assessment (test, quiz, essay test, or performance assessment) that you have recently used or taken. *If you are a current teacher, it must be one that you administered, scored, and recorded for use within the context of your teaching.* Using the "Classroom Assessment Quality Rubrics" in *Workbook* Appendix B, reflect on the quality of this assessment and write a brief analysis. What are its strengths? What could be improved?

   Write a brief comparison of the quality of all the assessments in your portfolio. Is the quality improving over time? How do you know?

3. *Recommended.* Take the "Classroom Assessment Confidence Questionnaire," in *Workbook* Appendix A, one final time. Is your classroom assessment confidence changing over time? Describe how.

4. *Optional.* Self-assess using the "Self-Assessment Developmental Levels" in *Workbook* Appendix C one final time. Do you notice any changes over time? Describe them.

5. *Optional.* Consider again the "Assessment Principles" in *Workbook* Appendix A. Now, which principles affirm your own beliefs? Why? Are there any with which you disagree either in part or in whole? Why? What concerns might you have about any of them? How has your opinion changed over time?

6. *Optional.* What else in your working folder or learning log might you put in your portfolio that demonstrates your increasing competence and confidence in assessment: quality, student involvement, and communication?

End of Book Preparation for Portfolio Sharing—Recommended

1. With your colleagues, set up a proper interpersonal communication environment:

   a. Establish clear and agreed-on reasons for sharing information—Why will you share your portfolios? Celebration? Certifying competence? Demonstrating Growth? Modeling the process in case you want to use it with students?

   b. Be sure you have a shared language for communicating about learning. Will you use the "Quality Rubrics" in *Workbook* Appendix B? Something else?

    c. Plan a focused opportunity to share. When will you share portfolios? With whom? Length? Format? Formal presentations to the whole group? Portfolio Fair? Pairs selected from a hat? Share with students?

    d. How will you check for understanding of the message receiver? What kind of feedback will be solicited?

2. Prepare your portfolio for the sharing session you have planned.

Write an overall self-reflection on changes in your competence and confidence in assessment during your period of study. Be sure to cite the evidence in your portfolio for each change.

    a. What specific evidence of improvement do you see in your own classroom assessments? Please comment on your proficiency in using as many different assessment formats as are relevant in your classroom. What criteria did you use to judge the quality of assessments? Can the reader tell?

    b. Did the nature and quality of your critiques change over time? How do you know?

    c. What are you doing differently in the classroom as the result of what you've learned? How does this relate to the "Five Standards of Quality Assessment" in *Workbook* Introduction Figure 2?

    d. What are you thinking about assessment now that is different from before?

    e. Did your self-ratings of competence and confidence (using Appendices A, "Classroom Assessment Confidence Questionnaire," and C, "Self-Assessment Developmental Levels") change over time? How?

    f. What is the impact of your learning on students? On colleagues?

    g. What questions from before can you now answer? What new questions do you have?

3. Write a "Dear Reviewer" letter. Tell reviewers a little about yourself as a classroom assessor and anything you would like them to notice about your portfolio. Be sure to include the purpose for your portfolio.

4. Be sure to have a table of contents listing all the pieces in your portfolio. Organize your portfolio in a way that makes it easy for reviewers to see your growth as a classroom assessor.

5. Is there a date on everything? Is there a statement for each piece on why it is included and what evidence it provides?

6. Analyze the content of your portfolio for how well it communicates in preparation for your portfolio conferences. (These questions link to *Workbook* Figure Intro IV-1, "Conditions for Effective Communication.")

    a. Is it clear what targets you are communicating about? Will the readers have a common understanding of these targets?

    b. How accurate a portrait of your growth and status is your portfolio?

Appendix A

Support Material

Classroom Assessment Confidence Questionnaire

Instructions: We designed this questionnaire for use by those involved in professional development or coursework using *Student-Involved Classroom Assessment*, 3d ed., by Richard Stiggins. It's designed to assist learners to track changing self-perceptions over time, as assessment learning proceeds. It's also designed to practice what we preach—that dispositions (such as confidence and attitudes) are worthy and useful learning targets. Confidence and attitudes, whether toward reading writing, science, or classroom assessment, can make or break learning. Therefore, it is in your best interests to be as honest as possible in your responses.

Complete the questionnaire by circling the number that corresponds to your answer. Many of us are reluctant to give ourselves a top score. Remember that when you choose "2" it does not imply that everything is perfect; it just means that you are well on your way or that you are feeling confident. No one but you will see your responses unless you want them to.

A. Clear Achievement Targets for Students

I can describe what it means to succeed academically in my classroom. I have . . .

	I'm uncertain if I've done this yet	I haven't done this yet	I've started	I'm well on the way
1. Outlined in writing the *subject matter content knowledge* my students are to master.	?	0	1	2
2. Differentiated content students are to *learn outright* from content they are to *learn to retrieve* later through the use of references.	?	0	1	2
3. Defined in writing the specific *patterns of reasoning* students are to master.	?	0	1	2
4. Articulated in writing the *performance skills* I expect students to learn to demonstrate (where it is the actual doing that counts).	?	0	1	2
5. Defined the key attributes of *products* I expect students to learn to create.	?	0	1	2
6. Thought through and defined *academic dispositions* (school-related attitudes) I hope my students will develop.	?	0	1	2
7. Considered whether there's anything about my learning targets or how they are written that will be unclear to some of my students.	?	0	1	2
8. Met with other teachers across grade levels to merge my expectations into a *continuous progress curriculum*.	?	0	1	2

B. Assessing Student Achievement

I can translate my learning targets for students into dependable assessments. I am confident that . . .

	I'm uncertain about my confidence	I'm not very confident	I'm somewhat confident	I'm very confident
9. I can define key standards of assessment quality in common sense, understandable terms.	?	0	1	2
10. I can develop high-quality *selected response/short answer assessments* (multiple-choice, true/false, matching, fill in).	?	0	1	2
11. I can develop high-quality *essay assessments* (traditional essay requiring a written response).	?	0	1	2
12. I can develop high-quality *performance assessments* (observation and judgment).	?	0	1	2
13. I can develop high-quality *personal communication-based assessments* (interviews, oral exams, etc.).	?	0	1	2
14. I can understand and use the results of *standardized achievement tests*.	?	0	1	2
15. I can select among assessment types based on the characteristics and strengths of my students.	?	0	1	2

C. Student-Involved Classroom Assessment

I am confident that I can turn the following assessment methods into instructional interventions by involving students in . . .

	I'm uncertain about my confidence	I'm not very confident	I'm somewhat confident	I'm very confident
16. Selected Response/Short Answer Assessments	?	0	1	2
17. Essay Assessment	?	0	1	2
18. Performance Assessment	?	0	1	2
19. Personal Communication Assessment	?	0	1	2

D. Communicating Effectively and Accurately About Student Achievement

I am confident that . .

	I'm uncertain about my confidence	I'm not very confident	I'm somewhat confident	I'm very confident
20. I understand and can apply *principles of effective communication* about student achievement.	?	0	1	2
21. I can use *report card grades* to communicate accurately and effectively.	?	0	1	2
22. I can use *other written reporting options* to communicate accurately and effectively.	?	0	1	2
23. I can use *portfolios* to communicate accurately and effectively.	?	0	1	2
24. I can use *parent-teacher conferences* to communicate accurately and effectively.	?	0	1	2
25. I can use *student-involved conferences* to communicate accurately and effectively.	?	0	1	2

E. Final Reflections

26. I have the most skill and confidence in the following assessment areas:

27. I want to work most on the following assessment skills:

28. I have the following burning questions about assessment:

29. Below are things I want to be able to do by the time I've finished my learning experience on classroom assessment.

Scoring Your Questionnaire:

For questions 1-25, add up the numbers you circled to determine your score. Before you begin your professional development or coursework, your score may be very low. However, as you learn about and implement effective assessment and communication procedures over time, your score should go up. Complete the Questionnaire at least twice—once at the beginning and once at the end of study. You can also complete the Questionnaire at the end of study of each major section of the textbook.

Assessment Learning Log

Directions: Fill out an entry whenever you want to remember an answer to a "Time for Reflection" embedded in textbook chapters or question at the end of a textbook chapter, when such an answer provides you with insight on your growth as a classroom assessor, when you want to remember something to share with a larger group as the result of an activity you've tried, or when a question comes up that you would like to think more about or get advice on from the group. (Modify the following format to fit your needs.)

Date	Good Ideas/ Things That Worked (Why?)	Don't Try This/ These Didn't Work (Why?)	I Made Progress on Mastering These Targets (How?)	I Still Need to Work on...	Other

Sample Working Folder/Portfolio Cover Sheet

Date: _____

Context for the sample: Workbook activity, learning log, another activity I tried, etc.

Target covered by this sample: (circle all that apply)

1. Standard 1-Clear and appropriate learning targets
2. Standard 2a-Clear and appropriate users and uses
3. Standard 2b-Sound communication about assessment
4. Standard 2c-Student involvement in assessment
5. Standard 3-Choosing the most appropriate assessment method
6. Standard 4-Sampling
7. Standard 5-Eliminating sources of bias and distortion

I chose this because:

❏   I am proud of it.

❏   It illustrates a problem that I overcame.

❏   This didn't work. Don't try it again. "I'd just as soon burn it."

❏   I said to myself, "Hey, I'm getting the hang of it."

❏   It illustrates a question I can now answer.

❏   It illustrates a skill I could improve on.

❏   Something happened that surprised me.

❏   I learned something.

❏   I want to keep working on it.

❏   It really shows how much I've learned.

❏   It illustrates a question with which I'm still struggling.

❏   Other:

Here's what I'd like you to know about my choice:

Sample Team Meeting Log

Date: _____   Location: _____

Leader: _____   Clarifier: _____

Recorder: _____   Timekeeper: _____

Goals:

Agenda:

1. *Opening* (5 minutes): Review group norms as needed. Review goals, agenda, and participant roles.

2. *Content/Ideas* (80-100 minutes): Review key ideas in the textbook and do selected *Workbook* activities. Emphasize discussion of applications. Share portfolio work as needed.

3. *Plan Homework for Next Time* (5-10 minutes): Decide on *Workbook* activities for next time. Review the textbook chapters to read and other work to be done for next time. This will form the "content/ideas" portion of the agenda for next time.

4. *Wrap-up* (5-10 minutes). Reflect on the meeting and appoint roles for next time. Record roles on the Meeting Log form for next time.

Materials Needed	**Preparation Checklist for Leader**
❏ Chart paper, pens, easel	❏ Agenda sent to participants
❏ VCR and monitor	❏ Meeting room prepared
❏ Post-It™ Notes, cards, paper	❏ Other: _____
❏ Worksheets	
❏ Other: _____	

Members in Attendance: _____

_____

Sample Learning Team Meeting Log (*Continued*)

Agenda Topic	Accomplishments	Interesting Issues Discussed	Actions Taken/ Next Steps

Meeting Evaluation

	LOW				HIGH
Were the results worth the time spent?	1	2	3	4	5
How well is the team achieving its goals?	1	2	3	4	5
Was group interaction positive?	1	2	3	4	5
Other	1	2	3	4	5
Other	1	2	3	4	5

What can be done to improve our working together?

Assessment Principles* *(one possible set)*

Principle 1

Learners need to find out often how well they are doing and teachers need to find out how successfully they are teaching. Therefore, regular assessment of student progress and achievement is part of good teaching.

Principle 2

The main purpose of assessment is to help students learn. When students are assessed well and given feedback about their performance, they find out what they have learned successfully and what they have not. Any weaknesses can then be reduced.

Principle 3

Assessment tasks should be designed so that most children in a group do well on most tasks. This takes the threat out of being assessed, and allows children to be motivated to learn by the regular experience of success and praise.

Principle 4

Design/selection of assessment tasks requires a clear idea of the curriculum objectives. Children should only be assessed on knowledge, skills and attitudes their teacher has given them opportunities to develop, and each task should be well within the capabilities of most students.

Principle 5

No single method of assessment can give information about achievement of the full range of learning objectives. Therefore a combination of different methods is vital if we are to get a balanced picture of student development.

Principle 6

Assessment tasks must be presented so that students are perfectly clear about what is expected, and grades or marks awarded so that students feel they have been fairly treated.

Principle 7

The language of assessment must match the language of instruction. If not, then assessment produces unfair and invalid results. Children must be fluent in the language in which they are to be assessed and the level of language used must match their stage of development.

Principle 8

The teacher's unbiased judgments are important in assessment, but students themselves can often be asked to assess their own level of achievement and the achievements of their classmates. They can be (surprisingly) accurate and honest.

Principle 9

Assessment should focus on each student's achievements, independently of how other students are doing. Constant comparison/ competition with classmates can damage the self-esteem and self-confidence of many students.

*These principles were developed by science teachers and specialists in the Federated States of Micronesia for the elementary science curriculum called FASE (FSM/Australia Science Education), 1996. This set of principles is intended as a discussion starter, not necessarily model principles that should be in place everywhere.

Seven Strategies for Using Criteria as a Teaching Tool*

1. **Teach students the vocabulary they need** to think and talk like _____ (writers, critical thinkers, mathematics problem solvers, etc.). In other words, teach students the criteria for quality.

    a. Ask students to brainstorm characteristics of good-quality work.

    b. Show students samples of work (both low and high quality) and ask them to expand their list of quality features.

    c. Ask students if they'd like to see what teachers think. (They always want to.) Show them how the student-friendly versions of the criteria match what they said.

2. **Practice scoring anonymous samples of student work.** Ask students to use the rubric(s) to "score" real samples of student work. Since there is no single correct score, only justifiable scores, ask students to justify their scores using wording from the rubric. Begin with single traits. Progress to multiple traits when students are proficient with single traits.

3. **Practice focused revision.** It's not enough to only ask students to judge work and justify their judgments. Students also need to understand how to revise work to make it better. Ask students to brainstorm advice for the author of the work on how to improve his or her work. Then ask students (in groups) to revise the work using their own advice. Begin with single traits; pick work that needs revision on a single trait. Revisions will almost always be better on more than just the single trait being addressed. For example, as students improve ideas (in writing), organization and voice tend to improve as well.

4. **Share professional examples.** Show students lots of samples from the real world—both strong and weak. Have them analyze these samples for quality.

5. **Model it yourself.** Ask students to analyze your work for quality and make suggestions on improvement. Revise your work using their advice. Ask them to again review it for quality. Students love doing this.

6. **Give students plenty of opportunities to show what they know.** People consolidate their understanding when they practice describing and articulating criteria for quality. Ask students to do such things as develop posters or drawings that illustrate the traits of quality; write a letter to their parents describing what they have done well and their next steps (using the language of the criteria); ask students to reflect on their work using the language of the criteria, etc.

7. **Teach lessons focused on the traits of quality.** Use the criteria and traits as organizers for lessons. For example, in writing you could teach specific lessons on organization—different organizational patterns and when to use them, transitions, catchy openings, good endings, etc. Make sure that students understand what particular trait(s) each lesson will help them improve. You already teach these lessons. The main difference is being very clear which trait(s) each lesson addresses.

*Based on work done at Northwest Regional Educational Laboratory, Portland, OR, and by Jan Chappuis, assessment consultant, Silverdale, WA.

Appendix B

Part 1: Fast-Tracked or Side-Tracked?—Classroom Assessment Quality Rubrics

Part 2: Sample Assessments

Part 3: Assessment Analyses

Part 1: Fast-Tracked or Side-Tracked? Classroom Assessment Quality Rubrics

Introduction

Before using any assessment, the user must ensure its quality. Any standardized test, state or district developed assessment, or classroom assessment must be evaluated through the careful application of specific quality control standards. Good consumers ask tough questions about quality.

Standards for Quality Assessments

On the following pages are the questions that an assessment user or author should ask in conducting such an analysis of quality. These questions are framed as rubrics that cover each of the "Five Standards for Quality Assessments" as described in *Workbook* Figure Intro-1:

1. **Standard 1**—*What:* A sound assessment arises from clear and appropriate student learning target(s)—achievement expectations are clearly and completely defined and are couched in the best current understanding of the field.

2. **Standard 2**—*Why:* A sound assessment serves clearly articulated and appropriate purposes—why are these targets being assessed, who will use the information, and what will the information be used for (2a)? This includes (2b) uses that have direct connections to opportunities for student learning and motivation, and (2c) communication that is appropriate for the audience and use.

3. **Standard 3**—*How:* A sound assessment uses a method appropriate for both the targets being assessed and the assessment's audience and purposes.

4. **Standard 4**—*How Much:* A sound assessment samples student achievement appropriately—it provides for gathering just the right amount of information, not too much and not too little.

5. **Standard 5**—*How Accurate:* A sound assessment is developed to avoid potential sources of bias and distortion—the results really do reflect what a student knows and is able to do.

Scored Samples

Sample classroom assessments evaluated using the "Classroom Assessment Quality Rubrics" appear in Part 1 of this Appendix. When learning any criteria for quality—from oral presentations in the classroom to teacher-made classroom assessments—scored samples help make the criteria and rubrics real. We've modeled this sound instructional practice by providing sample scored assessments in Part 2. The samples can be considered "models" or "anchors" for the rubrics.

Rationale for the Rubrics

The "Five Quality Standards" can be thought of as "traits" or dimensions of effective assessment. Therefore, the attached set of rubrics form an "analytical trait system" for assessing quality—a different analysis is carried out for each trait. This contrasts with "holistic" rubrics in which a single evaluation is carried out for a product for performance as a whole. Analytical trait systems are commonly considered to be more useful than holistic systems for teaching and learning the characteristics of quality of a complex product or performance because they help learners break down a complex whole into crucial subcomponents and practice them separately.

> *"One of the best examples of good teaching I have ever encountered was with a golf professional. On my first lesson, he said, 'Here is a bucket of balls . . . hit 'em.' A few minutes later he wandered back and quietly said, 'Keep hitting them, only this time keep your head down, eye on the ball.' By the next bucket of balls he had introduced one more skill for the day . . . no more. Before a few weeks were out, he had quietly attended to my feet, grip, shoulder level, and follow through. A few years later I realized with a start that every single one of my problems was visible on the first lesson. If I had attended to all of them that first day, I would probably have missed the ball entirely and resigned in disgust from ever playing golf again.'* (Donald Graves, *Writing: Teachers and Children At Work*, Portsmouth, NH: Heinemann. 1983)

Think of developing high quality classroom assessments akin to learning to play golf. If every detail of quality is presented at once, it can be overwhelming. Complex performances and products need to be broken down into essential subcomponents that can be practiced separately and then built back up into a whole. The attached analytical trait rubrics for assessing the quality of assessments attempt to model Donald Grave's sage observation.

Rationale for the Scale

We have used three-point scales in the rubrics—an assessment can be "fast-tracked," "on track, but needs work," or "side-tracked" for each dimension or trait. We decided that three levels of quality are probably enough for the purpose of helping educators understand the nature of quality assessment. The rubrics can, however, easily be converted into a five-point scale. Think of a "4" as having some qualities of a "fast-tracked" and some of an "on track." Likewise, a "2" can be thought of having some qualities of an "on-track" and some of a "side-tracked."

A Note of Caution

Do not think of these rubrics as checklists—it is not true that everything under a "fast-tracked" has to be present to get a high score. Rather, the statements in each level of the rubric represent the types of characteristics of an assessment at each level of quality. Use the rubric by finding the descriptors that most match the assessment you are reviewing.

Standard 1—
What: Clear and Appropriate Student Learning Targets

Fast-Tracked

- Targets are stated, selective, and easy to find.

- Targets are important—worth the assessment time devoted to them.

- Targets are related clearly to district/state standards/outcomes.

- There is an effort to define targets: examples of student work, references to definitions, references to performance criteria, and/or a table of specifications; it is clear that the author understands that such references help users define the targets.

- The targets are clear enough that educators would more or less interpret them the same.

- Target descriptions and definitions reflect an understanding of best thinking in the field.

- There is an appropriate mix of targets and/or there is evidence of long-term thinking—how the targets in the current assessment fit with the plan for the year.

On Track, But Needs Work

- Targets are listed, but they might be stated differently in different places, scattered, or require some work to find.

- Some of the targets are essential, but there also seems to be some dead wood that might profitably be cut; some targets seem to have been chosen because they were easy to assess.

- Targets seem to be retrofitted to an already existing test; as a result, one might feel somewhat dissatisfied that the assessment is not as well thought out, comprehensive, or as focused as it might have been had the targets been identified first.

- Although targets are stated, there is some question as to their meaning—different educators might define the targets differently.

- At first glance there appears to be a connection between stated targets and local content standards, but on closer examination the connection is not clear.

- Although the author provides local content standards, rubrics, etc., it is not clear that he or she knows that these help users understand the nature of the targets being assessed.

- Rubrics only partially help define the targets.

- Some of the targets represent the best thinking in the field; others do not.

Side-Tracked

- Stated targets are broad, general and vague; there is little attempt at clarification.

- No targets are stated.

- There is little focus; everything is listed.

- Statements of targets ramble; the author lists one and later seems to list others; targets have to be inferred from the assessment itself.

- Targets are stated, but seem trivial; why spend time assessing this?

- The description of targets doesn't reflect an understanding of best thinking in the field.

- There is a poor mix of targets; the author might, for example, have chosen only the easiest targets to assess; or, there is little evidence of long-term thinking—how the targets in the current assessment fit into the overall plan for the year.

- There is no connection made to district and state standards or outcomes.

- Targets and tasks are mixed up.

Standard 2a—
Why: Clear and Appropriate Users and Uses

Fast-Tracked

- It is clear who the intended users and uses are, and they are appropriate.

- Users and uses are focused—there aren't too many.

- There are statements relating assessment design to users and uses; these adaptations are appropriate, for example if an assessment is designed to report student progress to parents, parents actually do understand the report.

- Over several assessments the mix of users and uses is good, including tracking student progress toward important learning outcomes, planning instruction, student involvement, and evaluation of the success of instruction.

- It is clear how the assessment can be used to inform future instruction.

On Track, But Needs Work

- The author has considered several users and uses, but doesn't seem to have a feel for how assessment design might differ for these various audiences.

- Users and uses are implied, but not clearly stated; the reviewer has to infer them.

- The author is aware that users and uses are important considerations, but seems to be unsure what to do about it.

- Implications for instructional decision making are there, but they have to be inferred.

- Users and uses are stated, but there is a question about appropriateness.

- Users and uses are stated, but the author doesn't seem to understand the importance of stating them.

Side-Tracked

- There are too many users and uses; it would be impossible to satisfy all the stated purposes in a single assessment.

- No purposes are stated; it is not clear why the assessment is being given.

- The stated purpose doesn't seem to match the assessment.

- The only purpose, ever, is grading.

- The author doesn't appear to be aware that an assessment should be designed with users and uses in mind.

- It is not clear how the results would inform future instruction; or, the author seems unaware that this is important.

Standard 2b—
Why: Student Involvement

Fast-Tracked

- The author has considered how the assessment results, procedures, and/or materials can be used to promote instructional uses; if such student uses are not included, it is reasonable that they should not be.

- The assessment results, procedures or materials help students understand the nature of the learning targets they are to hit through such things as practice with criteria and rubrics, student-friendly versions of rubrics, student development of assessment, or student cross-referencing of assessment questions to targets.

- The assessment results, procedures, or materials assist students with self-assessment in a meaningful way—not as an afterthought that appears to have been tacked on to look good, but with no real substance.

- The assessment results, procedures or materials promote student self-tracking of achievement toward the desired goal; this is meaningful, not an afterthought that appears to have been tacked on to look good.

- The assessment results, procedures, or materials promote student communication about achievement progress; this is meaningful, not an afterthought that appears to have been tacked on to look good.

- There are likely to be other positive side effects for students, e.g., increased student interest in the topic being assessed, increased student motivation to learn, or increased student ability to take control of her or his own learning.

On Track, But Needs Work

- The assessment results, procedures, or materials can be easily adapted to promote student involvement, but the author has not included assistance with such use, e.g., there might be an adult rubric but no student-friendly version; or, the author just uses a rubric for assessment and has not considered how to use it in instruction.

- Student uses are scattered throughout, but have to be searched for or inferred; such use might not be consciously stated.

Side-Tracked

- There is no student involvement.

- Student-involved uses appear to have been tacked on to look good; suggestions don't promote meaningful student involvement.

- The assessment might have negative side effects for students, e.g., embarrassment, a feeling of being a failure, or turning students off to learning.

- The author does not seem to believe that students have the ability to assess themselves, nor sees the profit in their trying.

Standard 2c—
Why: Communicates Effectively To Users and Uses

Fast-Tracked

- The author has anticipated the needs of the users—type of information, timing, understandability of reports.

- A description of these considerations is easy to find.

- There is evidence that the message sender and receiver agree on the meaning of the achievement targets being communicated about.

- There is evidence that the symbols used to convey meaning mean the same thing to the message sender and receiver.

- There is evidence that the author has checked with users to make sure they understand the message and how to act on it.

On Track, But Needs Work

- The author has considered the communication needs of users, but it still needs work.

- Communication seems to be all right, but the information needs to be inferred or searched for.

- The author has theoretically considered communication issues, such as common meaning for symbols and a common understanding of the targets being communicated about, but still needs to pilot test the plan.

Side-Tracked

- Reporting mechanisms don't seem to fit the needs of the users—the stated users might not understand the information, it is not presented clearly, it is not timely, etc.

- The author has not considered communication at all.

- The author has not seemed to consider his or her own information needs, let alone those of students, parents, or others.

Standard 3—
How: Target-Method Match

Fast-Tracked

- The assessment method matches purpose and target.

- There's a reasonable rationale for the method(s) used and where/why compromises had to be made.

- There's a table of specifications showing how each target is to be measured and its relative importance; this table makes sense.

- There is an appropriate mix of assessment methods; there is balance.

- The author has chosen carefully when and how to use performance assessments; there is clever use of simpler methods.

- There is a good match between the targets the author says are emphasized, instructional emphases, and what is actually on the assessment.

On Track, But Needs Work

- The author has used a variety of assessment methods, but it is somewhat unclear why; or, some of the methods might be improved.

- The author seems to have overused performance assessment when a simpler method might be cleverly applied.

- Matching seems to be all right, but this information has to be inferred or searched for.

- There are some matches and some mismatches among targets, instruction, and methods.

Side-Tracked

- The method doesn't seem capable of doing the job—one finds oneself asking, "Why did they assess the target *that* way?"

- One type of assessment is used for everything, when various formats would be more appropriate.

- There is no rationale for the methods used.

- The method seems to be "overkill" for the target; for example, performance assessment is used for everything.

- There is overreliance on assessing only the higher-level skills, without consideration of assessing prerequisite skills which might require a simpler method.

- There is a mismatch between what the author lists as the targets being assessed, the targets emphasized in instruction, and the targets assessed; or, targets don't match criteria.

- There are many missed opportunities for assessment.

Standard 4—
How Much: Sampling

Fast-Tracked

- The author has defined the domain from which the specific tasks on the assessment have been sampled; this is an appropriate definition. (Note: this is where sampling overlaps with clear targets.)

- The sample of student performance will accomplish its purpose.

- There are enough samples of student performance to get a stable estimate of achievement.

- There are not too many tasks, nor too few, but just enough.

- The tasks cover the learning targets (domain) well.

- The sample matches the breadth of the target and/or the importance of results.

On Track, But Needs Work

- The author seems to have covered the learning targets (domain) well, but has not made a clear enough description of the domain to know for sure.

- There is some overkill; the author has students doing more tasks than are necessary to get a good estimate of student achievement.

- There is fairly good coverage of the domain of skills needed to make a stable estimate of achievement, but the assessment would benefit from a few additions; for example, a writing assessment plan might ask students to write stories and informational text, but no persuasive pieces.

- Although the sampling might be acceptable for some uses, the stakes are such that additional samples would be beneficial.

- Sampling seems to be acceptable, but this has to be inferred or searched for; it is not explicitly addressed.

- Some outcomes are sampled well, some are not.

Side-Tracked

- There are not enough tasks to draw the desired conclusion, e.g., the author attempts to draw a conclusion about student ability to read critically on the basis of a single reading passage.

- The tasks do not cover the ground well, e.g., the author wants to know how well students understand the characteristics of fables, but only asks students to write a single fable—there is no assessment of prerequisite knowledge in other formats, and no practice with writing fables over time.

- The author doesn't seem to be aware that all assessments sample from a domain and that this domain needs to be defined.

- The sample doesn't match the breadth of the target nor the importance of the results.

Standard 5—
How Accurate: Avoiding Sources of Bias and Distortion

Fast-Tracked

- It is clear what students are to do during the assessment—instructions are clear.

- Tasks seem to match the targets and criteria—complex target, complex task; simple target, simple task.

- Possible sources of bias and distortion are described or acknowledged; caveats on use are given.

- The author seems to have sought out assessments with certain features in order to minimize bias and distortion; e.g., a portfolio system having clear and appropriate performance criteria, a clear purpose, and clear guidelines for when items are included and who selects them.

- Performance criteria, when present, are clear, well defined, and cover the most salient features of a performance.

- Paper and pencil methods adhere to standards of quality.

- Students of equal ability will have an equal opportunity to excel regardless of cultural or gender differences.

- Tasks and exercises are feasible—it is possible for students to complete tasks successfully.

- The reader can't identify any obvious sources of bias and distortion.

On Track, But Needs Work

- The author is aware that bias and distortion can be a problem, but doesn't completely address potential problems in the assessment.

- Although tasks might have a few features that are vague or confusing, they are generally sound and just require some adjustments or rewording.

- Although criteria may be a little vague or confusing, they are generally sound and just require some adjustments or rewording.

- The assessment might work well for one group of students, but might need to be re-worked for use with other groups.

- Information about bias and distortion is included, but has to be inferred or searched for.

Side-Tracked

- Tasks are vague or confusing, and it is difficult to see how they might be fixed.

- Tasks (multiple choice to performance based) don't adhere to standards of quality.

- It would be hard to do the task successfully, e.g., a task requires specialized equipment that might not be equally available to all students.

- The author seems to be unaware of possible sources of bias and distortion.

- The reader can readily identify several possible sources of bias and distortion.

- Criteria for performance assessments don't cover important elements of performance, are vague or confusing, miss the point, or are missing entirely.

- Tasks and procedures might unfairly cause different groups of students to do poorly even when their skills and knowledge are the same.

Part 2: Sample Assessments

In this part of Appendix B, we provide sample assessments. These samples represent a range of grade levels and subject areas. Analyses of these samples, using the rubrics from Appendix B, Part 1, appear in Part 3 of this Appendix. The following sample assessments are included:

- Reading Rate, Grade 3: performance assessment

- Mathematics Problem Solving (math), Grades 3-12: performance assessment

- Setting up a Tropical Fish Tank (science), Grade 5: selected response and essay

- Exhibition of Mastery (social studies), Grades 8-9: performance assessment

- Emerson Test (literature), Grades 10-12: essay

- Interview (school to work), Grades 11-12: performance assessment

Assessment Sample 1: Reading Rate—Performance Assessment

Intended Grade Level: Grade 3

Description

The teacher assesses the reading rate of students once each quarter using a book that she judges is at an appropriate reading level. All students read the same book each quarter, but the books might differ as the year progresses. The students read for one minute while the teacher marks miscues. Reading rate is defined as the total number of words read in one minute minus the number of words that were skipped or misread.

The results for two students appear below. The teacher's handwritten notes are in italics next to where they occurred in the text. These notes show miscues and provide other information. An upward arrow (↑) denotes how far each student read in one minute. The original text had pictures and was printed in primary-sized type. We've reproduced it here in smaller type for ease of use.

The teacher uses the information to report progress to parents. Copies of the letter she sent in October and April follow the student results.

Student Reading Protocols

Watch Out, Ronald Morgan! *(2.2 level)*[1]

It all started when the bell rang. I raced *(rushed)* across the schoolyard and slid *(slide-self corrected OK)* over a patch of ice.

"Watch out, Ronald!" Rosemary yelled, but it was too late. I ↑ slid into her and she landed in a snow pile.

John 10/97:30 - 1 = 29 wpm

Watch Out, Ronald Morgan! *(2.2 level)*

It all started when the bell rang. I raced across the schoolyard and slid over a patch *(path)* of ice.

"Watch out, Ronald!" Rosemary yelled, but it was too late. I slid into her and she landed in a *(the)* snow pile.

When I got to my class I fed the goldfish. I fed Frank, the gerbil, too.

"Oh, no," Rosemary said. "You fed the gerbil food to Goldie."

"Oh," I said. "The boxes look the same. Billy shook his head. "Can't you read the letters? F is for fish. G is for gerbil."

At recess Miss Tyler wouldn't let us go outside. "You'll get snow in ↑ your sneakers." She said. We played kickball in the gym. The ball bounced off my head.

Lucy 10/97:105 - 2 = 103 wpm

---

[1]From *Watch Out, Ronald Morgan!* by Patricia Reilly Giff and Susanna Natti (New York, NY: Viking Kestvel, 1985).

Letters to Parents

October 1997

Dear Parent,

As part of the first-quarter assessment of your child, I checked your child to see how many words per minute he/she could read using a story at the **second-grade level.** The story was "Watch Out Ronald Morgan!"

Research shows that when an individual can read at a rate of 150-200 wpm, they are reading proficiently and will comprehend at a high rate. Students should be able to reach that goal by the end of fifth grade. The goal for second graders is 80 wpm, and **the goal for third-grade students will be to read 110 wpm at the third-grade level.** It only makes sense that the more at ease we are in reading, the more we will understand what we have read.

Next quarter your child will again be tested, but at the third-grade level instead of the second grade.

Please read your child's results and see where they are and how they compare with his/her peers. Oral reading at home will greatly improve your child's reading rate.

_____ is currently reading second-grade material at a rate of _____ wpm.

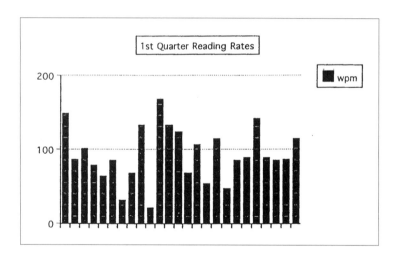

Figure B-1

April 1998

Dear Parents,

Your child was tested last week on the story "The Recital," a story that every child has read twice. It is a story from our third-grade reading book.

Please remember that our goal is to read 110 words per minute by the end of the year. As you can see we have quite a range, from 37 words per minute all the way to 208 words per minute.

Who has it easier in school? Yep, you got it . . . those who can read at a good rate have a much easier time, it only makes sense. Those of you who faithfully listen to your child or read with your child, pat yourself on the back. I applaud you.

Keep reading with your child this quarter. Let's see what percentage of our class can make that 110-word goal.

_____ is currently reading third-grade materials at a rate of _____ wpm.

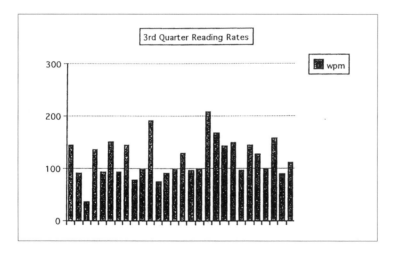

Figure B-2

Assessment Sample 2:
Mathematics Problem Solving*—Performance Assessment

Intended Grade Levels: Grades 4-12

Description

Everett School District has, for several years, conducted a district-wide mathematics assessment in several grade levels. Although the major purpose for the assessment is to provide a "snapshot" of the problem-solving skills of students, they strongly feel that the materials used in the assessment—especially the rubrics and scored samples of student work—are very useful instructionally to help teachers teach the very skills also being assessed. In 1998 they published a handbook for use by teachers, which contains the following parts:

- A rationale for and description of the performance assessment (excerpted in the next section).

- Suggestions for teachers on how to use the assessment materials instructionally. These suggestions include how to use the sample scored student problems and rubrics with students to illustrate the characteristics of sound problem solving, sample problems for students to solve, general ideas on how to teach mathematical problem solving, and a sample lesson plan (excerpted in "Suggestions for Instruction," below).

- Problem solving materials for students. These include steps to follow when problem solving and a student-friendly version of the rubric (excerpts included below).

- Sample scored student work from several grade levels. Each sample is annotated with the reasons why the paper was scored as it was (two-eighth grade responses are included below).

Rationale for and Description of the Approach

The authors provide information about this assessment in the first portion of their report. The following are excerpts:

"For the past three years students in Everett School District have participated in a district-wide math problem solving assessment. Results of this assessment provide a "snap shot" picture of the problem solving skills of Everett students. Group data from this assessment inform us of program strengths and weaknesses; individual student data provide teachers with information for making instruction decisions about what to teach, re-teach, emphasize, and practice." (p. 1)

"The purpose of this booklet is to provide teachers and students with models of math problem solving responses that exemplify the five levels (scale points) on the scoring rubric. These models, taken from actual student work from the 1997-98 district assessment, serve as 'exemplars'—showing by example what the rubric means in terms of student work. Particularly in the case of the level 4 and 5 papers, they can be effectively shared with students to give them an idea of what they can aim for in their own work." (p. 2)

---

*Abstracted from Everett Public Schools Comprehensive Assessment Program, *District Math Problem Solving Assessment*, Curriculum & Assessment Department, P.O. Box 2098, 4730 Colby Ave., Everett, WA 98203.

"The importance of providing students with exemplars of quality work cannot be over-emphasized. Standards-based teaching and learning focuses upon the use of exemplars because they provide clear, visible targets that are embedded in the day-to-day work of the students. Students can use the rubrics and exemplars as tools for evaluating their own and others' work and identifying what is needed to move toward the highest level of performance. Grant Wiggins states:

> *If you want students to do excellent work, they have to know what excellent work looks like. And the work that students produce has to be scored based on a pretty good knowledge of what excellence looks like. (Standards and Standardization,* ASCD video, 1991)" (p. 2)

"A few years ago, a large group of Everett teachers met over the course of a year and helped to develop the district's long range plan for district-wide assessment. They considered a variety of means of assessing math, including performance assessment, criterion referenced tests, and norm referenced tests. Based on their recommendations, we are currently using all of these assessments in the district. . . ." (p. 7)

"A wide variety of skills and content knowledge is represented in the district's curriculum standards. Many of the skills and much of the knowledge can be effectively assessed through multiple-choice items such as are found on norm-referenced tests and the district math criterion referenced tests. Some however, are broader and require actual samples of student work." (p. 7)

"Performance assessments such as the math problem solving assessment, allow students to complete a significant piece of work and show their ability to solve complex problems in a meaningful context. The problem solving traits of Communication of Reasoning, Conceptual Understanding, Processes and Strategies, and Accuracy and Reasonableness are each scored independently based on a rubric. . . . The results of this assessment give a snapshot of how well each student does in these important skills and allow the teacher to build on their strengths and help them in those areas in which they need more work. . . ." (p. 7)

"The committee and district assessment staff looked at a variety of ways to do performance assessment. . . . The current Everett rubric is an adaptation of the rubric developed for the Oregon State Department of Education. . . . The rubric was adapted to clarify the language and make it more aligned with the Everett Essential Learnings . . ." (p. 7-8)

"Our Mathematical Problem Solving Scoring Guide is consistent with what researchers such as Polya have suggested are the four phases of problem solving: understand the problem, devise a plan, carry out the plan, look back." (p. 4)

"The scorers are trained rigorously on the *Everett* scoring rubric. They work sample problems, score, and discuss their scores among themselves and with table leaders. They are then given 'anchor papers' to score, and if their answers don't match the official score they are retrained." (p. 7)

"During the scoring, the accuracy of the scoring is monitored and scorers who drift from the standard are retrained or replaced. An overall level of at least 80% exact match with anchor scores is maintained. They must be in 100% agreement plus or minus one point on the rubric. . . ." (p. 8)

Suggestions for Instruction (p. 2-3)

"Using the anchor/exemplar papers (scored examples of student's work). All or part of these steps might be used:

- "Spend some time going over the four 'traits' from the scoring guide, then give the students last year's question (without answers) to work on their own. Make sure that students have a copy of the scoring rubric while writing their response.

- "In pairs, have the students review each other's work, making suggestions and corrections, then rewrite their response individually.

- "Give the students copies of the anchor papers from last year, making sure that the scores are not indicated. In groups, have the students use the rubric to score each paper and to give reasons for the score. A discussion of the scores and reasons would help students better understand the expectations.

- "Have the students review and rework their own answer again, then use the rubric to score it. The goal is for each student to experience writing a '5' solution."

"Using the practice problems.

- "Have students write a response, then self-evaluate, using the rubric.

- "Have students work in pairs to review each individual's work using the rubric, then rewrite their response individually.

- "After students have worked the problem individually, have students show their work on the overhead or at the board.

- "Some problems may be given for practice only with no grade attached so that students can become more comfortable with the process."

Mathematics Problem-Solving Rubric

Everett Public Schools

MATHEMATICS PROBLEM SOLVING RUBRIC
SCORING GUIDE

	1	2	3	4	5
Communication of Reasoning	Does not use math terms; Does not explain thinking; Presents little or no work; Does not explain solution	Uses math terms incorrectly; Attempts to explain thinking; Presents work without logic; Explanation of solution confused	Uses some math terms correctly; Explains some of thinking; Presents work with some logic; Explanation of solution partially understandable	Uses most math terms correctly; Explains basic thinking; Presents clear work with some logic; Explanation of solution understandable by some	Uses all math terms correctly; Explains thinking deeply; Presents work in very logical and clear manner; Explanation of solution understandable by all
Conceptual Understanding	Demonstrates no understanding of problem; Does not use problem information/data	Demonstrates incorrect understanding of problem; Incorrectly uses problem information/data	Demonstrates partial understanding of problem; Uses most of problem information/data	Demonstrates basic understanding of problem; Uses enough problem information/data	Demonstrates thorough understanding of problem; Uses problem information/data clearly and well
Processes and Strategies	Graphs, pictures, models missing; Skills/strategy not evident; Plan is missing; Does not check work	Graphs, pictures, models not connected to problem solution; Skill/strategy inappropriate to problem; Plan does not apply to problem; Attempts check of work incorrectly	Graphs, pictures, models partially support problem solution; Skill/strategy partially supports problem; Plan applies to part of problem; Checks some of the work	Graphs, pictures, models support basic problem solution; Skill/strategy appropriate to problem; Plan applies to problem; Checks work the same way	Graphs, pictures, models very clearly support problem solution; Multiple skills/strategies appropriate to problem; Effectively implements plan to find solution; Checks work a different way
Accuracy and Reasonableness	Calculations/diagrams missing; No answer or answer only; Unsuccessfully attempts to justify or verify the solution; Makes no connections	Calculations/diagrams attempted but incorrect; Unsuccessfully attempts to justify or verify the solution; Attempts a connection	Calculations/diagrams partially accurate; Partially justifies, verifies, or extends the solution; Makes partial connection with solution	Calculations/diagrams basically accurate; Justifies, verifies, or extends the solution; Makes a basic connection with solution	Calculations/diagrams completely accurate; Justifies, verifies, extends the solution; Makes solution connections to general situations

NR (No Response) - no evidence provided   Curriculum & Assessment Department

8/1/98

Figure B-3

Student-Friendly Version of the Rubric

You may copy and cut this out. Students may use this as a quick way to score their own or each other's work.

Mathematics Problem Solving Scoring Guide

Communication of Reasoning	Conceptual Understanding	Processes & Strategies	Accuracy & Reasonableness
clearly explains what was done from beginning to end of the problem using pictures and words to communicate to others	shows an understanding of what the problem is asking	chooses strategies, carries out the process, and then checks the work	finds an accurate solution and shows why it makes sense
1 2 3 4 5	1 2 3 4 5	1 2 3 4 5	1 2 3 4 5

Figure B-4

Two Scored Eighth-Grade Student Responses
The Problem:

You have 100 congruent square pieces of paper to tack up on a bulletin board. Papers must be tacked at all corners. What is the fewest number of tacks you will need to tack the 100 papers? Explain your thinking at each step and your answer(s).

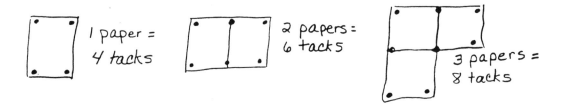

Student Response 1

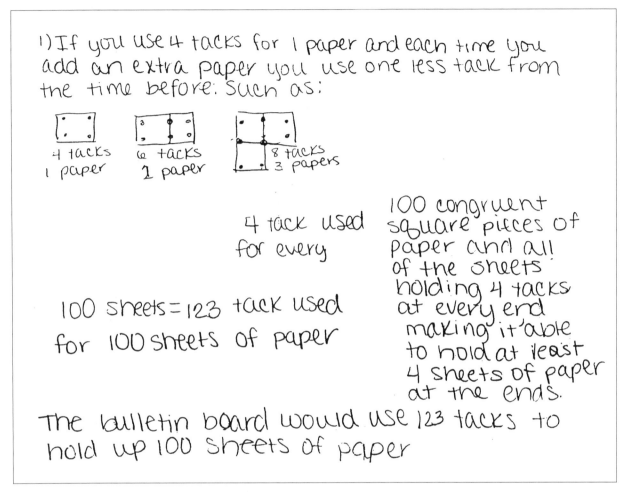

1) If you use 4 tacks for 1 paper and each time you add an extra paper you use one less tack from the time before. Such as:

4 tacks
1 paper

6 tacks
2 paper

8 tacks
3 papers

4 tack used for every

100 sheets = 123 tack used for 100 sheets of paper

100 congruent square pieces of paper and all of the sheets holding 4 tacks at every end making it able to hold at least 4 sheets of paper at the ends.

The bulletin board would use 123 tacks to hold up 100 sheets of paper

Figure B-5

Comments on student's response to problem:

- "The student does not explain what they are thinking. For the most part they are merely repeating what the problem states and then they give their solution with no explanation of how they got it. (Communication of Reasoning)

- "The diagrams used are only repeating what is drawn for them. They do not even continue it out showing the pattern developing further. They do state that 'each time you add an extra paper you use one less tack from the time before' which indicates that they saw a pattern. However, if they had carried this conjecture out further they probably would have realized that it doesn't work the way they stated it. (Conceptual Understanding and Processes/Strategies)

- "There is no indication what strategy they used to arrive at their solution. It is never stated what configuration they used for the 100 sheets of paper and therefore there is no evidence that their solution makes sense (even though their answer is close to the correct solution) since we cannot see what they did. (Processes/Strategies and Accuracy/Reasonableness)" (pp. 16)

Student Response 2

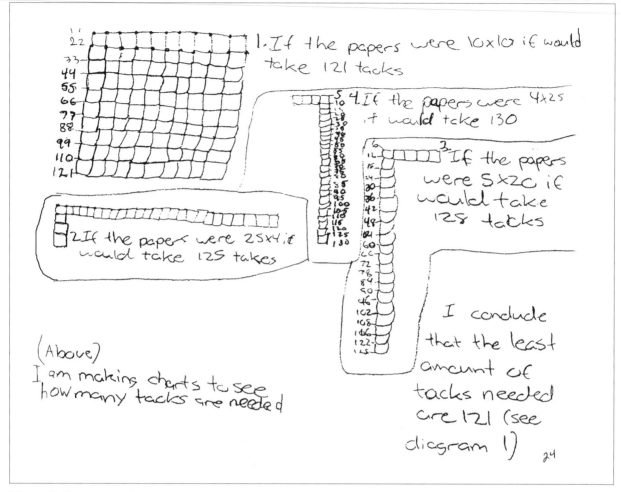

Figure B-6

"Comments on student's response to problem:

- "The student showed their first diagram in full labeling the number of tacks needed for each row. After that they just showed one row or column but still showed the number of tacks necessary. It was clear what they were doing and was easy to follow. (Communication of Reasoning)

- "The student showed several possible rectangular paper configurations using 100 papers. (Conceptual Understanding)

- "In the diagrams, they consecutively add up the number of tacks needed in each row and show the total number of necessary tacks for each solution. (Processes/Strategies)

- "The student explains that the charts shown are being used to see how many tacks are necessary and then summarizes the results by choosing the answer with the least number of tacks. Each solution shown has the correct number of tacks that would be necessary to make the particular configuration. A verbal recognition that the square shape leads to the fewest tacks would show a generalization of this problem. (Accuracy/Reasonableness)" (p. 23)

Assessment Sample 3:
Setting up a Tropical Fish Tank*—Selected Response and Essay

Intended Grade Level: Grade 5

Description

The following lesson/assessment is about how to set up an aquarium. The lesson has two parts. In part one the students read an information sheet and then observe the instructor actually setting up a new tank. In part 2, students work in small groups to actually set up a tank using the directions provided by the instructor. We have attached the information sheet, a set of test specifications to guide the development of a test, and the test the instructor developed to assess learning.

Setting up a Tropical Fish Tank-Information Sheet

Have you ever thought of setting up a fish tank as a hobby? It's fun and easy to do. To get started, you need seven things: a tank, some gravel, a pump, an underwater filter, a light, a heater, and water. Of course, you also need a place to put the tank and a place to plug in the heater, pump, and light. That's it. You don't need fish. They come later. Don't be in a hurry to put fish into a new tank. If you rush things, you'll kill them.

Don't buy any tank smaller than 20 gallons. Bigger is better. A 10-gallon tank will only hold a very few small fish. Figure out where you want the tank before you set it up; it's tough to move later. You don't have to buy a special stand, but make sure that whatever you set the tank on will hold plenty of weight. A 20-gallon tank filled with water weighs well over 150 pounds. Put the tank somewhere away from light. Even small amounts of natural light encourage the growth of algae which, though actually beneficial to some fish, will also cloud the water and turn it an unattractive murky green.

When you have your tank where you want it, install the filter. This needs to go in before anything else. Do not plug anything in yet, however. Next add the gravel. You need 10 pounds for every 10 gallons of water in the tank. You don't need to rinse or clean gravel from a pet store; it's ready to go.

Once the gravel is in place, add the water. Use clear water from your tap. It's a good idea to add dechlorinator to neutralize any chemicals in the water before adding fish. Dechlorinator is available from any pet shop. Fill the tank close to the top, remembering that you will need to add the heater.

Next, hook up the heater and set it to 80 degrees. Make sure it's well submerged in the tank. Most heaters are fully submersible, cord and all. Be careful not to set the temperature too high; not all fish can stand water temperatures of 90 degrees or more.

Now, turn on the light, admire how nice everything looks, and plug in the pump to start your filter system. Keep in mind that the pump forces air through the system. As you turn it up you add more air to the water. You also move the water around more. Some species of fish do well with all that commotion but others do not, so keep this in mind later when you choose your fish.

Finally, let the tank "cure" for five to ten days-or even more, if you can stand the wait. This allows for establishment of healthful bacteria to deal with pollution in the tank. When you're finally ready to add the fish, add just a few-perhaps one (or two at most) for every five gallons until you are sure the bacteria are sufficiently well established to keep your fish alive.

*This assessment is fictitious but based on several real classroom assessments.

Test Specifications Chart (Blueprint)

Content	Knowledge	Analysis	Inference	Evaluation
Setting up a new fish tank	4	2	6	1

Unit Test

Multiple Choice

1. About how much gravel is needed in a new tank?

    a. About 10 pounds.
    b. *About 10 pounds for every 10 gallons of water.
    c. It depends on the size of the tank.
    d. About 1,000 pounds.

2. Of the seven basic items you need to start up a new fish tank, which of the following is not one of them?

    a. *Fish.
    b. Gravel.
    c. A filter.
    d. All of the above.

3. The first step in setting up a new fish tank is to

    a. Buy a fish.
    b. Buy the tank.
    c. *Put the tank where you want it.
    d. Put in the water.

4. The main purpose of dechlorinator is to

    a. To kill algae in the water.
    b. Encourages the growth of beneficial bacteria.
    c. It cleans the gravel.
    d. *Make the water safe for the fish.

5. If you add fish to a new tank too soon, which of the following undesirable results will occur?

    a. The fish will get sick.
    b. *The fish will die.
    c. The fish will grow rapidly.
    d. Healthful bacteria will begin to grow.

6. The main purpose of the air pump is to

    a. *Pump air into the water.
    b. Empty water from the tank.
    c. Keep the fish moving at a fast pace.
    d. Stir up the water so it will look cloudy.

7. It would probably be a good idea to set up a new fish tank
    a. Near a window.
    b. On a small bookcase
    c. *Slowly, taking your time.
    d. Close to an electrical outlet.

                                                    *Correct answer

True/False

8. It is a good idea to not put a new fish tank too far away from natural light.   True   False

9. Natural light can stimulate the growth of algae, thus killing some fish.   True   False

Fill in

10. You should set the temperature in your tank at _____ _____

11. After your fish tank has cured for _____ weeks, add _____ fish for every
     _____ gallons of _____

Matching

12. Match items on the left with those on the right. Use each item on the right once or more
     than once.

a. Pump   _____ 1.   Cleans the water
b. Filter   _____ 2.   Reduces pollution
c. Algae   _____ 3.   Adds air to water
d. Heater   _____ 4.   Dangerous to fish
e. Bacteria   _____ 5.   Turns water murky
f. Filter   _____ 6.   Harmful to fish
g. Dechlorinator   _____ 8.   90 degrees
h. Pollution   _____ 9.   80 degrees
i. Light   _____ 10. Don't add too soon
j. Gravel   _____ 11. Helpful to fish
                      _____ 12. Kills fish
                      _____ 13. Add last
                      _____ 14. Add first
                      _____ 15. Causes algae
                      _____ 16. Ready to go
                      _____ 17. Helps show off fish attractively

Essay

13. Choose one of the following and write a one-paragraph answer (30 minutes, 50 points).

    a. Explain why it is important not to add new fish to your tank too soon.

    b. Do you agree or disagree that setting up a new fish tank is a simple process?
        Explain your reasons.

Assessment Sample 4:
Exhibition of Mastery*—Performance Assessment

Intended Grade Levels: Grades 8-9

Description

The following assessment is given at the end of middle school social studies courses to document competence in the skills listed. Students write a paper and give an oral presentation. A group of teachers rate the research paper. Presented here are the exit outcomes, a description of the research project, and a rubric that the raters use for the research paper. No information is provided on scoring the oral presentations.

Exit Outcomes

Skills and Habits of Mind	Content
• Research • Writing in a variety of modes • Analytical reading • Working cooperatively in a group setting • Working independently • Effective listening • Ability to speak publicly • Effective time management • Organization of materials, readings, etc. • Good study habits • Effective questioning • Group discussion	• The L.E.A.R.N.S. analytical model (Law/government, Economics, Arts, Research, News/current events, Science/technology) • Analytical thinking • Cause and effect thinking • Inferential thinking • Deductive thinking • Evaluative thinking • The origins of western civilization
Attitudes/Dispositions	**Essential Questions**
• Good citizen • Respectful • Open minded • Curious • Reflective • Persevering • Lifelong learner • Positive academic self-concept	• How does change occur? • What does "human rights" mean? • Where do governments come from? • Where do economic systems come from?

Description of the Research Project

Students will pick a topic, write a research paper at least 10 pages long (and with 10 references), and give an oral presentation at least three minutes long.

*This assessment is fictitious but based on two real classroom assessments.

Rubric for Research Report

Criteria:

Neatness, spelling, punctuation, grammar, capitalization, understanding.

Rubric:

Distinguished—Writing shows creativity in theme and development. It is correct in all mechanics.

Proficient—Writing correctly uses information and supportive details. Few errors in mechanics are apparent.

Apprentice—Writing does not have a theme and/or few supportive details. Errors in mechanics are common.

Novice—Research report is begun but not concluded. Writing shows lack of understanding. Contains several errors in mechanics.

Assessment Sample 5: Emerson Test[1]—Essay

Intended Grade Level: Grades 10-12

Description

This test is intended to assess mastery of content knowledge (knowledge of Emerson) and reasoning skills. The test consists of predicting Emerson's stand on various issues and citing evidence from various sources to support the prediction. This was practiced during class using statements different from those on the test. The author teaches and assesses Emerson in this fashion because he has found that students have trouble understanding Emerson and relating what he says to their own lives.

Students get one point for the right answer to each of the statements in the test and one point for their rationale. However, the author notes that even if a student doesn't provide the "right" answer as denoted in the scoring key, he will still give credit if the rationale for the answer is compelling. Results are used as 10 percent of the final grade in a literature class.

The Test

"Read each of the statements below and put a check if Emerson would most likely complete the activity or put an X if he would disagree or not do the listed activity. For each answer, find a statement from Emerson's work to support your check or X. Be sure to quote the statement directly and give the page number in parentheses. Use the introduction to Emerson, *Nature*, and 'Self Reliance.' Emerson would:

1. _____ reject organized religion.
2. _____ look to the past for guidance.
3. _____ claim that religious truth comes from intuition.
4. _____ rely on others for his success and happiness.
5. _____ join a popular civic organization.
6. _____ take solitary walks in the woods.
7. _____ dress in the most popular style of the day.
8. _____ speak boldly his opinions and thoughts.
9. _____ attend a seminar, 'How to Get Ahead and Reach Financial Success.'
10. _____ ask advisors what to do with his career."

Assessment Sample 6: Interview[2]—Performance Assessment

Intended Grade Level: Grades 11-12

Description

The purpose of this assessment is to "simulate as closely as possible the job application and interview process." Each student prepares a cover letter, resume, job application, and

[1]From Thomas Mavor, Brother Martin High School, 4401 Elysian Fields Ave., New Orleans, LA 70122.
[2]From Anna Lipski, Grossmont High School, P.O. Box 1043, 1100 Murray Drive, La Mesa, CA 91944.

followup letter. Business people who have experience in the human resource field conduct mock interviews on the high school campus during the first-semester final examination period. A few weeks before the interview assessment, all materials listed, a rubric to use for evaluation, a map, and a schedule of interviews are mailed to the interviewers. Interviewers are given no training on using the rubric to score interviews or application letters.

Students are given a list of receptionist's duties, rubrics, application forms, instructions for the interview process, and an evaluation form for the class.

On the day of the interview, the library is converted in to the Human Resources Department of a large company complete with receptionist. Approximately 20 minutes is allotted for each interview. When the student's interview is over, the interviewer gives the student immediate feedback, including why the person would or would not be hired. All materials are then returned to the receptionist. The student then returns to the classroom to debrief with the teacher and write a thank-you note to the interviewer.

About this process, the author says,

> *I have taught a job application skill unit in my English class for several years. Before I began this assessment process, students were not as interested in preparing the documents. At that time we simply discussed the interview process and how to answer difficult questions; they did not participate in a job interview.*
>
> *Involving business people in the assessment and requiring each student to participate in a job interview has piqued the students' interest. They realize the documents they are preparing will be evaluated not only by me but also by their interviewer. Having the opportunity to interact with someone from the community who is knowledgeable about the hiring process makes the assessment more meaningful. . . .*
>
> *Student feedback about this assessment has been gratifying. Several students have said that it is one of the most valuable things they have learned in high school. . . . After completing this assessment students have more self-confidence and poise. . . . The community interviewers are impressed with the quality of the students' documents and their presentation of themselves during the interview. . . . Grossmont High School has had the honor of representing California [in a national interview competition] for the past three years. Two Grossmont students have been national winners . . .*

Achievement Targets

- Prepare error-free job application documents: cover letter, resume, application form, and followup letter.

- Take an employment screening test.

- Participate in a job interview: use good communication skills, answer questions appropriately, demonstrate self-confidence, and dress appropriately.

Rubric for Application Letter

Name_____

Period_____

Row_____

Letter includes applicant's

Street address			
City, State Zip			
Date written out			
Followed by 3 blank lines			
Full name of person to receive letter			
Title of person, if known			
Name of person, if known			
Name of company			
Address			
City, State Zip			
Followed by a double space			

Letter:

Opens with a strong, positive statement about applicant or his qualifications			
or			
Opens with a statement naming a person known by the addressee who advised the applicant of available position			
Highlights the best items from applicant's background which directly qualifies him for the job			
States why applicant wants to work for this organization			
Requests an interview			
Suggest how applicant will follow-up or where he can be reached to schedule an interview			
Includes a proper closing followed by a comma			
Closing followed by four hard returns			
Applicant's full real name is typed below closing			
Applicant signed letter in ink between the closing and his name			
Letter is one page			
Sentences and paragraphs are short and easy to read			
No misspelled words or grammar errors			
Printed on high-quality paper			

Figure B-7

Rubric for Resume

Name_____

Period_____

Row_____

Personal information has been included Name, address, phone number			
Objective is clear and well stated			
Education Name of schools and special training			
Courses relating to position sought			
GPA if helpful			
Work Experience Full name of each company			
City and state where company is located			
Job title			
Month and year you began employment			
Month and year you left			
Specific results (use action words)			
Specific accomplishments (use action words)			
Activities Clubs			
Offices you have held			
Sports you have played			
Honors and Awards Specific name of award and date			
Special Skills Keyboarding, operating specific computers, knowledge of various computer programs, operating specific machinery and equipment, bilingual			
References None listed on your resume			
Available upon request			
Resume is Typed in attractive format			
Correct in every detail			
Printed on quality paper			
Limited to one page			

Figure B-8

Part 3: Assessment Analyses

In this part of the appendix we have analyzed and "scored" each of the sample assessments in Part 2 using the rubrics provided in Part 1. Remember, there is no such thing as a "right" score, only a justifiable score. We have tried to justify each of our scores using language from the rubrics. (This process attempts to model good performance assessment practice in which rubrics are provided to describe quality work and scored samples are provided to illustrate the rubric.)

Analysis of Assessment Sample 1: Reading Rate-Performance Assessment

Intended Grade Level: Grade 3

> **Standard 1: Sound assessment arises from clear and appropriate achievement targets.** Has the developer clearly specified the achievement targets to be reflected in the exercises? Do these represent important learning outcomes?

Yes, the target is clearly stated as being reading rate. The developer even gives a specific target reading rate and the formula for determining rate—number of words read in a minute minus any words read incorrectly. It is stated, selective, and everyone would interpret the target the same.

However, we have some questions: Is reading rate the most important thing to assess in reading? Is it the only thing the teacher assesses in reading? Is it worth the time devoted to it? What about comprehension? The developer's assertion about the relationship between reading rate and comprehension is probably true, but one might read pretty fast in Spanish and not understand much. So, the developer may need to review her mix and relative emphasis of targets.

For an overall evaluation of how this teacher assesses reading, we would want to explore these followup questions.

Rating: We would give this assessment a "3-4" on the trait of clear and appropriate targets on a scale of 1-5, where 1 is low and 5 is high. Although this target is very clear, we have some questions about its importance (appropriateness). Does this target represent the best thinking in the field on what is important to accomplish with students in reading? Is it the only thing assessed? If the answers to these questions are "yes" then we'd raise our rating.

Standard 2a: A sound assessment serves a clearly articulated purpose. Did the author specify users and uses, and are these appropriate? Will this assessment help inform instruction?

Although the assessment developer didn't specifically list users and uses, it is easy to figure out. The intended purposes appear to be to (a) help the teacher continuously track student progress toward a well-defined target—110 words a minute, and (b) keep parents informed of the progress of their children about their ability to read grade-appropriate material. In this case, ability to read is measured by reading rate. The users and uses are focused and clear.

This assessment would give the teacher a good idea of reading rate that could be used to continuously monitor performance over time to determine if students were meeting the well-defined target. So, the teacher would get good information from this assessment (if the questions in previous sections were answered satisfactorily).

Rating: We would give this assessment a "5" on the trait of clear and appropriate users and uses on a scale of 1-5, where 1 is low and 5 is high.

Standard 2b: Student involvement. Is it clear how students might be involved in the assessment as a way to help them see and understand intended achievement targets, practice hitting those targets, see themselves growing in their achievement, and communicate with others about their success as learners?

The developer does not mention using the assessment in this way, but we can certainly see how it might be so used if students were to monitor their own rates, track their own progress over time, and describe that progress to their parents. We would like to ask the author if the assessment is used in this manner. If not, why not? Is it because there are other, more important skills that students are monitoring, or the author hasn't thought of it, or, the author doesn't think students are capable of self-monitoring?

An additional question for the author—Do students know the importance of rate? Do they know the target rate? The answers to these questions might imply "next steps" for this assessment.

Rating: We would give this assessment a "3" on the trait of student involvement on a scale of 1-5, where 1 is low and 5 is high—the potential is there, but we are not sure if the potential is realized or intended. This rating could be higher depending on the author's answers to the questions posed.

Standard 2c: A sound assessment communicates effectively for the intended users and uses. Is it clear how this assessment helps communication with others about student achievement? Will others understand the message?

The developer appears to have thought this out carefully. The developer has made it very clear what the target is and has set up procedures for continuous reporting to parents. The overall idea is sound.

However, is the graph, as given, the best way to communicate with parents? Will they understand it? Is it useful to have every student listed separately so that parents can compare their child to all others? Might the average for the class be more useful? Or, maybe the teacher could graph the percentage of students meeting the standard and the percent not meeting it. We would like to ask the author whether she has made sure parents understand and find useful the way reading rate is reported.

Rating: We would give this assessment a "4" on the trait of communication. We have questions about the format in which the information is presented to parents. If the author demonstrates that parents understand and appreciate this reporting format, we would raise our rating.

> **Standard 3: A sound assessment relies on an appropriate assessment method.** Is it clear why the developer of the assessment chose the method(s) used? Does the selection of that method make sense given the targets and purposes?

It is clear that the developer picked the best procedure for assessing reading rate—performance assessment. If one wants to see how fast students can read, the best way to tell is to have them read something and time it.

The developer has also provided a reasonable rationale for the method chosen. Our only question would be whether the formula for reading rate should be total read in one minute minus number of words read incorrectly. Are there other formulas? Other miscues that might be taken into account?

Rating: We would give this assessment a "4" on the trait of target-method match on a scale of 1-5, where 1 is low and 5 is high. Certainly to assess reading rate, timing students is the most appropriate method. Our only question would be about the formula used to calculate rate. If, indeed, the best thinking in the field says that this is the way to do it, then we would raise our score.

> **Standard 4: A sound assessment provides an appropriate sample of achievement.** Is it clear to you how the exercises (tasks, questions) included in the assessment under consideration cover the domain of achievement that falls within the target? Are all the important aspects of the target covered?

The reading rate activity described does not cover the domain of achievement implied by the target. It appears that the developer relies on a single one-minute sample of a single reading selection. Might the average rate over several minutes result in a more stable measure of rate? Might reading rate averaged across several different selections of various types result in a more valid measure? This assessment, as stated, might be one good measure of rate, which, when combined with others, might provide a stable estimate of overall reading rate.

Additionally, there is the lingering question about the role of reading rate in reading comprehension. If the real goal of the assessment is to provide an estimate of reading comprehension using reading rate as a surrogate measure, then the method and sample described is probably not enough to draw a conclusion.

To understand the issue, think about writing. There is a high degree of relationship between scores on a multiple-choice language arts test and scores on a writing sample. Thus, some would argue that the multiple-choice test is an adequate surrogate measure of ability to write. This is okay as long as the test doesn't become the curriculum. If the skills on the test become the only targets of instruction then the test is no longer an adequate surrogate for the larger domain of ability to write coherent prose. Likewise, if reading rate is to become the target of instruction (because that is what is assessed), then it might no longer be a good surrogate measure of reading comprehension. As mentioned before, if we know that our competence in reading Spanish is how fast we can read it, then we'll go for speed; but, that doesn't mean we understand what we read.

Remember, we're not saying that this *is* an issue with this assessment, only that it might be, so further scrutiny of the author's reading assessment methods is in order.

Rating: We would give this assessment a "1" on the trait of sampling on a scale of 1-5, where 1 is low and 5 is high.

> **Standard 5: A sound assessment avoids distortion of scores due to bias.** Are the exercises (tasks, questions) of high quality, given the assessment method used? Would all students have an equal opportunity to excel? When the assessment is constructed response (essay, performance assessment, or personal communication) are the performance criteria of high quality?

The task is certainly clear and aligns with the target. There are, however, several questions with respect to the task. First, how did the developer determine that the selection to be read was at the second- (or third-) grade level? If the determination of level of reading passage is off, then reading rate will be affected. If the selection is too easy, then reading rate might be too high; if the selection is too hard, then reading rate might be too low. We would like to ask the author how the books are selected.

Second, are the books selected appropriate for all students? Might knowledge of snow, for example, affect the likelihood of miscues? If so, might students from the South Pacific be at a disadvantage even if their reading rates were the same as students who do know about snow? We're not saying that this *is* a problem, just that there is no evidence that the assessment developer has asked this question. A solution might be to have several books, equivalent in difficulty, that are matched to students.

Now, on to the performance criteria (since this is a performance assessment). This assessment attempts to measure a fairly straightforward target, so long, extensive rubrics are not needed—simple target, simple rubric. The procedure for determining rate is certainly reasonable. However, we'd still like to do a little more research on the formula used to determine rate. Is total number of words read in one minute minus number of words read incorrectly the commonly accepted way to determine reading rate?

Finally, general thoughts about bias and distortion. The developer has not addressed possible sources of bias and distortion. Again, we're not saying that bias and distortion *is* a problem, just that we don't know—the assessment developer doesn't discuss it. For example, does she pick times of day that will let students do their best? Are students at ease when they do their assessment? If the developer were to tackle such issues directly, then we'd be much more assured that she has thought through some of these issues and taken them into account. We'd like to ask the author these questions.

Rating: We would give this assessment a "3" on the trait of bias and distortion on a scale of 1-5, where 1 is low and 5 is high. If we were to use this assessment, we would want to corroborate the developer's conclusion on the formula and reading level of books, and supplement the list of selections students can read.

Overall Judgment

There is definitely enough here to warrant use. The overall idea is good, the communication aspects are strong, the procedures are clear, and the potential for student involvement is great. We'd like to see more justification for the procedures used, more attention given to sampling, and more of an idea how this fits into a whole program for assessing reading. We'd give this assessment a "3-4" on a scale of 1-5, where 1 is weak and 5 is strong.

Analysis of Assessment Sample 2: Mathematics Problem Solving-Performance Assessment

Intended Grade Levels: Grades 4-12; Grade 8 reviewed

> **Standard 1: Sound assessment arises from clear and appropriate achievement targets.** Has the developer clearly specified the achievement targets to be reflected in the exercises? Do these represent important learning outcomes?

The authors have clearly specified the achievement target to be assessed and it is selective and easy to find. They note that the focus is math problem-solving and include rubrics for defining what they mean. The rubric is illustrated with samples of student work. So, the authors have attempted to clearly define the target. The authors made an attempt to describe how they determined that these traits define the essential dimensions of math problem-solving and reflect the best thinking in the field. The target to be assessed is important and worth the time devoted to it.

The authors acknowledge that a comprehensive assessment program would address other aspects of math performance than problem solving, and make it clear that this assessment just addresses the problem-solving portion. So, the authors have addressed an appropriate mix of targets.

There is evidence that teachers (and other users) can be taught to score student work in a consistent fashion; this is evidence that educators can more or less interpret the target the same.

We would want only to clarify or modify three things:

- Perhaps it would be worthwhile to gather other rubrics and descriptions of math problem solving to make sure that the rubric and statements of targets really do represent the best thinking in the field.

- The definition of *targets*, as defined in the rubric, is sometimes a little vague. For example, in the trait of "conceptual understanding," the main difference between a "5" and a "4" rating are the words "thorough" and "basic." What is the difference? Would teachers interpret them the same? Since this relates more to "Standard 5-

potential sources of bias and distortion," and "Standard 2b-student involvement," we'll take this into account in our rating there.

- The link to local standards. We would guess that there is a good link, but this has to be inferred from context.

Rating: We would give this one a "4-5" on clear targets on a scale of 1-5, where 1 is low and 5 is high. The targets are important and fairly clear.

> **Standard 2a: A sound assessment serves a clearly articulated purpose.** Did the author specify users and uses, and are these appropriate? Will this assessment help inform instruction?

The authors clearly articulate the purposes for both the large-scale assessment and the classroom assessment ideas presented. The large-scale assessment is to "provide a 'snap shot' picture of the problem solving skills of Everett students. Group data from this assessment inform us of program strengths and weaknesses; individual student data provide teachers with information for making instructional decisions. . . ." The purpose is to provide students and teachers with samples of quality work that can be used instructionally to teach the very skills also being assessed.

Users and uses are focused, there aren't too many. Additionally, the authors distinguish between the designs for large-scale assessment and classroom use. The authors appear aware of various users and uses and state why the focuses are as stated.

Rating: We would give this one a "5" on clear and appropriate uses and uses, on a scale of 1-5, where 1 is low and 5 is high. The users and uses are appropriate, varied, and clear.

> **Standard 2b: Student involvement.** Is it clear how students might be involved in the assessment as a way to help them see and understand intended achievement targets, practice hitting those targets, see themselves growing in their achievement, and communicate with others about their success as learners?

This is the real strength of this assessment. The purpose of the rubric is to help teachers use the assessment as a tool for learning in the classroom. The authors give several suggestions for using these materials in instruction, many of which involve students. The result of this use is clearly stated when the authors quote Grant Wiggins: "If you want students to do excellent work, they have to know what excellent work looks like." The authors describe procedures to help students understand the achievement targets they are to hit, practice hitting the target, and communicate effectively with others about their success.

The authors supply the rubric and samples of student work for use in the classroom. There is no assistance with helping students "see themselves growing in their achievement over time," but this could easily be added.

Rating: We would give this assessment a "5" on the trait of student involvement on a scale of 1-5, where 1 is low and 5 is high.

Standard 2c: A sound assessment communicates effectively for the intended users and uses. Is it clear how this assessment helps communication with others about student achievement? Will others understand the message?

Although there is no "evidence" that the message sender and receiver agree on the meaning of the achievement targets being communicated about, the whole goal of the rubric is to build this understanding on the part of students.

Rating: We would give this assessment a "4" on the trait of communication on a scale of 1-5, where 1 is low and 5 is high. A little more could profitably be said about the communication potential of the assessment.

Standard 3: A sound assessment relies on an appropriate assessment method. Is it clear why the developer of the assessment chose the method(s) used? Does the selection of that method make sense given the targets and purposes?

The assessment method matches the purpose and target. The authors are assessing reasoning, problem-solving, and communication in math. These are all assessed well with essay ("explain your thinking at each step and your answer(s)") and performance assessment (communicating in math is a skill).

Further, the authors provide a reasonable rationale for the method selected and have made judicious use of essay/performance assessment.

Finally, there is wonderful alignment between the targets to be addressed, instruction, and the actual assessment. The link illustrates exactly how to use large-scale performance assessment materials in the classroom to build the very skills also being assessed.

Rating: We would give this assessment a "5" on the trait of target-method match on a scale of 1-5, where 1 is low and 5 is high.

Standard 4: A sound assessment provides an appropriate sample of achievement. Is it clear to you how the exercises (tasks, questions) included in the assessment under consideration cover the domain of achievement that falls within the target? Are all the important aspects of the target covered?

The weakest element in the assessment, as described, is sampling. To decide on a good sample one needs to consider the breadth of the target, the coverage of the task(s), and the stakes attached to the results.

First, the large-scale assessment: It seems that students are only given one problem to solve. Since the single problem is small in scope, this is unlikely to adequately cover either the eighth-grade content to which problem-solving might be applied or the range of possible problem-solving strategies. This is true whether the results are being applied to a large group (to get a "snapshot" of skills) or to an individual student. Additionally, the stakes are moderately high—to provide a snapshot of problem-solving ability of the group, and to provide information to make instructional decisions about individual students. There is hardly enough information from a single problem to do either.

Second, the classroom assessment use of the materials: The implication in the materials is that students should be using the process, and the rubric, on a range of problems. However, the piece could be strengthened by a specific reference to sampling, and other things teachers could/should do to ensure adequate sampling for decision making.

Finally, only having a single set of samples to illustrate quality is bothersome. If students only see models of quality based on a single problem, they are not likely to be able to generalize to a broad array of other problems. And, they might think that the way shown in the single problem is the only acceptable way to solve a problem. This restricts students' vision of the real target. Students should have the opportunity to critique lots of examples of problem solving that cover a variety of content and problem-solving strategies.

On further questioning, it might well be the case that all these considerations are taken into account. But, anyone other than the developers using this document might well fall into the sampling trap.

Rating: Based on the document, we would give this assessment a "1" on the trait of sampling on a scale of 1-5, where 1 is low and 5 is high.

> **Standard 5: A sound assessment avoids distortion of scores due to bias.** Are the exercises (tasks, questions) of high quality, given the assessment method used? Would all students have an equal opportunity to excel? When the assessment is constructed response (essay, performance assessment, or personal communication) are the performance criteria of high quality?

The single task that is provided as an example is fairly clear, although the sentence, "Explain your thinking at each step and your answer(s)," might be confusing. First, the wording is awkward. Second, students might not be clear that the manner in which they communicate their thinking is important. Actually having the rubric in hand while solving the problem helps make the task clearer. And, indeed, that is what the authors suggest.

The rubric might be fine tuned. Although the four dimensions, or traits, represented in the rubric are fairly common, the detail provided to describe score levels is sometimes vague. For example, a "5" in "communication" includes "Explains thinking deeply." A "4" is "Explains basic thinking." A "3" is "Explains some of thinking." A "2" is "Attempts to explain thinking." This raises some questions. For example, what exactly is the difference between "explains some of thinking" and "attempts to explain thinking"? Also when is explanation of thinking deep enough to warrant a "5?" What does "explains basic thinking" mean? There are similar questions with many of the other descriptors in the rubric.

The problem is not necessarily that teachers (or other raters) might not agree on the ratings. (After all, the document cites that teachers can be trained to be very consistent in their scoring.) The real issue is whether students will understand what it means and what to do about it.

We prefer rubrics that have descriptive detail over those that rely on vague comparative terms. For example, here are some statements that might help clarify the idea of "explains thinking deeply": the writer anticipated the information needs of the reader; mathematical representations helped clarify the solution; and, the format used for communication was effective and fit the problem. Similarly, instead of saying "attempts to explain thinking," one might use these descriptive phrases: the writer did not seem to have a sense of what the reader needed to know; the writer did not pick and choose what to write; and, the mathematical representations did not help clarify meaning, and even served to confuse meaning.

The only issue of bias and distortion the authors describe is rater bias. While important, there are other things that could potentially result in a distorted picture of student ability to solve problems. For example, if students couldn't write well in English, they might not be adequately able to explain their thinking. An oral interview would be better.

Rating: We would give this assessment a "3-4" on the trait of bias and distortion on a scale of 1-5, where 1 is low and 5 is high.

Overall Judgment

This assessment procedure has many strengths. The major things that could be fine tuned relate to sampling and the wording in the rubric. We would give it a "4" on a scale of 1-5 where 1 is low and 5 is high.

Analysis of Assessment Sample 3: Setting up a Tropical Fish Tank-Selected Response and Essay

Intended Grade Levels: Grade 5

> **Standard 1: Sound assessment arises from clear and appropriate achievement targets.** Has the developer clearly specified the achievement targets to be reflected in the exercises? Do these represent important learning outcomes?

This assessment has several strong features relating to targets. The developer has attempted to delineate test specifications. This helps to clarify the learning targets the developer intends for this assessment. The targets are stated, selective, and easy to find. Further, there is a mix of target and a conscious attempt to assess more than recall of facts.

We have several questions, however, relating to the importance and clarity of the target: Are the targets worth the instructional time devoted to them? Would teachers interpret them the same? How do they relate to district/state content standards? Do they represent best thinking in the field? How do they relate to the teacher's overall learning plan for the year? Does the blueprint offer a good testing plan, given the content of the lesson?

Rating: This assessment represents a balance of strengths and weaknesses on the trait of targets, therefore we would give it a "3" on a scale of 1 to 5, where 1 is low and 5 is high. This rating might be raised depending on the answers to the questions listed.

> **Standard 2a: A sound assessment serves a clearly articulated purpose.** Did the author specify users and uses, and are these appropriate? Will this assessment help inform instruction?

The author did not specify users and uses. It is not clear why the assessment is being given. It is not clear how the assessment would inform future instruction. We would want to ask the developer several questions to clarify what was intended: Why is this assessment being given? How will the results be used?

Rating: As presented, we would give this assessment a "1" on the trait of users/uses on a scale of 1-5, where 1 is low and 5 is high.

> **Standard 2b: Student involvement.** Is it clear how students might be involved in the assessment as a way to help them see and understand intended achievement targets, practice hitting those targets, see themselves growing in their achievement, and communicate with others about their success as learners?

The assessment developer did not indicate any student involvement. We would want to ask the developer several questions. It might be okay that students are not involved, depending on the use and the pattern of student involvement on other assessments.

Rating: As presented, we would give this assessment a "1" on the trait of student involvement on a scale of 1-5, where 1 is low and 5 is high.

> **Standard 2c: A sound assessment communicates effectively for the intended users and uses.** Is it clear how this assessment helps communication with others about student achievement? Will others understand the message?

The author has specified no plans for communication. We would want to ask several questions: Who are the users and uses? How will information be communicated to these users? It might be that there is no need for a formal plan, but we don't know.

Rating: As presented, we would rate this assessment a "1" on the trait of communication on a scale of 1-5, where 1 is low and 5 is high.

> **Standard 3: A sound assessment relies on an appropriate assessment method.** Is it clear why the developer of the assessment chose the method(s) used? Does the selection of that method make sense given the targets and purposes?

Target-method match is one of the strengths of this assessment. The focus is on knowledge and reasoning. Selected response and essay formats are good matches for this type of learning target. Further there is a mix of methods. However, the actual test questions don't represent the intended breakdown in the table of specifications.

Another strength is the apparent plan to assess student knowledge of how to set up a fish tank before actually asking students to do it. This indicates that the developer thought through a sequence of instructional tasks and assessments and how they relate. There is, however, no attempt to actually assess the extent to which students actually *do* adequately set up a fish tank. This gets back to the clarity and importance of the targets being assessed. It probably isn't worth the time to do a performance assessment on how well students actually can set up an aquarium. Therefore, why is this task being done at all? Are there other important learning targets being addressed: group skills, for example? If there are other important targets, why aren't they listed?

Rating: There is a balance of strengths and weaknesses, so we would give this assessment a "3-4" on the trait of target-method match on a scale of 1-5, where 1 is low and 5 is high. The score might be modified depending on responses to clarifying questions regarding the learning targets being emphasized.

> **Standard 4: A sound assessment provides an appropriate sample of achievement.** Is it clear to you how the exercises (tasks, questions) included in the assessment under consideration cover the domain of achievement that falls within the target? Are all the important aspects of the target covered?

This assessment probably does test the knowledge and understanding of students on how to set up a fish tank. That's the strength of selected response—you can assess a lot of material in an efficient manner.

Rating: We would give the assessment a "5" on the trait of sampling on a scale of 1-5, where 1 is low and 5 is high.

> **Standard 5: A sound assessment avoids distortion of scores due to bias.** Are the exercises (tasks, questions) of high quality, given the assessment method used? Would all students have an equal opportunity to excel? When the assessment is constructed response (essay, performance assessment, or personal communication) are the performance criteria of high quality?

Many of the test questions don't adhere to standards of quality for selected response and essay formats. For example, in question 4, at least two responses are ruled out due to grammar. The answer to question 6 is given away because of the repetition of words from the question in the right answer. In 8, the use of a negative makes the question harder to answer.

In question 10, the intended answer is 80 degrees, but this may be very unclear. Does the author mean for the student to write "80 degrees" in the two spaces?

In question 11, there are too many blanks. Students could fill in lots of things and be correct. For example, "After your fish tank has cured for more than a week, add a few healthy fish for every 10-20 gallons of liquid." These answers are not wrong but probably are not what the author is expecting.

In the matching section, there are several problems. Some options have more than one correct answer. For example, the filter (b) cleans the water (1), reduces pollution (2), helps fish (11) and goes in first (14). Some options are confusing. For example "ready to go" probably refers to the gravel because the lesson text uses these very words. But it's hard to be sure; lots of other things on the left hand list also come "ready to go." This list of options is very, very long. Who can sort through this much information effectively?

In question 13, the student is told to spend about 30 minutes and is also told that the essay is worth 50 points. This raises some immediate questions: 50 points out of what total? 30 minutes out of what total time? Also, the student is told specifically to write one paragraph, so 30 minutes seems excessive. Further, options 1 and 2 are not equivalent. Option 1 can be answered in a statement or two. Option 2 requires a more detailed response. Also, the nature of the task is different. One calls for a simple response based mainly on inference. The other calls for a detailed evaluation based on extensive information and application of good judgment. Not only is the second task more difficult, it is likely to require a much longer, more complex response than the first.

Rating: Because of the numerous technical glitches in the questions, we would give this assessment a "2" on the trait of bias and distortion on a scale of 1-5, where 1 is low and 5 is high. It doesn't get a "1" because it is clear to see how the glitches might be fixed.

Overall Judgment

The weaknesses outweigh the strengths in this assessment, but there *are* some strengths—a table of specifications, and good target-method match, for example. The biggest problems relate to importance of targets. We'd give it a "2" on a scale of 1-5, where 1 is low and 5 is high.

Analysis of Assessment Sample 4: Exhibition of Mastery-Performance Assessment

Intended Grade Levels: Grades 8-9

> **Standard 1: Sound assessment arises from clear and appropriate achievement targets.** Has the developer clearly specified the achievement targets to be reflected in the exercises? Do these represent important learning outcomes?

The author has listed targets and they are easy to find. The targets seem to be important and worth the assessment time devoted to them. There is an appropriate mix of targets. There is some evidence of long-term thinking—the overall big picture of the skills, knowledge, and dispositions to be developed in students. However, the statement of targets has some serious problems:

- Targets tend to be very general and vague. Educators are likely to interpret the targets differently. For example, what does "good study habits" entail? Or "group discussion?"

- Everything is listed. Granted, this is a culminating activity, intended to assess overall student mastery of the skills outlined in the social studies curriculum for grade 8 or 9, but, on first glance, it appears that it's going to be challenging to fit them all into a single assessment. Plus, the fact that it's a culminating activity has to be inferred from its title, "Exhibition of Mastery."

- There is no effort to relate targets to local content standards. We have inferred that they are related based on other statements in the assessment ("Exit Outcomes" is the title for the targets).

- The assessment itself doesn't really help to clear up the nature of the targets. For example, the rubric provided only helps define a very small part of the targets listed.

Rating: We would give this one a "2" on clear and appropriate targets on a scale of 1-5, where 1 is low and 5 is high. The targets are important, but are not well defined. Additionally, there are so many listed that it is difficult to see how they can all be assessed in the context of a single assessment. Perhaps the task really does require all these skills, but that is different from actually *assessing* them.

> **Standard 2a: A sound assessment serves a clearly articulated purpose.** Did the author specify users and uses, and are these appropriate? Will this assessment help inform instruction?

The author states the purpose of the assessment—to document competence. But, there is no real statement of how the results will be used and who will use them. Will this result in a grade? A judgment of overall mastery? Is this a barrier exam—do students have to do well to progress to the next grade? Is this purely for information—teachers might use it to plan instruction and parents might use it to judge the progress of their children? We simply don't know.

Rating: We would give this one a "2" on clear and appropriate users and uses on a scale of 1-5, where 1 is low and 5 is high. The users and uses simply are unclear.

> **Standard 2b: Student involvement.** Is it clear how students might be involved in the assessment as a way to help them see and understand intended achievement targets, practice hitting those targets, see themselves growing in their achievement, and communicate with others about their success as learners?

There is no student involvement and no acknowledgment that student involvement might be a desirable thing. There is no evidence that students understand the targets nor are involved in self-assessment, tracking progress, or communicating about learning. This is especially problematic because this is intended to be a "culminating activity."

Rating: We would give this assessment a "1" on the trait of student involvement on a scale of 1-5, where 1 is low and 5 is high.

> **Standard 2c: A sound assessment communicates effectively for the intended users and uses.** Is it clear how this assessment helps communication with others about student achievement? Will others understand the message?

The author has not considered communication at all. There is a rubric for one of the products in the assessment, but other than to assess the quality of the research report, we don't know how it might or might not be used to communicate achievement. Further, the rubric provided is incomplete—it is hard to see how communicating with this rubric would help. Finally, the author doesn't provide any mechanism for reporting on any of the other targets listed.

Rating: We would give this assessment a "1" on the trait of communication on a scale of 1-5, where 1 is low and 5 is high.

> **Standard 3: A sound assessment relies on an appropriate assessment method.**
> Is it clear why the developer of the assessment chose the method(s) used? Does the selection of that method make sense given the targets and purposes?

The complex nature of the targets require a complex assessment, as outlined. So, some sort of performance assessment is in order. But, this is outweighed by several major problems:

1. There is no stated rationale for the method used.

2. There are many missed opportunities here. There might be occasions during the research and preparation for this exhibition during which many of the listed exit outcomes can be assessed. For example, if students are working together, the teacher might assess "respectful," "working cooperatively in a group setting," "effective listening," and "group discussion" during one or more work sessions. Or, students could continually self-assess their own progress. (But, where are the rubrics for these?)

3. Similar to item 1, we are nervous that the author is not adequately assessing the prerequisites needed to do well on this task. There is an overreliance on assessing the higher-level skills, without consideration of prerequisites. For example, if the student does poorly on the exhibition is it due to poor writing skills? Or is it due to the student's inability to apply the proper analytical and comparative reasoning? Or, is it due to nervousness at speaking in front of a group? Assessing prerequisites could involve a series of simpler assessments and would make interpretation of the results of the exhibition assessment much easier.

4. Many targets aren't assessed at all. How does this assessment, for example, get at the targets listed under "Essential Questions?" Is application of this knowledge an important part of the task? If so, where? If it is an important part of the task, where are the rubrics to judge application of this knowledge in the context of this task? Performance assessments require both tasks and criteria.

5. There are a lot of eggs in this one basket.

Rating: We would give this assessment a "1-2" on the trait of target-method match on a scale of 1-5, where 1 is low and 5 is high.

> **Standard 4: A sound assessment provides an appropriate sample of achievement.** Is it clear to you how the exercises (tasks, questions) included in the assessment under consideration cover the domain of achievement that falls within the target? Are all the important aspects of the target covered?

We are very nervous about the sampling here. The assessment aims at very broad targets and the stakes are, seemingly, high. This requires careful sampling to ensure that inferences about student capabilities are accurate. Granted, the task is complex and requires application of lots of skills; it does cover a lot of ground. But it's still one shot, sink or swim.

We would feel better if we knew the students had practice opportunities before the "real" exhibition, and if they had, embedded into instruction all year, opportunities to demonstrate prerequisite skills. We might presume this is true, but we really don't know.

Also some of the targets don't seem to be covered very well even by the broad task outlined in the assessment, especially "Attitudes/Dispositions," "Essential Questions," and group skills.

Finally, the author does not seem to be aware that sampling is a consideration.

Rating: We would give this assessment a "1-2" on the trait of sampling on a scale of 1-5, where 1 is low and 5 is high, mostly because of these unanswered questions.

> **Standard 5: A sound assessment avoids distortion of scores due to bias.** Are the exercises (tasks, questions) of high quality, given the assessment method used? Would all students have an equal opportunity to excel? When the assessment is constructed response (essay, performance assessment, or personal communication) are the performance criteria of high quality?

It is only partially clear what each student is to do—the tasks are only partially explained. Since this is such a big task, there are lots of opportunities for lack of clarity.

The author doesn't address issues of bias and distortion at all. In fact, the author doesn't seem aware that it is important to consider such issues. Is this an equally appropriate task for a diverse group of students? Are the reading, writing and presentation requirements equally appropriate? Might there be some features of the task that will mask students' true ability? For example, the major products are a written report and an oral presentation. Those are legitimate targets in and of themselves, but having to write and present such a long piece might mask student ability to read, understand, and reason. The opportunity to present research orally, one on one with the teacher, might be a more valid way to assess reading, understanding, and reasoning for some students. Then students' ability to write about their knowledge could be assessed separately. This would enable the teacher to better tease apart the strengths and needs of each student.

Is the task developmentally appropriate for middle school students? Has the needed instruction, and learning, occurred that puts in place prerequisite skills? Or, is this too much to ask of middle school students?

But, the rubric and criteria are the real problem here. Does the author really believe that all of the student effort put into the task, and all the "exit outcomes" listed, are adequately reflected in the rubric?

Rating: We would give this assessment a "1" on the trait of bias and distortion on a scale of 1-5, where 1 is low and 5 is high.

Overall Judgment

This assessment is weak. It would require a lot of work to make it usable. It would be better to look elsewhere. We would give it an overall rating of "1" on a scale of 1-5, where 1 is low and 5 is high.

Analysis of Assessment Sample 5: Emerson Test-Essay

Intended Grade Levels: Grades 10-12

> **Standard 1: Sound assessment arises from clear and appropriate achievement targets.** Has the developer clearly specified the achievement targets to be reflected in the exercises? Do these represent important learning outcomes?

The developer has stated that the targets are knowledge of Emerson and reasoning skills. These are selective, easy to find, important, and a good mix. We would have the following questions for the developer: How do these targets relate to local content standards? How is reasoning defined? Is reasoning developed through different activities as the course progresses?

Rating: This assessment is definitely strong. We would give it a "4" on a scale of 1-5, where 1 is low and 5 is high. This rating might go up depending on the author's responses to the questions posed.

> **Standard 2a: A sound assessment serves a clearly articulated purpose.** Did the author specify users and uses, and are these appropriate? Will this assessment help inform instruction?

The purpose is clearly stated—summary assessment. The users and uses are therefore implied to be the author and the student. The users and uses are focused and it is clear how results might inform future instruction. We would have the following questions for the author: Do students understand the results? Are the results actually used to reflect on instruction?

Rating: Again, this assessment is strong on the trait of users/uses. Descriptors under "fast-tracked" seem to apply best, although some information needs to be inferred. We'd give it a "4-5" on a scale of 1-5, where 1 is low and 5 is high.

> **Standard 2b: Student involvement.** Is it clear how students might be involved in the assessment as a way to help them see and understand intended achievement targets, practice hitting those targets, see themselves growing in their achievement, and communicate with others about their success as learners?

We realize that not every single assessment needs to include student involvement, but there are some questions we'd like to ask the author: Do the students understand the type of reasoning they are to perform? Can they define it? Would it be profitable for students to track their reasoning progress over time and assignments? Do the students self-assess on reasoning? Do they understand why the Emerson Test is designed as it is?

Rating: We'd give this assessment a "3" on student involvement on a scale of 1-5, where 1 is low and 5 is high. Although student involvement is not specifically included, it is clear how such a component could be added.

> **Standard 2c: A sound assessment communicates effectively for the intended users and uses.** Is it clear how this assessment helps communication with others about student achievement? Will others understand the message?

The author does not directly discuss issues of communication, although the scoring and grading procedure is described and it is reasonable. We'd like to ask the author whether the students understand the meaning of the final test score.

Rating: This assessment seems to represent a balance of strengths and weaknesses on the trait of communication, therefore we'd give it a "3" on a scale of 1-5, where 1 is low and 5 is high.

> **Standard 3: A sound assessment relies on an appropriate assessment method.** Is it clear why the developer of the assessment chose the method(s) used? Does the selection of that method make sense given the targets and purposes?

The assessment method matches purpose and target, there is a rationale for the method(s) used, this is a clever use of essay, and there is a good match between the targets, instruction, and assessment.

Rating: We'd give this assessment a "5" on the trait of target-method match on a scale of 1-5, where 1 is low and 5 is high.

> **Standard 4: A sound assessment provides an appropriate sample of achievement.** Is it clear to you how the exercises (tasks, questions) included in the assessment under consideration cover the domain of achievement that falls within the target? Are all the important aspects of the target covered?

There are enough samples of student performance to get a stable estimate of achievement, and the sample matches the breadth of the target and importance of results.

Rating: Again, we would give this a "5" on a scale of 1-5, where 1 is low and 5 is high.

> **Standard 5: A sound assessment avoids distortion of scores due to bias.** Are the exercises (tasks, questions) of high quality, given the assessment method used? Would all students have an equal opportunity to excel? When the assessment is constructed response (essay, performance assessment, or personal communication) are the performance criteria of high quality?

It is clear what students are to do; in fact, they've practiced it. The tasks match the targets and they are feasible. We would ask the following questions: Might some students be able to reason adequately but score low because of their writing skills? Might the lack of criteria for reasoning be problematic?

Rating: the assessment is stronger than it is weak—we'd give it a "4" on a scale of 1-5, where 1 is low and 5 is high.

Overall Judgment

This assessment has many more strengths than weaknesses—we would give it a "4" on a scale of 1-5, where 1 is low and 5 is high.

Analysis of Assessment Sample 6: Interview—Performance Assessment

Intended Grade Levels: Grades 11-12

> **Standard 1: Sound assessment arises from clear and appropriate achievement targets.** Has the developer clearly specified the achievement targets to be reflected in the exercises? Do these represent important learning outcomes?

Mostly, yes. The author clearly identifies that she is trying to assess job application documents (products) and job interview skills (communication, self-confidence, and appropriate dress). The targets are selective and important, within the context of her course. There is an effort to define the targets through the use of performance criteria. The rubrics would assist students to understand the nature of the targets being assessed and add needed detail to make the targets clearer (although the rubrics could be improved—see the Standard 5 discussion).

The statement of targets could be refined a little. First, the developer tends to mix up tasks with targets. For example, under "Achievement Targets" the developer lists: "participate in a job interview" when she means "develop job interview skills."

In addition, it might be profitable to relate targets to local content standards so it is clear how this instance of assessing oral communication fits into a complete picture of student ability to communicate orally. This assessment represents only one audience and purpose for oral communication—not the range required in most oral communication standards. So, depending on the context, it may or may not be enough. For example, if you, as a teacher, were teaching a business class, or something having to do with school-to-work, this assessment would help you help students develop communication skills related to important content standards in the context of your class. This might then contribute to a cross-disciplinary collection of work that could be used to demonstrate mastery on communication standards in general. (Performance on this assessment only would not provide enough evidence to judge overall mastery of the communication standards; thus there might be a sampling problem—see Standard 4, Sampling.)

Rating: We would give this one a "4" on clear targets on a scale of 1-5, where 1 is low and 5 is high. The targets are important and rubrics are provided to make it clear what is meant. The statement of targets could stand one more draft.

Standard 2a: A sound assessment serves a clearly articulated purpose. Did the author specify users and uses, and are these appropriate? Will this assessment help inform instruction?

The author is fairly clear about users and uses, even though they have to be inferred from the text. The purpose of the assessment is to "simulate as closely as possible the job application and interview process" so that students will be more motivated to do a good job preparing interview materials. The implication is that students will learn more if they "realize the documents they are preparing will be evaluated not only by [the teacher] but also by their interviewer. Having the opportunity to interact with someone from the community who is knowledgeable about the hiring process makes the assessment more meaningful." These are essentially instructional and learning purposes.

The users and uses are also focused-there aren't too many. This implies that the author is aware that different users and uses might require different assessment designs. But, this has to be inferred.

Rating: We would give this one a "4" on clear and appropriate uses and uses, on a scale of 1-5, where 1 is low and 5 is high. The users and uses are appropriate, but must be inferred.

Standard 2b: Student involvement. Is it clear how students might be involved in the assessment as a way to help them see and understand intended achievement targets, practice hitting those targets, see themselves growing in their achievement, and communicate with others about their success as learners?

Even though the developer has not done so, it is easy to see how the assessment could be used to enhance student achievement through their involvement:

- One could ask students to "re-create" (or add to) the criteria for quality by looking at previous samples of student job applications and video clips of interviews.

- One could ask students to critique the job applications or video clip interviews of others.

- One could ask students to practice with feedback from the teacher and their peers.

- One could ask students to keep track of their performance over time and analyze how first attempts differ from current ones.

These procedures would help students see and understand the intended achievement targets, practice hitting the targets, and self-assess. They would probably also help students be more confident in the job interview and knowledgeably discuss the criteria by which they will be judged. In fact, the developer might already be doing this, but just didn't mention it.

Rating: We would give this assessment a "4" on the trait of student involvement on a scale of 1-5, where 1 is low and 5 is high. Although the author does not state such uses, they can be easily added. This rating would go up if the developer actually did these things.

> **Standard 2c: A sound assessment communicates effectively for the intended users and uses.** Is it clear how this assessment helps communication with others about student achievement? Will others understand the message?

The communication aspects of this assessment are strong. Students get immediate feedback and they have an opportunity to critique the experience. The performance criteria help extensively in this regard (although the process might be fine tuned using the suggestions in Standards 2b and 5).

Rating: We would give this assessment a "5" on the trait of communication on a scale of 1-5, where 1 is low and 5 is high. It is easy to find statements about communication, and these statements are on target.

> **Standard 3: A sound assessment relies on an appropriate assessment method.** Is it clear why the developer of the assessment chose the method(s) used? Does the selection of that method make sense given the targets and purposes?

Yes, the developer implies this clearly—to have a good assessment in this case, real life has to be simulated as closely as possible. This means that the assessment is not only performance based, but set in as realistic a context as possible by having real business people review real application materials and conduct mock interviews with students, and then discuss with the students whether they would have been hired. The only thing more realistic would be to participate in an actual job interview.

The targets specified for the assessment, the assessment tasks or exercises, and the scoring criteria used to evaluate performance all reflect the same thing-they are aligned.

Rating: We would give this assessment a "5" on the trait of target-method match on a scale of 1-5, where 1 is low and 5 is high.

> **Standard 4: A sound assessment provides an appropriate sample of achievement.** Is it clear to you how the exercises (tasks, questions) included in the assessment under consideration cover the domain of achievement that falls within the target? Are all the important aspects of the target covered?

Adequacy of sampling has to be determined in the context of the targets being assessed and the purpose for the assessment. For example, a job interview is only one small piece of the "various audiences and purposes" implied by most oral communication content standards. Therefore, if the purpose of the assessment is to demonstrate competence on communication standards in general, this assessment, although part of a bigger picture, is not enough.

However, since the course in which the assessment is embedded is business related, the domain is covered pretty well. Context is everything. (This issue was also addressed in Standard 1, Clear Targets.) In this case, the author is using oral communication in a very narrow sense. But, even in the narrower sense, one has to ask about sampling. Students only get one chance. There might have been something in the interaction with the particular interviewer, or how the student felt that day, etc., that caused the single performance not to represent their true ability to do a job interview.

Additionally, we would feel better if students had practice opportunities before the "real" interview. One sample of performance, sink or swim, might not accurately represent what a student can do.

Rating: We would give this assessment a "3" on the trait of sampling on a scale of 1-5, where 1 is low and 5 is high, mostly because of these unanswered questions.

> **Standard 5: A sound assessment avoids distortion of scores due to bias.** Are the exercises (tasks, questions) of high quality, given the assessment method used? Would all students have an equal opportunity to excel? When the assessment is constructed response (essay, performance assessment, or personal communication) are the performance criteria of high quality?

In general, we feel that if students had mastered the relevant content standards, they would be able to perform well on this assessment. A particular strength is the clarity of the task-it is clear what each person (student or interviewer) is to do.

However, the author doesn't directly address issues of bias and distortion, and there *might* be a few things that mask student ability. Examples: if the students have had no practice, nervousness might mask ability; there might be unconscious rater bias due to gender, ethnicity, cultural differences, or disabilities; raters aren't trained, so there is no assurance that two different interviewers watching the same interview would rate students the same.

The criteria need a bit of fine tuning. First, the criteria for the **application letter.** The list of things to be evaluated is a little daunting. Since many of the listed items seem to go together, one might want to group them into five general categories, or "traits":

1. *Content.* Does the letter cover what it needs to cover? Is the information accurate? Has the applicant done her homework? Does the letter cover the skills needed for the job? There are several items on the rubric that relate to content.

2. *Voice/style/flair/penetrability.* Is the letter written in such a way that the interviewer wants to read it? Does it have a professional, earnest, sincere voice? There is not much in the current rubric that relates to style.

3. *Organization.* Is the letter organized well? Currently there are no items in the developer's criteria that relate to organization. There is not much on the current rubric that relates to organization.

4. *Format/presentation.* Is this, in fact, a job application letter? Does it have the proper format, opening, etc.? The criteria, as listed, are very heavy on format. Is this the emphasis desired?

5. *Mechanics/conventions.* Is the letter free of spelling, capitalization, punctuation and grammar errors? Only one item in the current rubric relates to conventions. Might there also be other conventions to look for, such as paragraphing, capitalization, and punctuation?

Second, as written, it seems that the criteria for the trait of content might be limiting and might result in some good letters being called "bad." For example, the criteria only allow two possible openings for the letter—"opens with a strong, positive statement about applicant or his qualifications or opens with a statement naming a person known by the addressee who advised the applicant of available position." What if neither of these is appropriate for the particular job being applied for? Or what happens if the student comes up with a very catchy, yet highly appropriate, way to begin? Thus, the trait of "content" might need to be reworked.

Finally, will all raters agree on the score (1-3) for these traits? Is it possible that one person might think that, for example, the applicant has "highlighted the best items from the applicant's background which directly qualifies him or her for the job" while another person thinks the student has not? Because the intent is instructional, will students understand what to include?

Now for the criteria for the **business interview.** Again, these are a good start, but also could use a little work. First, the criteria for "letter of application and resume" include organization, conventions, and format, but do not include content or style (as do the criteria the teacher and students use). Also, the interviewer might be somewhat adrift on how to assign points. Do we care if the number of points the student gets depends on the interviewer?

All the unclear aspects noted would be helped by having samples of student letters (and maybe video clips of interviews) that illustrate the criteria. Maybe a panel of business folks could be persuaded to work together for a day to agree on some "anchors." This would be especially important if the assessment is to help students learn (perhaps even to understand the differences and vagaries among job classifications and interviewers).

Rating: We would give this assessment a "4" on the trait of bias and distortion on a scale of 1-5, where 1 is low and 5 is high. In general, this looks like an assessment that could be worked with to eliminate possible sources of bias and distortion.

Overall Judgment

Overall, with some fine tuning, this is a good assessment. The major revision would relate to the criteria. We would give it a "4-5" on a scale of 1-5 where 1 is low and 5 is high.

Appendix C

Self-Assessment Developmental Levels

Standard 1—
Clear and Appropriate Learning Targets

The Self-Assessment Developmental Levels are yet another way that you can track your own learning and growth as a classroom assessor. These Levels describe the levels of performance skill gone through by learners as they progress from beginners to skilled practitioners. You have the option of self-assessing using the Levels at the end of each Part of the textbook, *Student-Involved Classroom Assessment*, 3d ed. Your self-assessments using these Levels (and your self-reflection on your growth) would make good growth portfolio entries. There is a Self-Assessment Developmental Level for each of the Five Standards of Quality Classroom Assessment (Workbook Introduction, Figure 2). This once again reinforces the link between the learning targets we have for you, the instruction in the textbook and *Workbook*, and assessing your own progress.

Skilled

I know and can articulate the enduring skills and knowledge important for students to master. I am, myself, a master of the learning targets I teach. The following statements describe me:

- I know local definitions of such terms as *content standards*, *performance standards*, and *benchmarks* and I can provide examples. I can analyze content standards for their implied learning targets. I can relate content standards to classroom instruction and assessment.

- I can, without hesitating, answer the question, "What are your learning targets for students?"

- I can describe the five kinds of learning targets in the textbook *Student-Involved Classroom Assessment*, 3d ed., and regularly use this (or a similar scheme) to organize my instruction and assessments. I can list specific examples of each kind of target.

- I consider the targets of instruction before I develop a unit of instruction or assessments.

- My learning outcomes for students represent the best thinking in the field with regard to what students need to know and be able to do.

- I can provide thorough descriptive details about the student knowledge, skill or ability associated with each of my learning targets. For example, if the learning target is to become a fluent reader, I can define what a fluent reader knows and is able to do.

- I understand how the achievement targets in my own setting lay the foundation for students' success in later grades.

- I can explain to students, parents, and others, in terms they can understand, which learning targets I plan to achieve during instruction. I can spell it out so that students, parents, and others can accurately explain it back in their own words.

- I can describe the various levels of student development toward the learning target—for example, the stages of development in becoming a fluent reader or a strong math problem-solver. I can describe the appropriate level(s) for the grade I teach.

- I model the skills that students are to master. I am, myself, a confident master of the achievement targets students are to master.

- I can show specifically where during instruction each learning target is addressed and how a sequence of instructional activities develops the required knowledge and skills over time.

- I have students who can use precise and common terminology to describe the quality of their work, articulate the criteria for success, explain what I expect them to learn, and describe how the work they're doing is applicable to their lives.

- I have posted performance criteria for complex learning targets.

Practiced

I know what it takes to be a master of the targets of instruction, but I need help with the details. The following statements describe me:

- I can define in broad terms words like *content standard*, *performance standard*, and *benchmark*, and I sometimes have trouble identifying examples.

- I have tried to explain to students, parents, and others which learning targets they are to achieve in their instruction, but I am sometimes not entirely successful at the explanation.

- I link specific learning targets to instructional activities in general terms, but need to stop and think about specifically where in an instructional sequence I emphasize these various learning targets.

- I plan instruction by identifying activities that would be engaging for students and then I go back to identify which learning targets are emphasized.

- I can list features of a quality performance, but I need some assistance to distinguish levels of performance. For example, I can state that a piece of writing needs to have voice, but I need assistance to articulate what *strong* or *weak* voice looks like.

Aware

I know that it is important to be clear on student learning targets, and that it is important to have a good "mix" of learning targets, but I am not sure where to begin or what needs to be done. The following statements describe me:

- I need help to clearly state learning targets for students. I need to develop a better sense of when a learning target is "clear."

- I need help to relate goals for students to instructional activities.

- I need help to differentiate between goals for students and the instructional activities designed to achieve them.

- I need help to describe characteristics of strong performance on a learning target.

- I'm not always sure if my target statements can be easily understood by all of my students. Sometimes I can't see potential barriers to their understanding.

- I need help to distinguish between levels of quality (or levels of development), and identify those student words or actions that indicate level.

- I know I need clear criteria for student success; but I'm not sure that I have them.

- I know a good mix of learning targets is important, but I'm not sure I've achieved this.

Beginner

I am not sure what learning targets are. The following statements tend to describe me:

- I'm not sure I could define what a *learning target for students* is. I don't know various types of targets.

- I count on the textbook, or a series of prepackaged instructional materials, to define and address the important learning targets for students.

- I design instruction mostly on what I like to teach. I'm not sure how it relates to local content standards.

- I am not convinced that it is necessary to have clear learning targets.

- My students have difficulty self assessing, describing what quality work looks like, and explaining why they get the grades they do.

- I feel uncomfortable teaching certain subjects because I don't understand them myself.

- I don't understand the issue regarding cultural diversity and stating learning targets in terms all students can understand.

Standard 2—
Clear and Appropriate Users and Uses of Assessment

Skilled

I understand the various purposes (users and uses) of classroom assessment and successfully balance them. Several of the following describe me:

- I can describe uses of classroom assessment information other than grading and believe that these purposes are not only useful, but essential.

- I monitor student performance and adjust instruction accordingly.

- I sometimes gather assessment information just to help refine instruction.

- I can explain the important aspects of standards-based education/instruction and the role of day-to-day classroom assessment in this process.

- I plan assessments with the end user(s) in mind. For example, if feedback to parents on student status and progress is important, I design assessments (and reporting mechanisms) to communicate clearly to parents. If assessment materials are used with students as instructional tools, they are "student friendly."

- I consider the cultural differences of parents and students when planning communication about achievement.

- I can describe the impact assessment has on students and I know how to design assessments to involve students to improve motivation and maximize achievement. For example, I teach students to use rubrics, and/or involve students in student-led conferences.

- I recognize that instructional support staff and policy makers have legitimate needs for information and that the type of information they need might be different from the type I need in the classroom. I advocate balance between large-scale and classroom assessment.

Practiced

I know about the various users and uses of classroom assessment, and am experimenting. More than one of the following describes me:

- I know about many uses for assessment information other than grading and I'm attempting to implement some, but I'm not sure I completely understand these uses yet.

- I try to involve students in their own assessment, but I'm not totally successful yet.

- I generate assessment information to fine-tune instruction, but I need to do more.

- I generally know the important aspects of standards-based education, but I need to fill in some of the details.

- I try to plan assessments with the end user(s) in mind, but I'm only partially successful.

- I try to take cultural background of parents and students into consideration when planning communication about achievement, but I have only been partly successful.

Aware

I am aware of the need to have clear and appropriate users and uses for assessment, and I know that assessment is more than grading, but I need assistance in articulating my thoughts. The following actions and behaviors describe me:

- I want to use assessment information for more than grading, but I'm not sure how or what questions to ask of whom.

- I know that student involvement in their own assessment is important, but I don't know how to begin.

- I would like to make reporting about achievement more powerful, but I'm not sure how to go about it.

- I know that different users need different information, but it is unclear to me how needs differ.

- I know that cultural differences affect the ability to communicate effectively about achievement, but I'm not sure what to do about it.

Beginner

I have not yet considered various users and uses for assessment. The following statements describe me:

- I use assessment mostly for grading.

- I have not thought much about or analyzed my own information needs, nor those of students, parents, or others.

- I'm unsure that it makes sense to consider home language, culture, and so forth in planning communication about assessment. Why would their information needs be different?

- I'm not sure students have the ability to assess themselves, and I'm not convinced that self-assessment is useful. I have not considered involving students in developing assessments.

Standard 3—
Matching Methods to Targets and Users/Uses

Skilled

I understand the broad range of assessment options and when to use each. I use all types of assessment on a regular basis. The following statements describe me:

- I can describe various assessment methods (multiple choice, matching, short answer, essay, performance assessment, personal communication) and show examples.

- I can articulate when to use each assessment method—how to match methods to targets and purposes. The verbs in my student learning targets match the verbs in my assessment approach; for example, active verbs in an outcome imply performance assessment. I know how to balance an ideal choice of method against a practical choice of method.

- I use all types of assessment methods.

- I use test blueprints that indicate how each learning target will be assessed and its relative importance.

- I experiment with new methods to find better ways to assess.

- I use "prepackaged" assessments only when I'm sure they'll do the job for me.

Practiced

I am trying many different types of assessments, but I need to fine-tune what I am doing. The following statements describe me:

- I can list various assessment methods, but sometimes I have trouble defining them or identifying examples.

- I use various assessment methods, but sometimes I have difficulty explaining why.

- I sometimes feel afraid of using "traditional" assessment methods because of the recent focus on performance assessment.

Aware

I am aware of the need to match assessment methods to learning targets and purposes, and I have the desire to be more intentional about selecting assessment methods, but I'm not entirely sure what needs to be done or where to start. The following statements describe me:

- I have the nagging feeling that I should be using a variety of assessment methods, but I'm not sure what they are.

- I want to try more performance assessments, but I'm not sure how.

- I think I might already be using performance assessments, but I'm not sure.

- I think I might overuse one form of assessment, but I'm not sure.

Beginner

I'm not sure what is meant by matching targets to methods. The following statements describe me:

- I use mostly prepackaged assessments that come with instructional materials. I'm not sure what to look for to make sure these assessments match my learning targets for students.

- I tend to use the same assessment method all the time.

- My major consideration when selecting an assessment method is that tests are easy to correct.

- I concentrate on using assessment methods that match our standardized tests.

- I mostly use the methods used by other teachers; I'm not sure why.

Standards 4 and 5—
Sampling and Eliminating Potential Sources of Bias/Distortion

Skilled

I understand the importance of both sampling student performance well, and eliminating potential sources of bias and distortion in my assessments. I have skill in both these areas. The following statements describe me:

- I can define *sampling* and *bias and distortion* and describe why they are important to consider when designing classroom assessments.

- I can readily list and describe potential sources of bias and distortion in assessment.

- I can show examples of assessments with various problems and can describe which problems can be fixed and which have to be lived with.

- I have a feel for how many samples of performance are needed to draw reliable conclusions about student achievement.

- I seek out assessments that have certain features and avoid assessments with certain other features. For example, I seek portfolio systems that have clear and appropriate performance criteria and avoid portfolio systems with skimpy or no performance criteria.

- I can analyze existing assessments to identify linguistic and cultural barriers and can adjust and adapt these assessments to remove the barriers to accuracy.

- I modify my assessments if I don't get what I want from students.

- I plan for multiple assessments of complex targets and use a variety of assessments so that all of my students have opportunities to demonstrate their learning fully.

- I have modified assessments developed by others because of observed problems such as unclear instructions, obvious answers, wording that is too difficult, or features that might not allow each student to do their best.

- I have pilot-tested assessment questions to make sure they work. I discard questions that don't.

- I have asked others to critique my assessments.

Practiced

I have tried many of the things in the "skilled" category, but I need to fine-tune. The following statements tend to describe me:

- I can describe at least some of the most common potential sources of bias and distortion, but I don't always understand how to address these issues.

- I can identify potential problems in real assessments and I have tried to fix them, but I may not always know the best solution.

- I'm experimenting with alternative ways to assess the learning of students whose language, culture, or other characteristics differ from my own without losing vital information about the target, but I'm not sure if I'm doing it right.

- I don't use assessment results I know are biased, but I'm not sure what to do to compensate for the bias.

- I have tried to sample student performance, but I'm not sure I do it well.

Aware

I understand that sampling and bias and distortion can be a problem, and I want to improve my classroom assessments, but I'm not quite sure how to proceed. The following statements tend to describe me:

- I'm not sure I can define *sampling* and *bias and distortion*.

- I have noticed possible problems in some of the assessments I use, but I don't quite know what to do about them, or even if they are *real* problems. (I tend to think, "The assessment developers must know what he or she is doing; I'm probably wrong.")

- I am uncertain about how to prevent problems.

- I don't know what to look for to determine if sampling or bias and distortion are problems.

- I think there are some problems in prepackaged assessments, but I'm not sure what to do about it.

- I know that assessments can contain barriers that mask some students' learning, but I'm uncertain what to do about it.

Beginner

I know that such things as sampling and bias and distortion exist, but I don't quite see how this issue applies to me. The following statements tend to describe me:

- I think that sampling and bias and distortion are problems primarily with large-scale assessments.

- I use prepackaged assessments uncritically.

- What's *sampling*? What's *bias and distortion*?

- Why should assessing students from different cultural or linguistic backgrounds be any different than assessing any other student?

Appendix D

Universal Classroom Assessment
Course Description

Program Overview

Many participants in learning team based professional development on classroom assessment will be interested in receiving credit for completing this in-depth program of study. This generic course description details that program of study in a manner that will permit review and evaluation by higher education institutions considering this course for credit in their graduate programs.

There are two ways this description might come into play. The institution might initiate contact with its students and alumni to advise them that they can receive credit for completing this program by contacting the institution before they begin their studies. Alternatively, a teacher/graduate student might contact the college or university where they are studying to initiate credit arrangements. In either case, this description can facilitate the process.

Overall Course Goal

The _____ School District is providing resources for teachers and administrators to complete a program of professional development in classroom assessment. The professional development program seeks to build a deep and far-reaching understanding of the difference between sound and unsound classroom assessment, promoting the effective use of assessment as a teaching tool. The means selected to reach this goal include having educators study the textbook, *Student-Involved Classroom Assessment*, 3d ed., (2001) by Richard J. Stiggins of the Assessment Training Institute, Portland, Oregon, and work with its associated print and video training materials. (The text is published by Merrill/Prentice Hall Publishing; it and its associated learning materials may be obtained directly from the Assessment Training Institute, 1-800-480-3060.) A list of instructional materials is attached.

Specific Course Objectives

Educators who succeed in completing this course of study will

1. *Know and understand* five (5) standards of assessment quality and how to use assessment to promote maximum student achievement.

2. *Reason* through when to use various assessment methods and how to use them effectively to promote success at individual student, classroom, building, and district levels.

3. *Skillfully develop* and use sound assessments to maximize student motivation and achievement.

4. *Produce* assessments that meet specified standards of quality.

5. *Invest* the time and energy needed to become assessment literate and to develop and use only high-quality assessments.

Program of Study

The primary organizational structure of this program of study is the *learning team*. Working in groups of three to seven, participants take responsibility for their own professional development. They proceed chapter by chapter through the text, relying on assignments described in the ancillary publications, *Practice with Student-Involved Classroom Assessment: A Workbook and Learning Team Guide,* by Judith Arter and Kathleen Busick and supplementary videos. The learning teams are coordinated at the local district level.

The amount of work to be completed will require a time investment of three to six hours per text chapter, including reading, reflecting, completing associated assignments, classroom practice, and team work. Thus, the total work time will be about 50-75 hours. Of this, two-thirds involves individual study, reflection, and experimentation in the classroom, and one-third involves cooperative efforts within the learning team.

Evaluation of Achievement

Each higher education institution offering credit for completion of this program will need to take responsibility for inserting its own standards, assessment, performance criteria, and grading procedures into this course. These will vary from program to program. Thus, a professor of record will need to be identified. However, be advised that educators participating in this program are completing a number of activities as part of their studies that provide an excellent basis for this evaluation.

It is a very high priority in this professional development program that individuals and teams take responsibility for monitoring their own improvement as classroom assessors of the essential learning achievement targets. In this way, the program models for teachers and administrators exactly the kinds of self-assessment experiences recommended for use in the classroom with their students.

1. *Learning Log.* Participants are asked to keep a learning log, in which they record their responses to the following:

   a. "Times for Reflection" interspersed throughout the text.

   b. Personal insights, breakthroughs, achievements, frustrations, etc., as they apply information in the classroom.

   c. Exercises at the end of each textbook chapter designed to promote reflection and further learning.

2. *Classroom Assessment Confidence Questionnaire.* Participants are asked to complete this questionnaire at least twice—once at the beginning and once at the end of the program of study.

3. *Analyzing Assessments for Quality.* Participants regularly analyze their own assessments for quality using rubrics supplied for the purpose.

4. *Developmental Levels.* Participants periodically self-assess their status using developmental continuums.

5. *Classroom Assessment Professional Growth Portfolio.* Over the full term of study, each participant gathers and presents to the team evidence of increasing mastery of the essential learnings and mastery of assessment literacy. The individual record of improvement takes the form of a portfolio.

Any one or some combination of these can provide the professor of record with evidence of achievement on which to base judgments of student performance. However, decisions about appropriate standards, criteria, and grading practices are left to the credit-granting institution.

Instructional Materials

Textbook: *Student-Involved Classroom Assessment*, 3d ed, Rick Stiggins, Merrill/Prentice Hall (2001)

Workbook: *Practice with Student-Involved Classroom Assessment: A Workbook and Learning Team Guide*, Judith Arter and Kathleen Busick, Assessment Training Institute (2001)

Training Videos:

Imagine! Assessments That Energize Students—This video workshop is vital to understand how student-centered classroom assessment enhances teacher effectiveness and student motivation. Rick Stiggins argues that the key to success for students and teachers in today's standards-driven educational environment hinges on our ability to maintain and rebuild student confidence through intensive student involvement in classroom assessment.

Creating Sound Classroom Assessments—This video is designed for both teachers and administrators. First, you'll learn what quality assessment means. Then, you'll discover how to achieve it in your own school or district. Rick Stiggins reveals five, critical quality assessment standards that you can use to check the reliability of your assessments and to turn the assessment process into an effective teaching tool.

Common Sense Paper and Pencil Assessments—Implementing student-centered assessment methods doesn't mean you have to toss out traditional paper and pencil tests. This interactive video shows you how to design better paper and pencil tests and use them to build student motivation and achievement.

Assessing Reasoning in the Classroom—Building on the information in *Creating Sound Classroom Assessments*, this video provides valuable insights into exactly what it means for students to be proficient reasoners and effective problem-solvers. Using clear illustrations and focused instruction, the video guides you through a variety of practical, effective ways to use assessments to teach reasoning to your students and to help them succeed at problem-solving.

Report Card Grading—Through insightful discussion and valuable, hands-on activities, you'll explore the 'ins and outs' of report card grading. You'll examine a variety of student grading factors and discover which ones are key to accurate grading. Rick Stiggins will guide you through a discussion of the most effective evidence of achievement. Is it tests and quizzes? Performance assessment ratings? Homework scores? Class participation? Or even your own intuition about the student? You'll discover the answers with the help of this highly interactive video.

Student-Involved Conferences—This engaging video workshop will help you take maximum advantage of student-involved conferences to help students learn. Guided by Rick Stiggins and Anne Davies, both well-respected assessment trainers, consultants, and authors, you'll learn the most effective ways to involve students in and prepare students for conferences with parents.

Appendix E

Supplemental Readings on Classroom Assessment for Learning Teams

Assessment and Student Motivation

Covington, M. (1992). *Making the Grade: A Self-Worth Perspective on Motivation and School Reform*. New York: Cambridge University Press. To order: 914-937-9600. #34803X, ISBN 0-521-34261-9.

Kohn, A. (1993). *Punished by Rewards*. New York: Houghton Mifflin. To order: 800-225-3362, ISBN 0-395-65028-3.

Assessing in Diverse Classrooms

Farr, B. P., and Trumbull, E. (1997). *Assessment Alternatives for Diverse Classrooms*. Norwood, MA: Christopher Gordon. ISBN 0-926841-50-51-X.

Regional Educational Laboratories (2000). *Making Assessment Work for Everyone: How to Build on Student Strengths*. San Francisco, CA: WestEd.

Thurlow, M. L., Elliott, J. L., and Ysseldyke, J. E. (1998). *Testing Students With Disabilities: Practical Strategies for Complying With District and State Requirements*. Thousand Oaks, CA: Corwin. To order: order@corwin.sagepub.com. ISBN 0-8039-6551-6.

Learning Targets

Erickson, H. L. (1998). *Concept-Based Curriculum and Instruction: Teaching Beyond the Facts*. Thousand Oaks, CA: Corwin. To order: order@corwin.sagepub.com. ISBN 0-8039-6580-X.

Wiggins, G., and McTighe, J. (1998). *Understanding By Design*. Alexandria, VA: Association for Supervision and Curriculum Development. To order: 800-933-2723. ISBN 0-87120-313-8.

Student-Involved Communication About Achievement

Austin, T. (1994). *Changing the View: Student-Led Conferences*. Portsmouth, NH: Heinemann. To order: 800-541-2086. #08818, ISBN 0-435-08818-1.

Davies, A., Cameron, C., Politano, C., and Gregory, K. (1992). *Together Is Better: Collaborative Assessment, Evaluation & Reporting*. Courtenay, BC, Canada: Classroom Connections. To order: 800-603-9888, ISBN 1-895411-54-8.

Gregory, K., Cameron, C., and Davies, A. (2000). *Knowing What Counts: Self-Assessment and Goal-Setting For Use in Middle and Secondary School Classrooms*. Courtenay, BC, Canada: Classroom Connections. To order: 800-603-9888. ISBN 0-9682160-2-1.

Guskey, T. R. (Ed.). (1996). *Communicating Student Learning: 1996 ASCD Yearbook*. Alexandria, VA: Association for Supervision and Curriculum Development. To order: 703-549-9110. Stock No. 196000.

O'Connor, K. (1999). *How to Grade For Learning*. Arlington Heights, IL: Skylight. To order: 800-348-4474. ISBN 1-57517-123-6.

Dispositions Assessment

Anderson, L. W., and Bourke, S. F. (2000). *Assessing Affective Characteristics in the Schools*. Mahwah, NJ: Lawrence Erlbaum Associates. ISBN 0-8058-319-3.

Mathematics Assessment

Stenmark, J. K. (1991). *Mathematics Assessment: Myths, Models, Good Questions and Practical Suggestions*. Reston, VA: National Council of Teachers of Mathematics. A handbook of assessment guidelines and strategies in mathematics. To order: 800-235-7566. ISBN 0-87353-339-9.

Performance Assessment

Arter, Judith A., and McTighe, Jay (2001). *Scoring Rubrics in the Classroom: Using Performance Criteria for Assessing and Improving Student Performance*. Thousand Oaks, CA: Corwin.

Reading Assessment

Valencia, S., Hiebert, E. H., and Afflerbach, P. (Eds.) (1994). *Authentic Reading Assessment: Practices and Possibilities*. Newark, DE: International Reading Association. To order: 800-336-READ. ISBN 0-87207-765-9.

Science Assessment

Brown, J., and Shavelson, R. (1996). *Assessing Hands-On Science*. Thousand Oaks, CA: Corwin. A handbook of performance assessment guidelines and strategies in science. To order: 805-499-9774. ISBN 0-8039-6443-9.

Writing Assessment

Northwest Regional Educational Laboratory (1999). *Seeing With New Eyes: Writing Assessment for the Primary Grades*. Portland, OR: Author. To order: 503-275-9500.

Spandel, V., and Culham, R. (1995). *Putting Portfolio Stories to Work*. Portland, OR: Northwest Regional Educational Laboratory. To order: 503-275-9500.

Spandel, V. (2001). *Creating Writers: Linking Assessment and Writing Instruction*, 3d ed. New York: Addison-Wesley Longman. To order: 800-822-6339.